KEN JONES

Boots and Spikes

KEN JONES

Boots and Spikes

Steve Lewis

SPORTS
BOOKS

Published in Great Britain by
SportsBooks Limited
1 Evelyn Court
Malvern Road
Cheltenham
GL50 2JR

© Steve Lewis 2011
First Published September 2011

Cover designed by Alan Hunns.

A catalogue record for this book is available from the British Library.

ISBN 9781907524 05 9

Printed and bound by Jellyfish Print Solutions, Hampshire

For the town and people of Blaenavon,
always close to Ken Jones' heart

CONTENTS

FOREWORD

Ken was not only murderously fast and fearless in the tackle but he possessed a razor-sharp sense of anticipation. When you watched him play you felt the tingling of the spine – the prickling of the scalp. He was world class.' These were the priceless words of that immortal centre of Wales and the world, Bleddyn Williams, in memory of Ken Jones.

For me, Ken left an indelible fingerprint on everything he touched in his life. He was modest, unassuming, had great charm and never wore his abundant and creative talents on his sleeve. His love of virtue and his sense of duty and loyalty to his fellow man singled him out as a special person. His life touched not only those who were close to him but the many thousands he thrilled and entertained in sprinting for Wales and Great Britain and winning a silver medal in the 4x100m relay at the Olympic Games in 1948 in London. Then there were the many thrilling tries he scored for Newport and Wales and again for the Lions in 1950 in New Zealand.

I was proud and fortunate to have played with him and against him for there was little to compare in those days with the Newport and Cardiff fixtures. We actually played against each other four times every season in the 50s to packed houses. We all felt privileged to be part of something special. I remember with enormous warmth, after my first game for Cardiff at Rodney Parade, Ken taking me and John Phillips to the tearoom. 'I can promise you the most delicious cup of tea and a scrumptious meal – all made by the wives and sweethearts of the Newport club,' said Ken. It was, indeed, for me wonderful and unforgettable.

I was lucky too, to play many international matches with Ken and still have vivid memories of the 1952 England match at Twickenham when Wales were not expected to win. I always hoped to get into the same compartment as Ken when we were travelling, be it to Edinburgh, Paris, Dublin or London, for I knew there would be good conversation and treasured stories. En route to Twickenham, the day before the match, Ken said he would like to score a try that would be as famous as the one scored in 1936 by the Russian, Prince Obolensky, playing for England against New Zealand. The great Obolensky sped from one touchline, across the field to the other. 'It will, for ever be talked about,' said Ken. In all the good record books you can now read that the very next day, Ken Jones ran from our own 25-yard line (these were in the days before metres), outstripped the England defence and scored near the corner flag. A few weeks later in Dublin, he repeated that 70-yard run from our own line and dived over to score and Wales won the Triple Crown; and how many times in the past 50 and more years have I retold the story of those two magnificent tries!

In 1953, the last time Wales beat New Zealand, it was Ken who scored the try that gave us the win. Clem Thomas cross kicked, Ken Jones chased and gathered the ball, side-stepped Ron Jarden and touched down under the posts. He shone like a glittering star and his passion for rugby never faltered.

Ken was, indeed, the complete athlete but I also admired his true sense of values. He adored his role as a teacher and firmly believed in education and felt that caring for young people was a most honourable and rewarding job that could help to set standards for the future generation. He firmly believed that bad behaviour, jealousy and greed were destructive emotions and that mediocrity was second rate. Ken was first rate.

He felt exactly the same about the craft of journalism, which he also mastered. He was a natural presence in the press box and his articles on rugby made you think that the game was worthwhile – a game of chance so dramatically and romantically played. In fact the stuff of which dreams are made.

In the autumn of 1977, we were both at a match at Newport and in the clubhouse later, in our usual gathering for a chat and the cool comfort of a few beers, Ken asked me to relate a story about Jesse Owens, of the United States, one of the greatest Olympians of all time. I had been at a press conference at the 1976 Olympics in Montreal when a young journalist challenged Jesse, asking him if there was any future in pursuing the principles of the Olympic Games when there was so much cruelty, greed, jealousy, starvation and poverty all around the world. Was the Olympic Games worth preserving? This is what Jesse Owens replied: 'Take a look at what's happening out there on the field today. This is where youngsters break bread together, they sing together, they dance together and they play together. The only body in the world where you can find the youth of the world that can come together on a friendly field of competition. You've got the United Nations and they haven't solved a damned thing but you do solve something here. You solve a championship of the world and you're not breaking heads, you're breaking records and this is why it is going to endure because the youth of the world is going to be the leadership of the world in not too many years from today and the things that he learns right here today he is going to take back to his land in his own mind and they are going to live for ever because they are great moments. Whether you win, whether you qualify, in the finals or not – you were here. You broke bread with the rest of the world.'

As I told that story Ken smiled, for though I had told him this tale before he wanted to hear it again. For Ken, the supreme athlete, the dedicated teacher, the talented journalist

3

and, above all, a loving and caring family man, the words of Jesse Owens very much reflected his own philosophy on life.

I am proud to call Ken Jones my friend and he will live in my heart for ever. I am sure when you have read this book you will understand why.

Cliff Morgan

ACKNOWLEDGEMENTS

When considering who might lay claim to being Wales' finest all-round sportsman the name Ken Jones must be on every shortlist and after much discussion it would be difficult to come to any conclusion other than that the man from Blaenavon should top the list. Strange then that the life of such an outstanding performer on both the rugby field and running track was not to be found among the many biographies that dominate the sports sections in shops and libraries. When the opportunity to write an autobiography was presented Ken declined politely, which says much about the man; but his is a story that needs telling, such is the magnitude of his many achievements.

Before setting out on such a project it is vitally important to receive the total support of the subject's nearest and dearest. For this, the interest shown from the outset by Ken's widow Irene and son Philip never faltered. Without their commitment the story could not be told. It is easy to reminisce about the international caps, the athletics medals and much else but revisiting the darker days that followed Ken's stroke could not have been a comfortable experience. I am indebted to them both.

When researching an earlier work, I was fortunate to meet Ken. This was after he had suffered the stroke, a time when he found it difficult to speak, but with Irene's assistance he was able to reflect on his years as an international rugby player, particularly the match against Scotland for which he was appointed Welsh captain. Similarly, I previously interviewed Onllwyn Brace, John Gwilliam, Jack Matthews, Malcolm Thomas and Bleddyn Williams, discussions that covered the highs and lows of Welsh rugby during the late 1940s and 1950s with many references made to the man ever present on Wales' right wing.

Jack Kyle welcomed me to his home in County Down and was more than equal to the task of recollecting those heady months spent in Ken's company touring New Zealand and Australia with the British Lions in 1950. There was time to get sidetracked by some Benny Goodman recordings before we were entertained by Ethel and Ronnie Chambers at their nearby home. Ethel certainly knows her way about a kitchen and it comes as no surprise that Ronnie bears little resemblance to the man who once contested 100yds sprints with Ken Jones.

At Newport Rugby Club everybody of a certain age has a story to tell about Ken. When it became apparent that there was some contradiction and that many of the tales might have been favourably embellished over the years I decided to focus on Bobby Owen and Brian Jones for extended comment and opinion. Both played alongside Ken and continued to enjoy his company long after the boots had been hung up. Brian would later read the eulogy at Ken's funeral. Then there is Doug Ackerman, who can always be relied upon for a good story. He is a great raconteur when it comes to life on tour and his memories of Newport's visit to France in 1951–52 are particularly illuminating. But as they say – what goes on tour stays on tour!

Ken Jones was first and foremost a Newport player. Phil Stallard provided some useful material relating to Ken's years at the club and the excellent website put together by members of the Friends of Newport Rugby confirmed or disproved the inevitable conflicting statistical information to be found in other source material. Phil Grant also found some interesting photographs which are included. Ken certainly was first and foremost a Newport player but he did appear for other clubs. There was no one better to turn to when seeking information on his matches in the colours of Pontypool RFC than Ray Ruddick, and Stuart Farmer confirmed details of his one appearance for Leicester RFC.

Just as rugby football has a network of statisticians who can satisfy the most obscure enquiry so too does the world of athletics, where the detail recorded is perhaps even more impressive. A chance meeting with Clive Williams at the Millennium Stadium led to a copy of his impressive tome on Welsh Athletics arriving at my doorstep a few days later. Therein lies a wealth of statistical information, among which are to be found all Ken's performances and times at the Welsh Championships and much else. Walter Nicholls, Honorary Secretary of the Amateur Athletic Association, also provided useful material relating to Ken's involvement in the AAA Championships and appearances for Great Britain.

The world of academia played an important part in Ken's life. I am particularly grateful to Derwyn Whent who was a pupil at West Mon School during Ken's time there, played with him in the colours of Priestley House and 'taught him to tackle'. Later the two would reunite in the clubs and bars of Blaenavon following their return home at the end of the Second World War. West Mon still stands proud, looking over the town of Pontypool, and deputy headmaster Clive Jackson and head of history Christine James were both generous with their time in allowing me access to the inner sanctum that can lay claim to putting the young Ken Jones on the straight and narrow.

That road led to St Pauls' College of Education, now part of the University of Gloucestershire, where archivist Lorna Scott unearthed some fascinating material and took me on a comprehensive tour of the campus. Jenny Clark fills a similar position at Loughborough College and some of the photographic material she supplied is included.

When Ken returned to Newport in 1949 to take up a teaching post at Newport High School for Boys he joined a staff that included geography master Herbert Lewis among its number. His input on the machinations of the famous old school were of particular interest to an old boy, albeit one of more recent vintage.

At a time when the local library appears to be under threat, the service these institutions provide cannot be underestimated. Alex Jarvis and the staff in the reference department at Newport Central Library once again guided me through the comprehensive collection of books, microfiche and microfilms in my search for the all-important details I needed. Pat Sanderson at Pontypool Museum allowed me access to the archive of the *Free Press* newspaper, among the pages of which were to be found many features covering Ken's schooldays and early appearances for local clubs.

Researching Ken's service record with the RAF proved to be less productive. Air Commodore Keith Minton (rtd) pointed me in the right direction but despite an appeal for information in the pages of the *RAF News* courtesy of editor Simon Williams, no feedback was forthcoming.

I am particularly grateful to Cliff Morgan, who provides the foreword. Cliff played alongside Ken in the Welsh team on 22 occasions, including the famous victory over New Zealand in 1953. The players were also opponents many times when Newport and Cardiff clashed in the most eagerly anticipated club matches of the season. They developed a friendship that would last well beyond their rugby-playing days and it would be difficult to find someone more suitably qualified to introduce Ken than Cliff Morgan.

Randall Northam at SportsBooks deserves special mention. Without his enthusiasm and love of sport in general many worthwhile projects would never see the light of day. His years of experience at the sharp end of sports journalism give him an uncanny instinct which I readily fell back on when necessary.

Finally, my wife Catherine played her usual role of nuisance, cajoler, critic and enthusiast to the hilt – she is well practised! I would like to be able to state that any errors found in the text are down to her but, as is usual in such circumstances, they are mine and mine alone.

Explanatory Notes

1 Newport Athletic Club was a body that encompassed a wide range of sporting activities with sections dedicated to athletics and rugby football. When mention is made of Ken Jones running for Newport Athletic Club it is the section rather than the umbrella name that is referenced. Newport Rugby Football Club was also a section of Newport Athletic Club but more easily identified as such.

2 Now recognised as the Commonwealth Games, there have been other names under which the event was held. Ken Jones turned down the opportunity to compete in the Empire Games in 1950 but ran in the British Empire and Commonwealth Games in 1954 and was involved in the similarly named tourney when it was held in Cardiff in 1958. The names applicable at the relevant time are used throughout.

3 In 1950, rugby players selected to represent the four home unions on overseas tours were known as the British Lions. In recent years this has been extended to the British and Irish Lions but the name recognised in 1950 is used here.

4 Llanelli is the correct spelling of the west Wales town and its famous rugby club. In the 1950s the variant Llanelly was regularly used and appears in the text.

INTRODUCTION

In February 1956 Ken Jones received a letter from London publishing house Herbert Jenkins Ltd in which JD Grimsdick, a director of the company, discussed the imminent publication of *The Bob Scott Story*, the autobiography of the famous New Zealand full-back. More pertinently, the letter also put forward the suggestion that possibly Ken Jones would consider allowing his life story to be told through the pages of a book. Previous ventures by leading Welsh rugby players were thin on the ground and those in print were not complete autobiographies or biographies, but rather general observations on the sport which included a brief resumé of the subject's playing career. Not exactly what Grimsdick had in mind. A second letter dated 1 March refers to a telephone conversation in which the matter was discussed and goes on to consider a possible meeting between the two parties. Ken was obviously interested, certainly enough not to have dismissed the suggestion out of hand, but there was no further correspondence and the project was abandoned.

Later that year *Rugger My Life*, the autobiography of Bleddyn Williams, arrived in the shops. Published by Stanley Paul, the book was a resounding success and can possibly be identified as the template for the many volumes written in a similar vein over the following years. Just as Bleddyn Williams had a story to tell that would garner interest not only within Wales but further afield, so too did Ken Jones, particularly as his would extend beyond the game of rugby football and include many successful years as a track athlete. But there was a stumbling block: where Williams had retired from the game Jones was still actively involved. Quite simply, association with any project that appeared to capitalise on his name would be seen as a breach of the strict amateur code to which rugby union conformed and he would become persona non grata with immediate effect, an outcast banned from playing the game. It was not in the nature of the man to allow his sporting career to end in such contentious circumstances; he and he alone would decide when it was time to call it a day. There would be a further two seasons of first-class rugby which Ken would have forfeited if he had gone in search of the silver lucre and, as he had been put on this earth to play the union game and set the world of athletics alight with his blistering pace, such financial incentives were never going to carry the day.

Things may have been different if retirement had beckoned. Ken had brought his distinguished athletics career to an end in 1954 following a successful British Empire and Commonwealth Games in Vancouver and European Championships in Berne, Switzerland but he continued to play rugby football and would do so for a further four seasons.

In February and March 1956, Ken Jones won the Welsh caps that took him into the record books as not only Wales' most capped rugby international, but also the most capped player in the world game. Onlookers may have been predicting the imminent retirement of one of Wales' greatest players but he continued to belie his 34 years, knowing there was some petrol remaining in the tank and intent on running it dry.

From humble beginnings in Blaenavon, a town famous for its association with the iron and coal industries, to becoming Wales' most capped rugby player and champion sprinter suggests a journey of some note. Schoolboy rugby international and victor ludorum at the annual sports day; college rugby and track star; champion sprinter at the All India

Olympics, drawing comparisons with Jesse Owens; winner of 16 titles at the Welsh Athletics Championships; medallist at the Olympic Games, British Empire and Commonwealth Games and European Championships; captain of the Great Britain athletics team; member of the British Lions party that toured New Zealand and Australia in 1950; winner of 44 Welsh caps, 43 consecutively; scorer of a record number of tries for Wales; Welsh captain; stalwart of Newport Rugby Football Club; member of the Order of the British Empire; and all-round good egg, a gentleman who remained modest in the extreme about his outstanding sporting achievements. Little wonder then, that the rights to his story were sought after.

Wales' greatest sportsman? An unequivocal yes. Welsh rugby has produced many fine players who can lay claim to more caps and more tries. Likewise, Welsh athletics has produced champions at the highest level of competition; medallists at the major games and world record holders. But only on a few occasions has someone performed at the highest level on both the rugby field and in the athletics stadium. And certainly with nothing like the level of achievement attained by Ken Jones during ten years of international competition. The arrival of professionalism at the top level of all major sports suggests that the chances of enjoying dual careers are a thing of the past, confirmation in itself that we shall never see his like again.

If JD Grimsdick had waited a few more years then perhaps an autobiography would have followed, Ken proving more than capable when required to put pen to paper, as his time as a frontline sports journalist would later confirm. But Grimsdick was left to rue what might have been with the matter apparently laid to rest. Until now, over 50 years on from that initial interest. It is unfortunate that while Ken Jones was a household name in the 1950s, certainly throughout Wales, such celebrity has a habit of fading. Beyond Wales, mention of his name may raise questioning eyebrows which makes it all the more remarkable that in New Zealand he is still remembered as the man who swept all before him in 1950 when touring with the British Lions and scored one of the greatest tries seen at Eden Park, Auckland. Then there was another try three years later, one for which he is equally remembered by followers of the game in the antipodes. One scored on a famous day in Cardiff when Wales defeated the All Blacks for the third time. That Wales have failed to repeat the victory in a period that has extended to 58 years and a further 24 matches does, however, guarantee that Ken's name remains in print whenever the two countries meet on a rugby field.

His athletics career also saw its share of controversy, none more so than the drama played out at Wembley Stadium in 1948 during the Games of the XIVth Olympiad: how Ken Jones together with Alastair McCorquodale, Jack Archer and Jack Gregory were presented with gold medals following the 4x100m relay, only to have to return them three days later. An appeal made on behalf of the disqualified USA team was upheld, the placings reversed with Great Britain having to settle for silver medals. In a reflection of a bygone era there were no recriminations, no complaints, no sour grapes from the British quartet, rather the recognition that justice had been done and the much superior USA team rewarded with gold. The incident confirms what was the accepted manner of all sportsmen and sportswomen at the time. Magnanimity in victory and generosity in defeat were synonymous with all sports and no individual epitomised these fine qualities more so than Ken Jones – Wales' greatest sportsman.

CHAPTER ONE

AN EDUCATION

FROM THE LATTER part of the eighteenth century through to the middle of the nineteenth, the landscape of Britain laid witness to a transformation of such magnitude that from being a nation once steeped in agriculture it became the most prosperous in the world. This was the time of the Industrial Revolution, years during which the eminent engineers George Stephenson, Matthew Boulton, James Watt, Thomas Telford and Isambard Kingdom Brunel helped change the landscape for ever. This was the period that witnessed the arrival of the steam engine, which led to the development of the railways; the construction of bridges and canals that in turn improved the transportation of goods; and the subsequent rapid growth of the shipbuilding industry which helped secure the important overseas markets. These were great innovations that encouraged the exploitation of what lay beneath the 'green and pleasant land' – coal and iron ore. Some of the largest deposits were found in South Wales, which led to the opening of a network of mines that straddled the valleys and became a major source of employment not only for the local population, but also for the thousands who came in search of work.

Blaenavon is a small town located at the source of the Afon Lwyd, five or six miles to the north of Pontypool in the south-east corner of Wales. Travellers passing through the area could be forgiven for dismissing Blaenavon as simply a valley town, albeit one of many with a proud history – but they would be wrong. Found nestling among the rolling landscape of surrounding hills and only a short distance from the southern boundary of the Brecon Beacons National Park, Blaenavon is also at the hub of an area of land approximately 19 square miles in size which on 30 November 2000 received global recognition.

The United Nations Educational, Scientific and Cultural Organisation (UNESCO) first introduced the concept of World Heritage Sites in 1978 and by 2009 there were 890 locations making up an impressive list. Nominations – and many are received by UNESCO's World Heritage Committee – are sites of particular historical, natural, cultural or industrial importance. The inclusion of the Great Wall of China, the Taj Mahal, Machu Picchu, Sydney Opera House and the Pyramids can be taken for granted, as can that of the Grand Canyon and Australia's Great Barrier Reef. Closer to home, Canterbury Cathedral, Blenheim Palace, Stonehenge, Hadrian's Wall and the Giant's Causeway on the Antrim coast of Northern Ireland have all been recognised as being of particular significance. And Bath joins Venice as a site reflecting the importance of society as a whole, both culturally and historically.

The suggestion that Blaenavon and its surrounding environs be proposed for consideration as a World Heritage Site was first put forward in 1999. As many as 500 sites in the UK had expressed an interest in being nominated but it was a shortlist of 25 that was presented to the World Heritage Committee for consideration by its members at their meeting in Cairns the following year. By 2000 the UK had 18 World Heritage Sites, a relatively low figure which confirms the elite membership of what has to be viewed as a particularly exclusive club. To be included on such a prestigious list, certain demanding criteria have to be met and when considering the nomination of a small area in South Wales it was criteria iii and iv that were particularly important. The area was found to 'constitute an exceptional illustration in material form of the social and economic structure of nineteenth century industry' and 'the components together make an outstanding and remarkably complete example of a nineteenth century industrial landscape'. In inscribing the Blaenavon Industrial Landscape as a World Heritage Site UNESCO confirmed that 'The area around Blaenavon bears eloquent and exceptional testimony to the pre-eminence of South Wales as the World's major producer of iron and coal in the nineteenth century. All the necessary elements can be seen in-situ; coal and ore mines, quarries, a primitive railway system, furnaces, the houses of the workers and the social infrastructure of their community...'

Such recognition revitalised the fortunes of a town in decline. Blaenavon now sees a constant flow of tourists wanting to learn about the early years of the Industrial Revolution. At Big Pit, the National Coal Museum of Wales, visitors can go down the mine shaft and experience the unforgiving working environment endured by the miners. Blaenavon Ironworks are recognised as the best preserved in the world and the Monmouthshire and Brecon Canal, originally constructed to take the coal and iron to the ports on the Bristol Channel, now plays host to a traffic of small pleasure craft and barges while the towpath is busy with cyclists and walkers. The Pontypool and Blaenavon Railway, the Workmen's Hall, Keeper's Pond and the continuing popularity of the books of Alexander Cordell, in particular *Rape of the Fair Country*, which is set in the town, serve as a constant reminder of a history that reaches back to the eighteenth century with the construction of Blaenavon Ironworks in 1790, and the production of the first pig iron.

Two Englishman and a Welshman joined forces to establish Blaenavon Ironworks. Thomas Hill and Benjamin Pratt from the Midlands and Welsh-speaking Thomas Hopkins leased land from Lord Abergavenny, invested £40,000 and by 1796 the works was the biggest producer of iron in Wales. But there was a problem. The level of phosphorus in the iron affected the quality of the steel produced, which was brittle and therefore limited in its use. It would be 80 years before a solution was found but it would prove to be the most significant development in the industry to date.

Sidney Gilchrist Thomas was born in London in 1850. In 1875, he was working as a clerk in Stepney while at the same time taking a chemistry course at night school. A chance comment by the lecturer to the effect that the person who could eliminate the phosphorus problem would become rich and famous set the young man thinking. Thomas came to the conclusion that the problem lay not so much with the ore but in the lining of the converter, which was made of bricks that contained a high level of acid. This appeared to prevent the removal of the acid content of the phosphorus and he concluded that a different lining should be introduced. His cousin Percy Gilchrist had started working for the Blaenavon Company as a chemist and Sidney Thomas became a regular visitor to the area, where the cousins conducted experiments with a lining made of limestone that had no acid content. It worked. Allowed the use of the Blaenavon Company's facilities, the theory was put to the test on an industrial scale and by the end of the decade the process had generated great interest from the major iron-producing areas of the world. Ten years later the patents were sold into Europe and America, making the cousins rich and famous, as predicted during that evening class at the London college.

Ground-breaking discovery it may have been but the real benefits would be seen elsewhere, in those countries where supplies of the raw material were seemingly inexhaustible. Mining for coal around Blaenavon had started at the end of the eighteenth century and with the volatility of the iron industry, a century later the pits had become the biggest employers. More than 2,000 men, women and children worked for the mining companies when the industry was at its peak and at the start of the twentieth century as many as 1,600 workers and their families were still dependent on the collieries.

The population of Blaenavon peaked at approximately 12,000 in the second decade of the twentieth century and the town had grown in both size and infrastructure to accommodate the quite unexpected number of residents. As early as 1854, a rail link with Pontypool was established which enabled people to travel to the bigger town and beyond with ease, but there was little need to look beyond Blaenavon for basic everyday requirements. A plethora of churches and chapels catered for what was a devout community and together with schools, a hospital, local police station, court house and numerous public houses the basic amenities of a working-class town were in place. Broad Street became the nucleus, with a variety of well-stocked shops and cafes which circa 1920 included Deakins and Hughes, a chemist's well known for its own chest, cough and lung remedy; Fowlers was a well-established drapers and milliners and general outfitters; for footwear it was Briggs Shoe Shop; and groceries and dairy products could be purchased at the Maypole Grocery or the local Dairy Company. Partly funded by the local workforce, the Workmen's Hall was opened in 1895 and catered for a variety of concerts, social gatherings and, in later years, the arrival of moving pictures.

Blaenavon may have been built around heavy industry and accommodated all the needs that a largely male-dominated workforce demanded but there was also room within the environs of the town for the pursuit of outdoor sporting activities. In 1921, a new recreation ground was opened which incorporated the local rugby club's playing field and in the summer it was there the cricketers and athletes would take centre stage. Later that same year Blaenavon welcomed the arrival of a new resident, one who in time would make good use of the local sporting facilities before moving on to display his unique talent at much bigger arenas around the world.

Kenneth Jeffrey Jones was born on 30 December 1921, the first child of John and Ella Jones (née Burland). The early 1920s saw the mining industry in crisis, which was of particular significance as John 'Jack' Jones worked for the Blaenavon Company, which operated the major pits in the area. Mines across South Wales were closing at an alarming rate and half the men who relied on the industry for work found themselves unemployed. Over the next decade men would be forced to leave Wales, some travelling overseas in their search for work, many of whom would never return. By the 1930s the problem had escalated with an estimated 250,000 men in Wales out of work at a time when the national figure topped two million. The financial crisis that threatened to bring the country to its knees heralded a change of government and saw the pound devalued, but more specifically it was the Treaty of Versailles, laid down following the First World War, that had a direct impact on the mining industry. Among its many provisions was the return to French sovereignty of the Alsace-Lorraine region, which had been incorporated into Germany in 1871. This region was particularly wealthy in mineral deposits and with France now able to develop an iron and steel industry based on the rich fields once again under her control, the need to import was eliminated. France had been one of the main importers of British iron and coal and with this market now effectively closed it was inevitable that the industry would suffer; and for areas such as South Wales, the impact was serious.

The mining companies continued to operate but with production at a much-reduced level. Fewer in number they may have been but men were still needed, and Jack Jones was among those fortunate enough to remain in full employment during this most difficult of times. When Ken was born,

Jack and Ella were living with Ella's parents and siblings at Greenfield Place, located at the top end of the town. Space was at a premium and shortly after the birth of their first child, Jack elected to up roots and take his family to a new home. They moved into a house on Lower Hill Street, only a short distance from Greenfield Place but at the bottom end of the town, in close proximity to the Lower Level railway station, which in time would play a big part in the formative years of the new arrival.

Life was hard during the 1920s and 1930s but for those growing up during these difficult years, youngsters who knew no different, life was good. If school proved to be something of an inconvenience there was always the recreation field and the swimming pool to look forward to. Ken Jones' introduction to the education system that he would later become a part of was at the Church Boys Endowed Junior School. It was there he learnt to read and write but it was at the recreation ground that he learnt to run. Do boys have to be taught how to run? Certainly not, but it was on the playing fields of Blaenavon that a young Ken Jones is believed to have first caught the eye of the man he would later credit with having had the biggest influence on his sporting career.

Bob Barwell was well known about town as the trainer of the local rugby team, who also took particular delight in finding young athletes in whom he saw a special talent, something that made them stand out from the rest. Whatever it was that Barwell looked for, he found it in the slim, angular frame of the dark-haired lad who lived on Lower Hill Street. The only known photograph of Bob Barwell and Ken Jones was taken circa 1935, by which time the 13-year-old Jones was a well-established junior sprinter in the eastern valley with many titles to his name. It shows the trainer and athlete standing either side of a table laden with medals and prizes, including the Boys' Championship Shield awarded to the winner of the 100yds at the annual Abertillery Police Sports. Ken Jones, hands on hips and looking very composed for one so young, is dressed in a short-sleeved running vest with trim at the neck and arms, black shorts, white socks and black running shoes. Barwell appears in collar and tie, waistcoat with shirt sleeves folded at the cuff and a towel casually draped over his right shoulder. It is unclear whether Ken was tall for his age or Barwell a particularly short man as both figures appear to be of similar stance, but everything about the picture suggests the archetypal pupil–mentor relationship, and so it proved to be.

The earliest record of Ken running competitively was at the Blaenavon Bank Holiday Sports in August 1932, held at the Recreation Ground. He won the boys' 100yds with some ease and the following year he took the 100yds and 220yds sprints at the Blaenavon School Sports, a comfortable winner of both. These performances are important when viewing the early career of a future Olympic athlete as they give a clear indication of his outstanding talent being identified at an early age, but at the same time they merely confirm that the ten-year-old was nothing more than a big fish in a small pond. How good he actually was would be found out when he came up against the fast boys produced in other areas of Wales.

For the first ten years of his life Ken enjoyed a somewhat privileged existence within the Jones household. He was an only child, which certainly had its advantages, but that was about to change. In 1931 there was a new addition to the family and things would never be the same again. Ken had a sister and history tells us that he and Phyllis not only enjoyed a loving brother–sister relationship, but would also become great friends.

Ken celebrated his 11th birthday on 30 December 1932, which meant his move to the second level of education would be in the following September. From the day he was first introduced to the regime of one of Wales' leading schools his real potential as a sprinter would begin to blossom. Likewise, the gentle introduction to rugby football he had experienced playing for Blaenavon Schools during the 1932–33 season would also move up a gear. The next seven years would turn a schoolboy prodigy into a serious contender, both on the running track and on the rugby field, and come 1940, the first stage in the development of Wales' greatest all-round sportsman would be complete.

Jones West Monmouthshire School (West Mon) was founded in 1898 but its history has to be traced back to 1615 and the last will and testament of one William Jones. Born in the county, William Jones led a varied life about which there is much conjecture. Unable to pay a small debt, he travelled to London before settling in Hamburg where he became a cotton merchant, from which trade he accumulated his fortune. A member of the Worshipful Company of Haberdashers, he bequeathed a sum of money to the Order with specific instructions as to how it should be used. Included among the many stipulations was the building of a school. Years of careful administration meant that the trust had sufficient monies to consider the funding of two educational establishments and it was decided that a school for girls should be built in Monmouth and a school for boys at a location west of the River Usk.

After much deliberation it was agreed that the new school for boys would be built in Pontypool on land acquired from Squire Hanbury. The landowner generously donated the sale proceeds to the trust to fund scholarships which would be awarded at the discretion of the school governors. On completion, West Mon looked down somewhat imposingly from its elevated position on the west side of Pontypool and continues to do so more than one hundred years after first opening its doors.

Such institutions were founded on solid moral and ethical codes. A high level of discipline was maintained and pupils strayed from the straight and narrow at their peril. For September's new intake, that first walk up the hill from the town must have been a daunting experience. The passing of time and familiarity with the way things worked would certainly help, but throughout their years at the school the boys would be expected to observe the high standards set at all times. Robert Ivor Jones, MA Oxon, was the second man to hold the prestigious position of headmaster following in the footsteps of James Henry Priestley, BA, who held the post between 1898 and 1912. Jones' tenure would extend to 30 years, 1912 to 1942, during which the school gained public school status in 1935. Reports suggest that the headmaster was a strict disciplinarian, giving added credence to the school motto – 'Serve and Obey'.

Joining Ken Jones on that first walk up the hill from the town in September 1933 were 84 other new arrivals, bringing the total number of pupils attending the school at the time to 334. West Mon had long since observed a system whereby boys were allocated to a specific house in which they would remain for the duration of their time at the school. Used in this context, the term 'house' referred to a collective of pupils of all ages who would join together with the common cause of bettering the performances of other houses in various fields of academic and sporting endeavour. This system was deemed to instil an element of competition, highlighted on the various fields of play, together with a sense of loyalty and allegiance to one's designated house and its fellow pupils.

For the start of the academic year in 1933 the number of houses was increased from four to six and Ken Jones found himself placed in Priestley, one of the new houses. Named after the first headmaster, Priestley was made up of boys from the Blaenavon and Talywain catchment areas while those who lived beyond the borough boundary to the south of Pontypool were drafted into Watson, the other new house, which took its name from a senior master who had taught at the school for 26 years. Three houses of long standing were Jones, named after the founder of the school; Hanbury, in memory of the squire who had effectively donated the land on which the school sat;

and Daniel, after a member of the committee that brought the school to the town who was also a school governor. The sixth house was School, which accommodated those pupils who were boarders, of whom there were 34 in 1933.

Pupils initially entered the school for a four-year period at the end of which the examinations took place for the School Certificate. Subjects taught were mathematics, English, French, Latin, biology, chemistry, physics, history, geography, religious instruction, woodwork and drawing. The school day extended between 9.00 and 13.00 and 14.10 and 15.40 on Monday, Wednesday and Friday and 9.00 to 13.00, Tuesday, Thursday and Saturday, on which days the afternoons were devoted to sport.

Living in Blaenavon, Ken Jones had to travel to and from Pontypool by train. The single-track line between the towns was opened by the Great Western Railway in 1854, and while there was a good bus service available in 1933, the train was the only realistic option for the boys and girls who travelled to Pontypool on a daily basis. Fortunately, for a boy notoriously difficult to prise out of his bed in the morning, something he would never improve on, Blaenavon's Lower Level railway station was a stone's throw from Lower Hill Street. But even living in such close proximity to the station rarely prevented the young Jones from being last to board the 8.00am departure. Pulled or shunted by what were known as 'coffee pot' engines, two carriages transported passengers between the two towns, stopping at Cwmavon, Cwmffrwyd Halt, Abersychan, Snatchwood Halt, Pontnewynydd, Crane Street, Pontypool and Blaendare, where the West Mon boys got off. Crane Street saw the girls heading for Pontypool Girls School, known locally as the County, leave the train, having observed one of the unwritten rules of the day by spending the journey in a separate carriage from the boys.

Irene Edmunds was born on 4 January 1923. The only child of Arthur and Mary Edmunds, she was raised in some comfort, the family home a substantial property located adjacent to The Park. It was here on the west side of town that the more affluent members of the community resided; the directors of the Blaenavon Company, other prominent businessmen and those with a professional standing in the town. Arthur Edmunds was employed as an engineer with the Blaenavon Company. He was one of 12 children, whose father, Isaac, had owned a thriving construction company which had built some of the town's chapels and many residential properties, including those located at Greenfield Place, the first home of Ken Jones. Irene attended St Peter's School before moving on to higher education and in September 1934 it became her turn to take the train to Pontypool, where she continued her studies at the County. It was at the Lower Level Station she first noticed the young man with whom she would spend more than 70 years, the one who day after day came running down to the station with seconds to spare before the train set off. Surely, this was the only time in his life that Ken Jones took an element of pride in coming last!

At the end of his first year at West Mon there was little to suggest Ken Jones was going to make his mark as an outstanding academic. The favoured 'could do better' best sums up his efforts in the classroom, but his name did appear twice in the 1933–34 edition of *The Westmonian*, the school magazine. West Mon continued to observe a long-standing tradition that saw the speech day proceedings held in the main hall before the pupils and guests made their way to the playing field for the end of term inter-house sports day. The athletics competitions were completed before tea was taken, following which the principals and guests would make their way to the school swimming pool for the finale of a long day. On this one day of the year, the practice of boys only being allowed in the pool in their birthday suits was dispensed with, all competitors suitably attired in the presence of many ladies, including Mrs Holmes Watkins of Griffithstown who presented the prizes.

The records included in the '33–34 edition of *The Westmonian* confirm that KJ Jones of Priestley House won the under-14 100 and 220 yards in 12.4 and 27.4 seconds. The age group categorisation tells us that Ken would have been competing against boys a school year ahead of him. The same would happen two years later when he competed in the under-16 age group events and again in 1938, when he was included in the 'open' category. Despite having to take on the older boys every other year, school records confirm that for six consecutive years Ken Jones won the 100yds in his particular age group at the annual sports day and the 220yds at every opportunity, the longer sprint not always included for each age group. In addition to his outstanding performances on the track there were also various victories in the high jump and long jump. The records also tell us that during his time at West Mon the times recorded by Ken showed consistent improvement. He trimmed his performances from 12.4 to 11.0 in the 100yds and from 27.4 to 25.6 in the 220yds. At a time when an even 10.0 was considered the benchmark for the shorter sprint the 17-year-old Blaenavon boy was certainly heading in the right direction. Then there was rugby – and girls!

Shortly after she began making the daily journey to and from Pontypool, Irene and Ken became what in modern parlance would be called an 'item'. In their wildest imaginings neither could have possibly predicted how long the relationship would last or where it would take them. For Ken there was little room for anything beyond his rugby and athletics but over weeks, months and then years the couple grew closer together. The local cinemas at the Workmen's Hall and the Coliseum on Lion Street provided weekend entertainments but very quickly Irene found herself taking an interest in rugby football and athletics as Ken continued to make his mark in the sports that would elevate him to superstar status.

For 25 years association football was the winter sport at West Mon. A radical change took place in 1923, when it was decided that the school would dispense with football and the boys would now concentrate on rugby union. This change was partly brought about by the fact that when it came to competing with other schools, the numbers playing association football were far fewer than those where rugby took priority. That most grammar schools favoured rugby football was a great help when it came to compiling fixture lists and by 1933, the school ran three teams; a First XV, Second XV and a Colts or Juniors which catered for boys under 15 years of age. Prominent on the fixture lists were Newport High School, Cardiff High School, Abergavenny Grammar School, Bassaleg Secondary School and Newbridge Secondary School.

In 1933, the school's honours board boasted five senior Welsh rugby internationals among its alumni but it is certain that all five acquired their rugby skills elsewhere. Clifford Charles Pritchard attended West Mon in the 1890s and his eight appearances for Wales included the famous 3-0 victory over the 1905 New Zealand All Blacks. The famous Jones brothers were also Old Westmonians; David 'Ponty' Jones won his only cap against Ireland in 1907; James 'Tuan' Jones toured Australia and New Zealand with the Anglo-Welsh team in 1908 before making his only Welsh appearance five years later against Scotland; and the youngest of the brothers, John 'Jack' Jones, also toured in 1908 and won 14 Welsh caps between 1908 and 1921, one of only seven players who represented Wales before and following the Great War. More recently Vince Griffiths had won three caps in 1924 and toured South Africa with the British Isles team in the same year.

A sixth name would be added to the list in 1947, but when Ken Jones first represented West Mon on a rugby field is not known. The *Free Press* was very supportive of the school, regularly reporting on First XV matches, but understandably the coverage didn't extend to the other teams. Neither did the school magazine review the Second XV and Colts' seasons beyond listing the results of matches played. All of which leaves us guessing a bit. What is known is that Ken played for the First XV during the seasons from 1937 to 1940 and it is a fair assumption that he was a Colts and Second XV player before being selected at the higher level. Newspaper reports confirm he played for the First XV against Caerleon College A on 12 March 1938 in a match that saw the school heavily defeated, 33 points to 5, but whether or not there were any earlier appearances remains open to speculation.

What we can say is that Ken was already familiar with the rudiments of the game when he started at West Mon. Under the guidance of Rees Jones and Miles Thomas, headmaster and games master at Blaenavon Church Boys Endowed School, he made his first tentative steps onto the field of play and in 1933, was selected for Blaenavon Boys against the youngsters of Mountain Ash. TW Dowson and JD Ridge were responsible for the Colts and Second XV at West Mon and must have played some part in Ken's development but once selected for the First XV he came under the watchful eye of Gilbert Garnett. A Yorkshireman, Garnett had graduated from Manchester University with a science degree in 1930, and added a physical education qualification before joining the school as PE master in 1931. Perhaps it was being brought up in the rugby league hotbed of Bradford that influenced his thinking on the 15-man game but his emphasis on players being able to tackle appears to have overridden any other skills the boys had to offer and it was in this crucial area that Ken Jones was once perceived to have shortcomings.

In 1938–39, Priestley House was captained by Derwyn Whent, another Blaenavon boy who was two years Ken's senior. Whent played on the right wing for both house and school, which meant Ken was selected on the left in house matches and it is highly probable that he continued in that role in his early games for the junior teams. Trial matches were a feature at the start of the term in September and Whent recalls facing Ken in one of the pre-season matches. 'I have always maintained that I taught Ken Jones how to tackle. During the trial match I had reason to tackle him hard and he ended up on the cinder running track that circled the playing field. He wasn't happy, downright angry in fact, and at the first opportunity he exacted his revenge by hammering me with a savage tackle and from that day on there were no weaknesses in his defence. Garnett was happy, because even if Ken had scored three tries, if his opposite number ran in four there would be no place for him in the team. Ken was eventually selected on his preferred right wing and I had to make way for him, moving to wing-forward before settling in at centre.'

Clearly Ken Jones was making a big impression on the school playing fields but in the classroom he was less of a leading light. At the end of his fourth year he passed the School Certificate examination, which allowed him to continue his formal education, and in September 1937 entered the fifth form with a reduced list of subjects on his timetable. Gone were chemistry, physics, French, Latin and religious instruction, leaving him to focus on what was classified as a general list of subjects as opposed to the two alternatives which stressed the sciences and arts. Ken would now concentrate on mathematics, English, biology, history, geography, woodwork and drawing – plus athletics and rugby.

By virtue of its elevated position, the grounds at West Mon were limited in scope and could not accommodate a rugby field. Home matches were played on the outskirts of Pontypool at the Skew Fields, Pontymoil. This necessitated the boys' changing at the school and walking down to the fields found half a mile away. The local community showed great interest in the fortunes of the First XV and it was not unusual for a crowd numbering several hundred to gather along the touchlines to cheer on the boys. It was also the place where representatives of local clubs would get a chance to cast an eye over any youngster who looked capable of holding his own in the lower levels of the senior game. Being at the centre of a thriving valley community there were many such clubs in the area, all of which had a place in the pyramid that saw the best talent eventually move on to a first-class club.

His name may have been put in several little black books as one to watch, but when Ken made his senior debut it was by accident rather than design. His mother's younger brother Lewis Burland lived and worked in Bristol, but this did not prevent him travelling home at weekends to play for Talywain, one of Blaenavon's greatest rivals. On 26 November 1938 Talywain were at home to Machen and Lewis took his young nephew to watch the match. Both teams were short of players and while the visitors set about their task with 14 men, Talywain invited Ken Jones to make up the numbers, the schoolboy still 34 days short of his 17th birthday. Ken may have had some experience in the school First XV but this was no preparation for the rough and tumble of the game at club level. Second-class rugby certainly didn't produce the highest quality of play but the endeavour and commitment was never less than total and the physical side could be brutal on occasion. It may not have been ideal grounding for a lad still wet behind the ears but it is pleasing to note that on his senior debut Ken Jones proved to be equal to the task. Two newspaper reports of the match confirmed he 'played a fine game. He is a strong runner with a safe pair of hands...' and 'Ken Jones of Blaenavon... showed that he has determination and speed...'

Talywain were keen to hold on to the young wing and there were further matches later that season against Crumlin, Blaenavon, Pill Harriers, Blackwood, Newbridge and Bedwas. All these matches had one thing in common – they were played on Saturdays when West Mon didn't have a fixture. After beating Machen 15-0, Talywain drew with Newbridge and Bedwas but Ken enjoyed only one victory in the club's colours. Despite appearing regularly in a losing team, the newspaper reports continued to report his progress favourably: '...another good game on the wing...'; '... promising display was given by Ken Jones on the wing but he had few chances... showed a good defence...'; 'showed speed but few chances...'; and he was even seen as being '... starved and wasted...'. In what appears to have been his final appearance for Talywain Ken scored his first try in senior rugby at Blackwood but it was not enough to prevent the visitors going down by 19 points to 3.

The rugby season fitted neatly into the school year, with matches played between 1 September and 30 April, but athletics did not conform quite as readily. The major meetings took place in July and August during the long summer holidays. In 1934, the South Wales & Mon AAA, the governing body of Welsh athletics prior to the formation of the Welsh AAA in 1948, organised what are recognised as the first schools championships, and in 1937, Glamorgan and Monmouthshire both formed county schools associations. Schoolboy athletes were now able to compete with their contemporaries from beyond the county boundary and by doing so a more realistic measurement of their ability could be assessed.

This was a positive step, but Ken knew that if he was to make progress in the highly competitive world of sprinting he would have to join a club enabling him to train and compete throughout the season. Just as the local rugby clubs were always on the lookout for the young talent being nurtured at schools, so too would representatives of the local athletic clubs keep their ears to the ground and follow up any positive recommendations. One of these, Vernon Parfitt, gained a reputation as an international rugby referee and would later serve the Welsh Rugby Union (WRU) with distinction, becoming its president in 1972–73. In the late 1930s, Parfitt was associated with Newport Athletic Club and it was on his recommendation that Ken Jones joined the famous club, firstly as a track star before his later involvement with the rugby section.

On 6 July 1939 Ken competed in what would prove to be his last sports day at West Mon. In the previous five years he had remained unbeaten over 100yds and 220yds. His final appearance would exceed all previous performances and see him win both sprints and the long and high jump competitions. He was without doubt the school's star performer, although he shared the victor ludorum with GR Hirst, who could not only run well but excelled at throwing things and was placed in several events. For the second time in his short life Ken had become a big fish in a small pond, but he knew that elsewhere in the Monmouthshire valleys there was another sprinter of outstanding ability, one who would prove to be his nemesis within the world of schoolboy athletics.

Eric Finney was a product of Ebbw Vale Secondary School and, like Ken, in recent years he had established himself as an exciting prospect. The two first met in 1939, at the Monmouthshire Secondary School Championships held at Abercarn. Finney won the 100yds with Ken runner-up and the same result was seen at the championships a year later. Coming up against boys from other schools in open events provided much stiffer opposition and Ken also had to be satisfied with second place in the long jump and hop, step and jump in 1939, but in 1940 there was cause for celebration when he won the hop, step and jump, his only Monmouthshire Schools title.

The 1940 Welsh Secondary Schools Championships held at Whitchurch High School, Cardiff, extended the boundaries further. Ken was relegated to third place in the 100yds behind Finney and a pupil of Canton Secondary School, Cardiff; he chased home Finney in the 220yds and was beaten into second place in the long jump and hop, step and jump competitions. This was the last time Ken Jones would compete in schoolboy athletics because he left West Mon before the end of term, missing the opportunity to compete in a seventh sports day. His last two athletics seasons had proved that beyond the environs of Pontypool there were others who could run faster and jump further, but on the rugby field during his last two seasons of schoolboy football Ken Jones had no peers.

At the start of that final year Ken was appointed captain of the First XV, succeeding GR Hirst, with whom he had shared the athletics victor ludorum in July. Hirst had led the team through two seasons but the school had not excelled, winning six and losing six of 12 matches played in 1937–38 and showing only a marginal improvement in winning eight, losing seven and drawing one in 1938–39. When Ken arrived at West Mon on Monday 4 September 1939 he knew the year would focus beyond the classroom as he had matriculated in the summer. Age was his problem; he wouldn't turn eighteen until December so his arrival at college had to be put on hold for a year. His priority in 1939–40 was to lead the school to success on the rugby field and there was the added incentive of winning a Welsh Schoolboys cap. Undoubtedly we are now talking about a person whose attitude had changed markedly since the day he had walked up the hill for the first time six years earlier. Looking at the three photographs of the First XV teams in which he featured, we see what appears to be a shy, unassuming boy in the back row mature into the confident-looking young man sitting next to the headmaster in his capacity as captain.

Less than 24 hours before the school opened its doors for the start of the new term, Britain had declared war on Germany. In the House of Commons at noon on Sunday 3 September Prime Minister Neville Chamberlain confirmed what the nation had been expecting following Germany's refusal to withdraw its troops from Poland. On 5 September the WRU suspended all senior rugby but the decision would not affect schools in the immediate future. Ken's season had actually started with a long overdue first appearance for

Blaenavon in a charity match played at the Recreation Ground against a team from John Morgan & Co, a local manufacturing company. He provided the highlight of the afternoon with a length-of-field run that saw him scorch down the touchline before making his way infield to score under the posts, the first of 30 tries he would register that season. There could have been more. Over the next eight months it was not the war that would have a disruptive effect on the fixture list, but a particularly harsh winter which caused the cancellation of five of the school's 18 arranged matches. Much improved from recent years, under Ken's captaincy West Mon First XV won 11 of the thirteen matches played. Notable among many outstanding team performances were three matches that took place in October. Cardiff High School were beaten 18-6, with two tries by the captain, and Abergavenny Grammar School were crushed 42-3, Ken crossing for six tries. But it was a first meeting with Monmouth School that produced the most exciting match of the campaign. Played at the Skew Fields on Tuesday 31 October, West Mon won a thrilling encounter 13-12 in front of a large crowd. Once again Ken got his name on the score sheet, bringing his total of tries to nine in three matches. This was form that could not be ignored and he maintained it in the new year when the Monmouthshire and national selectors began to consider their options for fixtures scheduled to be played against an Anglo-Welsh Public Schools team that would visit Wales during April. It would be selected from Welsh boys studying at English public schools and fixtures against West Wales, Monmouthshire and Mid-Glamorgan were confirmed before a meeting with Wales would take place at Cardiff Arms Park on 27 April.

Ken Jones made his first appearance for Monmouthshire Secondary Schools in a charity match played at Blaina against a combined Abertillery–Nantyglo Schools XV. The match took place on 6 April, and four days later the West Mon captain was included in the team to play the Public Schools at Newbridge. The combined Abertillery–Nantyglo team were beaten 13-0, Ken scoring two tries, and when the Public Schools were comfortably despatched 21-5, his name again featured as scorer of two of seven unconverted tries.

Ken Jones appeared on the right wing in each of his 44 senior appearances for Wales but for his first experience of international rugby he was selected on the left for the Welsh Secondary Schools against the Public Schools. The right wing berth was taken by G Williams of Newport High School but of the 15 players in the Secondary Schools team that day only Ken would play international rugby at the highest level. The same cannot be said of those who played for the Public Schools in Cardiff. Taking his place in the back row was a lad studying at Wellington College in Somerset. John Robins would tour with the British Lions in 1950, as would the young man who captained the team. With the scores tied at 6-6 and very few minutes remaining the 5,000-strong crowd were getting ready to head for the exits when the Public Schools skipper turned the match on its head. In the centre was a player of whom much was expected, one mature beyond his years, and in the final moments he scored two tries, both converted, to give the Public Schools a hard-fought 16-6 victory. Ken Jones would get to know Bleddyn Williams very well in the years to come, the pair striking up a life-long friendship, but it is certain that 27 April 1940 was the first of many matches in which they faced each other on the field of play. There would also be many memorable occasions when two of the greatest players of their generation joined forces.

Ken opted to finish his schooling after the spring term, spending time getting valuable work experience before heading off to college. For some years Panteg Steel Works at nearby Griffithstown had welcomed parties of sixth formers, who were given an extensive tour of the plant which introduced them to the intricacies of steel manufacture. He may have elected to favour subjects leading to a general qualification but Ken did have an interest in the sciences and his presence on one of the school visits appears to have created a favourable impression.

In 1952, the November edition of *Ingot*, the magazine for employees of Richard Thomas and Baldwins Ltd, produced an article on Ken's sporting achievements and confirmed that he had once worked as a laboratory assistant at the Panteg plant. He spent four months on the payroll, cycling to work regardless of which shift he was on. If there were any thoughts of abandoning his plans to pursue a career in teaching for one in the steel industry they were soon dispelled when a colleague confirmed that while it may have been a good job '…it was not good for the lungs…'. This was not what a young athlete with great sporting ambitions wanted to hear and in September 1940 Ken Jones set out for Cheltenham, where the air was guaranteed not to pose any such threat to his health.

CHAPTER TWO

FROM CHELTENHAM TO CAWNPORE

S t Paul's College, Cheltenham, had long been recognised as one of England's leading teacher training institutions. Together with St Mary's College, which catered for girls, St Paul's produced annually in excess of 150 qualified teachers after completion of a two-year course. Established in 1847, St Paul's is located in the centre of Cheltenham and although much has changed with the addition of new buildings and departments, the main body structure as designed by Samuel Daukes, a well-respected architect from the town, still dominates the campus. The original college building accommodated the comparatively small number of students in dormitories situated on the first floor overlooking the quadrangle and it was here that Ken Jones would spend much of the next two years.

From the discipline exacted on the pupils at West Mon the more mature students now came under the regime of dean of the college, Canon Wilfred E Beck, and his staff, who demanded a higher level of work ethic and responsibility from them than may have previously been experienced.

For example, the college operated a strict curfew policy, monitored with even greater diligence following the outbreak of the Second World War. Any chance of breaking the 10.30pm Saturday deadline was minimal as students would have to negotiate their way past the living quarters of the principle, vice-principle and college superintendent, each of whom resided in strategic parts of the main building. If any of these failed to notice any curfew breakers making their guilty way back to the dorms there was always 'Sarge' Harper, who served as porter at the college for more than 30 years, waiting in support.

In all probability, other than when working shifts at Panteg Steel Works, Ken had never spent a night away from his parents' home before leaving for Cheltenham in September 1940. Not only would he have to adjust to a new regime that would play havoc with his morning routine but he would also spend periods of two to three months away from his home town. Ken would not have appreciated it at the time, but the everyday routines and general way of life with which he was so familiar soon became things of the past on arrival in Cheltenham. He would never forget his roots and remained extremely proud of his association with Blaenavon, but apart from a few months at the end of the war, he would not live again in his place of birth. Such changes are much more readily accepted in the twenty-first century but were far from commonplace in 1940, and it would have been reassuring to see some familiar faces. The intake of students at St Paul's in 1940 included ten from South Wales, among them Eric Finney, the Ebbw Vale lad who had given Ken such a hard time on the athletics track in recent years. The journey to destinations new began at Lower Level and covered the familiar route to Pontypool, but this time Ken remained on board until the train reached Newport, from where he caught the connection that would take him through Chepstow, the Forest of Dean, and Gloucester before arriving at Cheltenham Spa station.

College education was relatively expensive in 1940, certainly when compared with the average wage. Firstly there was a £2 acceptance fee to be paid, which was followed by a payment of £48 made on admission that would cover the costs of board and lodging for the first academic year with a further payment of £50 to be paid at the start of the second. Ken Jones had been granted a scholarship, meaning the basic fees would be paid, but there were additional incidental costs still to be found. These included a £1 annual fee which allowed the student to partake in the various sporting activities on offer; 5/0 (five shillings – 25 pence) allowed use of the common room; and at the end of the two years there was a £2.10 (two pounds fifty pence) entrance fee for the final examinations set by the Western Joint Committee of the University of Bristol and Training Colleges. Other costs included the college blazer, a striking design of navy and light blue stripes manufactured by Thomas Plant & Co of Cheltenham, together with the accompanying tie, suitable trousers, shirts and shoes, all of which were supplied by The Famous, outfitters of long-standing experience and a Cheltenham institution. Students were also expected to finance any costs relating to visits home; not that there would be many beyond the normal end-of-term breaks.

There was a familiar structure about the week, with lessons, which included Saturday mornings, dominating the timetable. That aside, the curriculum made generous allowances for sporting activities and most Saturdays would see the First XV in action before the running track was marked out for the summer term. Additionally, students were expected to attend services at the chapel on Sunday and it was here that the young men of St Paul's would get the opportunity to cast an eye over the young ladies attending St Mary's as both colleges would observe the sabbath together under the guidance of Canon Beck. Strict segregation was observed, the male and female contingents arriving at the chapel separately before taking their respective places on either side of the nave, but it was difficult to monitor a large group of curious teenagers and following the service the Sims (female students at St Mary's) often had company on the walk back to college. At the start of his second year Ken would need no introduction to one of the new arrivals at St Mary's: Irene Edmunds had gained admittance to the college and the couple would both reside in Cheltenham during the 1941–42 academic year.

When Ken Jones arrived at Cheltenham to start his first year at college, the Second World War entered its second. The Luftwaffe had been making night raids over Britain for some time, with London the prime target, but as 1940 drew to a close cities beyond the capital were targeted, often with devastating effect. St Paul's Cathedral suffered a direct hit on 10 October, but it was Coventry that experienced the most damage and highest number of casualties. On the night of 14 November much of the city was flattened, with more than 1,000 civilians killed. The RAF responded with a raid on Hamburg during which 2,000 bombs were dropped but Goering maintained the air assaults on Britain, attacks centred on Birmingham and the surrounding Midlands bringing more misery. Liverpool, Manchester, Glasgow and Southampton were subjected to extensive raids by as many as 400 German bombers before the focus turned to Cheltenham, which came under attack for the first time on 11 December, with part of St Mary's College suffering a direct hit.

At the outbreak of the conflict the War Office had requisitioned St Mary's for immediate use should the need arise and the staff and students were relocated to Llandrindod Wells in mid-Wales. While the main college premises sat empty, work that had started in the summer of 1939 on a new building at Fullwood Park, which would eventually house new halls of residence, was allowed to continue and it was this unoccupied structure that received the direct hit. Plans to bring the staff and students back to Cheltenham were put on hold but normal service was resumed in January. Apart from a brief period of occupation by the Auxiliary Territorial Service, St Mary's College was not used by the War Office and the remaining years of the war passed without further disruption to the pursuit of knowledge at Cheltenham's colleges.

St Paul's College rarely had more than 150 students on its books but in 1940 two rugby XVs and three soccer teams played other colleges, universities and local clubs on a regular basis. During the latter months of the academic year it was the turn of cricket, tennis and athletics, each of which enjoyed equally strong fixtures. A gymnasium had been built over the assembly hall in 1914 but it wasn't until the late 1930s that PE started to gain some recognition as a serious discipline, one that had to be taught competently by trained teaching staff. St Paul's was among the first colleges to recognise this but it would be some years before a recognised qualification could be gained. For Ken Jones this would mean a further year in college at a later date, but that final chapter in his education was to be completed elsewhere. Meanwhile it was geography and English that became the focus of his attention, but rugby and athletics never failed to find their way into his itinerary with no opportunity to don the boots and spikes passed up.

With the experience gained at West Mon, a Welsh Secondary Schools cap and several appearances for a local club under his belt it is not surprising that within a short time Ken was involved in college rugby. Well known he may have been in the eastern valleys of South Wales but this counted for little at a new institution, one based in England no less, and one that attracted students from across the country. Age had never proved to be a barrier and while he may initially have been competing for a place in the First XV with students a year older, Ken quickly earned selection on the wing and would remain a regular first-team player during his two years at St Paul's.

With the recent introduction of physical education courses there was a need for staff with some experience in the field. Such personnel were a scarce commodity and it fell to Reg 'Buster' Riley, a student at the college between 1920 and 1922, to launch the new course. Riley was noted as an all-round sportsman but his only qualification to teach PE came via a course held at Scarborough during the summer holidays. Better than nothing maybe, but with the accent on advanced physical education qualifications, the search continued for someone who had attended a more recognised course. Harry Smith had gained his qualification in Denmark (Scandinavia long recognised as leaders in the field) and he joined the staff in 1938 to help establish a course that would eventually gain recognition. Ken's studies may have majored on geography and English but he also took the opportunity to study the new physical education course, which may not have taken him beyond a level commensurate with that attained in other subjects at grammar schools but would prove useful when he made the decision to make PE his first subject.

What we see now is a young man who had grasped the fact he needed to make a commitment not seen before if he was to make something of himself, and that St Paul's was where this would be done. After working his way through school without ever threatening to make a mark as an exceptional pupil in the classroom this was new territory. *The Westmonian* reported his many achievements on the fields of play but the entry KJ Jones, Priestley, is absent from the lists of School Prizes. Ken was never a recipient of the 'Stewart' Prize for General Knowledge, the Old Boys' Prize for General Proficiency or any of the other academically related awards presented at the annual speech day. Neither did he pick up any of the various form prizes on offer. Nor is there any mention of Ken having been involved in the debating society, the dramatic society or the chess club. Suffice to say that if looking for the name KJ Jones in the school magazine one should seek out the sports sections where it is ever present between 1933 and 1940.

That he entered further education at a well-respected college confirms that the substance was there even though it was yet to surface. It was at St Paul's that Ken finally realised that sooner or later he was going to have to make his way in the world and as his plans didn't include following his father underground, he was not going to let this opportunity pass. Every record of his two years in Cheltenham confirms a welcome change of intent and at 18 he at last began to make his mark in the academic world. There would be the occasional transgression from the straight and narrow but these instances were more frequent in his second year, when Irene may have led him astray; overall, we are talking about a model student. In his second year Ken became a proctor, a college prefect, and was also called upon to write a piece for inclusion in the 1941–42 *MS Chelt*, a large tome which tells the story of each academic year in the words of the students. As captain of the First XV he wrote three pages on the season in a hand best described as scholarly; the work of someone who took great pride in their handwriting, as autograph hunters would later confirm. Academic endeavour may have reached beyond anything seen before but this was not allowed to impact in any way, shape or form on his involvement in college sport, and not long after his arrival in Cheltenham it was business as usual – rugby football September to April and athletics in May and June.

The two-year course meant there was little age disparity between those students in their second year and the new arrivals. Whether a student was 18 or 19 years of age became of little significance when teams to represent the college were selected; all that mattered was how good he was. The Welsh Secondary Schools cap and a fast-growing reputation meant Ken could not be ignored and after leading the new entrants against the senior students in the annual 'Jam' match he was immediately fast tracked into the First XV. The 'Jam' match brought the two academic years together on the soccer and rugby fields. In 1940 the junior side won the soccer match 3-1 but under Ken's captaincy the rugby players could not secure a rare double, losing by three points to nil.

The College fixture lists were affected by the outbreak of war and saw a reduction in the number of matches played in previous seasons. Culham College, Dudley College and King's College London, which had been evacuated to Bristol, were all included, as was Caerleon College, giving Ken a rare opportunity to see family and friends when St Paul's travelled into Wales for the away fixture. Local forces camps also raised teams and there are records of matches against Staverton RAF, Little Rissington RAF and the 5th Battalion of the King's Regiment. Birmingham University, Goldsmith's College London and Rotol Airscrews, a local engineering company, were also included but it was the matches against Cheltenham Town that created the biggest interest. Usually played at the Athletic Ground, these were well advertised in the local press and there was always an admission charge. On 18 October 1941 spectators paid 1/- for admittance to a covered stand, 7d gained entrance to the ground and for HM Forces in uniform there was a concessionary charge of 3d – all good value to see what the local press promoted as 'Another Grand Match'.

The 1940–41 season had produced a mixed bag of results. Under the captaincy of EB Ebborn seven matches were won and eight lost, including those against Cheltenham Town, but a year later, on that October day, the students gained a rare victory. Ken took over the captaincy from Ebborn, who had completed his course, and appointed fellow Welshman Eifion 'Taffy' Davies, a hooker from Cwmavon, as his vice-captain. England schoolboy international Jimmy Morton was a regular in the pack and 'Conk' Norman, a prop forward who appears to have lost his way, had an outstanding season in the centre, scoring many barnstorming tries and on occasion taking over the place-kicking duties. It was Norman's try, converted by Davies, that secured the 5-0 victory over Cheltenham, one of many notable results in what was a grand campaign. Staverton RAF were beaten 73-0, Birmingham University 19-0, Little Rissington RAF 69-0 and the 5th Battalion King's Regiment 41-3, a match in which Ken ran in six tries. On the negative side there was a surprise defeat against Rotol, and later in the season Cheltenham gained revenge for the earlier defeat, winning the second encounter between the teams 11-0.

At the end of the season St Paul's entered a team in a seven-a-side tournament organised to raise funds for the Aid to Russia appeal. Held at the Athletic Ground, it was the first sevens tournament played in the town and attracted teams from the RAF, the Welsh Army and Cheltenham, who all entered A and B sides, together with Rotol, Smiths Ltd, Old Patesians, Lydney and St Paul's. On the back of a good season, and with a team that exuded pace in every position, the students were going to be difficult to beat and after defeating RAF B and Cheltenham B on their way to the final the college ran out 13-5 victors against the Welsh Army A team to win the tournament in some style.

Ken's involvement in athletics at St Paul's was limited due to the short period during which the summer term and the recognised season ran concurrently. His most reported performances came in a triangular match held at the college grounds, against teams from the universities of Birmingham and Bristol. The meeting received extensive pictorial coverage in the *Cheltenham Chronicle and Gloucester Graphic* and the report highlights Ken's great achievement in winning the 100yds, 220yds and long jump competitions, three events in which he created new College records before graduating in June 1942.

It is worth recording at this point Ken's close attachment to St Paul's, which continued long after he had finished his studies. He regularly attended reunions and in 1949 was present at the retirement of Canon Beck. Eight years later, in June 1957, he was invited to officially open the new pavilion at the Folley, the college's sports ground, and wasted no time in confirming his acceptance to the principal. The occasion was marked with a triangular athletics meeting between St Paul's, Old Chelts (college old boys) and Cheltenham and County Harriers. Before performing his duties, Ken, now 35, ran in the 100yds, coming second to D Drinkwater, another Old Chelt but eight years his junior. In a race started by 'Buster' Riley, both men recorded even times of 10.0, equalling the college record set by Ken in 1941.

Following the two years at Cheltenham there was only one direction open to Ken. He received his call-up papers within a matter of weeks of returning to Blaenavon and joined the RAF. The next few months were spent receiving basic training, firstly at RAF St Athan, a camp ten miles to the west of Cardiff, before being transferred to Kirkham in Lancashire. The following March, Leading Aircraftman Jones became a qualified instructor under the RAF's Educational and Vocational Training Scheme and was told to prepare for duty overseas.

When Japan attacked Pearl Harbor on 7 December 1941 the war in Europe became a global conflict. The following day Britain declared war on Japan and the War Office, aware that the Japanese effort would soon focus on South East Asia, immediately ordered troops to India. Japan's strike was both swift and successful. Hong Kong quickly fell as the offensive gathered momentum and the massive mobilisation of troops continued south towards the important naval base at Singapore; on 15 February 1942, the Japanese took control of the island. With the fall of Singapore, not only had the Allies lost an important link between the Indian and Pacific Oceans but Japan had gained a stronghold from which it could begin an assault through Thailand and Burma into India.

In March 1943 LAC Jones joined a troop ship preparing to set sail for the Far East. There were stops at Cape Town and Durban before it docked in Bombay (now Mumbai) at the end of April. He arrived in a country not only finding itself embroiled in war but one also experiencing massive internal turmoil as the fight for home rule continued regardless of issues elsewhere. The previous year Britain had presented a plan for independence which it was hoped would stabilise the country and allow the growing threat of Japanese invasion to be defended. Mahatma Gandhi advised rejection of the offer and even went so far as to suggest that the Japanese should not be resisted. It was in a country of 319 million people that the man from Blaenavon now found himself, one of thousands of British troops charged with defending the borders while the politicians tried to keep the peace within them.

LAC Jones was routed to RAF Chakeri, based near Cawnpore in the troubled north-east. The major threat from Japan lay along the Burmese border and since the fall of Mandalay in May 1942, the Japanese had made great advances towards it. In March 1944 an Allied operation of great daring saw a large contingent of men and equipment dropped 200 miles behind enemy lines. Flown in by gliders, the troops cleared a landing strip which allowed the main force access and the operation marked the beginning of the end for the invading army. A month later the Allies won a resounding victory at Kohima on the Imphal Plain, the Japanese army was forced back and India was reprieved.

On 7 May 1945, Germany's unconditional surrender, signed by General Alfred Jodl at General Eisenhower's headquarters in Rheims, marked the end of the war in Europe. It would be three months before Emperor Hirohito performed a similar duty to bring an end to the Second World War. Then the mammoth task of repatriation could begin, but for the now promoted Sergeant Jones, it would be another eight months before he returned home.

A natural athlete, Ken had maintained a high level of fitness during his time on the subcontinent. Throughout the campaign rugby matches were played between teams from the various RAF and Army units based in India and in

1944 Ken helped his division to victory in the India United Province Challenge Cup. In August 1945 he represented RAF (Chakeri) Cawnpore in the rather long-winded Cawnpore Rugby Football Challenge Cup Tournament. The knock-out competition played over two weeks saw RAF (Chakeri) defeat RAF (Phaphamau) Allahabad and La Martiniere Rugby Club, Lucknow before losing 12-8 in the final to the 16th Infantry Brigade, Dehra Dun.

Take a group of men, find them a suitable tract of land, give them a football or rugby ball and they will play to their hearts' content. Team sport will always prevail, but for an individual who performs alone the same criteria does not automatically follow. The search for serious competition will likely take him beyond the boundaries, away from the daily kickabout. In 1946, a series of athletics meetings saw Ken Jones leave his own individual mark on Indian sport. It all started at a local meeting held in Cawnpore where the Welshman won the 100yds title in even time and the 220yds in 23.0. He was also runner-up in the long jump and was selected to represent the province in the United Provinces Olympiad at Lucknow. Yards became metres but Ken continued to dominate the sprints, winning the 100m in 10.7 and the 200m in 22.2. Both times created new championship records, significantly improving on the previous bests of 11.0 and 23.0, and there was another second place in the long jump. Reporting on the meeting a journalist likened Ken to being 'somewhat of a Jesse Owens. His name is on everyone's lips...'.

The final meeting of the season was the prestigious All India Olympiad held at Bangalore. Selected to represent the United Provinces in the 100m, the only European in the team, Ken set out on a 1,000-mile journey that took three days to complete. It was in Bangalore that he met up with Dick Burland, his mother's younger brother who, hearing of his nephew's outstanding achievements on the track, was desperately keen to see him run in the Olympiad. How much travelling this entailed is not known but Dick's attendance at the track was rewarded when he saw Ken beat off the challenges of 26 other competitors representing 16 provinces. After making his way through the early rounds, the Welshman won the 100m title with a time of 10.8, only 0.2 outside the All India record. Comparisons with the great American athlete Jesse Owens may have been the excited opinion of one journalist but they were the first suggestion that Ken Jones may have the talent to compete on the sport's biggest stage. When there would be a resumption of the Olympic Games was yet to be announced but it was something upon which Ken could begin to focus and he had the additional experience under his belt of running over the metric distances favoured by the International Olympic Committee.

Ken Jones and Irene Edmunds had become engaged in February 1943, a month before he headed overseas. In the following months and years many letters made their way from the north-east of India to the south-east of Wales and an equal number had gone the other way, but the couple had not seen each other for over three years. On completion of her two years at St Mary's, Irene had accepted a teaching post at a school in the Birmingham suburb of Smethwick, and it was to the Midlands that Ken was instructed to go on his return, where the formalities of his demobilisation would be completed. The journey home was much quicker than the outward one, with the RAF bringing troops back via the Middle East with a fuel stop at Lydda (now Lod) in Palestine. Ken knew that his old house captain at West Mon was stationed in the area and with six hours at his disposal he set about finding Derwyn Whent, but to no avail. Their reunion would be put on hold until they were back in Blaenavon.

Irene was working with a class of pupils when she received word there was a phone call for her. This was not accepted practice at the school and she was concerned there may be a problem back home but when she picked up the receiver it was Ken's voice at the other end. They arranged to meet outside

Snow Hill Station in Birmingham, but when Irene arrived there was no sign of Ken. She gave only a passing glance to the tall, dark-skinned chap sporting a paper-thin moustache until he approached her. Three years was a long time and Irene could be forgiven for not immediately recognising her fiancé; the unassuming young man she'd bade farewell to in 1943 was no longer. In his place was the dashing, upright individual now standing in front of her. A little under six feet tall and weighing in at what would remain his fighting weight of 12 stone, Ken Jones was a welcome sight – but that moustache would have to go!

On his return to Blaenavon, Ken set about searching for a teaching post but with the long summer holiday approaching there was time to kill before he could expect to start work in September. The rugby season was coming to an end but after attending a training session, Ken made a first senior appearance for his home town; if one excludes the charity match against Jon Morgan's XV played before the war. Blaenavon beat Risca 9-0 at the Recreation Ground in a match postponed from earlier in the season and home supporters were treated to a fine display by the new man on the right wing. Ken scored his first try for the club, side-stepping inside two defenders before outpacing any would-be tacklers in a dash for the line. Rescheduled for a Thursday evening, this was the first of three matches played over the Easter holiday. Two days later Blaenavon entertained Blackwood and again it was the flying wing who caught the eye, Ken scoring four of his team's nine tries in a resounding 31-0 victory. Ebbw Vale were expected to provide much stronger opposition but Blaenavon were in fine form and the visitors from across the valley were comfortably despatched 19-3, Ken among the scorers.

Heady days they may have been but the one thing all the players, officials and supporters of Blaenavon RFC knew was that, come the start of new season in September, Ken Jones would be playing his rugby elsewhere. Nobody could go into denial; this outstanding local talent was going to make his name in the game but sadly it would not be in the town's colours. Before the season finished Ken was invited to play for Pontypool in the club's final match. This was not his first appearance in the famous red, black and white colours. During his last term at West Mon, Pontypool selected the recently capped schoolboy to play against a Midlands Counties XV led by Gwyn Bayliss, a former club captain, in a charity match in aid of the Area War Comforts Fund. His second appearance for Pontypool was against Cardiff, a totally different proposition to lining up against a scratch invitation team and a big step up from his recent experiences with Blaenavon. Unfortunately, Cardiff had entered a team in the Middlesex Sevens, also played on the last Saturday of the season, and as a consequence several leading players were missing. There was no Bleddyn Williams, Jack Matthews, Billy Cleaver or Cliff Davies, which improved the home team's chances of a rare victory over the Blue and Blacks, but a disappointing match ended in a 3-3 draw. Supporters and all those involved with Pontypool RFC would have been delighted if Ken had expressed an interest in playing for the club in the following season. The same could be said of Cardiff RFC but when the decision was made it would see him take up residence at a club of which he was already a member.

Also back in Blaenavon after serving in the Middle East was Ken's old house captain. Derwyn Whent had proved difficult to find in Palestine but he and Ken were not hard to track down in the town, the pair in the habit of spending mornings in the Conservative Club. A pint of beer, a game of snooker and a perusal of the racing pages became part of the day, Ken and Derwyn making use of a Pontypool bookmaker's runner who would collect bets in the surrounding towns. Nobody could deny them their extended leisure time but it could not continue. For Ken, no sooner had the rugby season drawn to a close than it was time to dig out the spikes and get back on the track. Vernon Parfitt had first introduced the young Ken Jones to Newport Athletic Club while he was still at West Mon and the members' list includes him in the junior section in 1935. It was only to be expected that when he felt ready to return to the track it would be at Newport and much of that summer of 1946 would see Ken take the train from the Lower Level to the town and club with which he was destined to become associated for the rest of his sporting life and beyond.

Newport Athletic Club occupied a 15-acre site alongside the River Usk. A short walk from the station led to the old town bridge, over which could be found the gates of Rodney Parade, home of Newport Athletic Club and Newport RFC. This became a well-trodden path for Ken as he began to put in the training sessions that would take him back to full fitness. Many hours were spent honing the muscles during that first summer home, time spent between the track and the gymnasium, mostly with only himself for company.

The first major athletics meeting of the season saw a renewal of the Welsh Championships, last held in 1939 at Newport Athletic club. The parcel of land that accommodated the running track was requisitioned by the military during the war and would not be handed back to the club until 1947. Interim arrangements had been made by marking out a running track around the rugby pitch and while it may have served the purpose of a young man going through his paces it did not meet the standards required by the governing body. In 1946 the championships were held at Sloper Road in Cardiff, where on 6 July Ken Jones first made his mark as a senior Welsh athlete, winning both the 100yds and 220yds titles. There were other meetings and other titles during the season but two issues were uppermost in Ken's thoughts. Firstly he needed to find a job, and secondly he still hadn't decided where he would play his rugby in the coming season, which would see the reintroduction of international rugby with the Five Nations Championship scheduled to begin with Scotland's visit to Paris on 1 January.

Life was about to get complicated. Ken accepted a teaching post at Bathwick Junior School in Bath, meaning he would have to move home. Fortunately his uncle Lew Burland was still living in Bristol with his family and had a spare room available if Ken wanted it. In fact Lew lived at Saltford, a small village to the south-east of the city which straddled the Bath Road and was a short bus ride from the famous city with its Roman Baths and Regency architecture. Getting to work would not present any problems. Irene was still working in Birmingham, but with Ken having found a job in the West Country she could now start searching for something suitable in the area. All that remained was to find a rugby club that would appreciate his services, and of course it was there, staring him in the face every time he trained at Newport Athletic Club.

CHAPTER THREE

CAPS, CUPS AND A PRIZE CATCH

Newport RFC played a limited number of matches during the early years of the Second World War but a structured fixture list was put together for the 1944–45 season. Under the captaincy of Jim Hawkins, 27 matches were played and in addition to the more familiar Cardiff, Bristol, Wasps and Abertillery, also included were Cardiff Medicals, Filton, Rotol, Brecon ITC and RAF St Athan; clubs that would not appear on the fixture list again. The following season Swansea, Neath, Leicester and Gloucester were among those clubs renewing fixtures and by 1946–47 there was a very familiar look about the list of scheduled matches; Blackheath, Llanelly, London Welsh, Cross Keys together with Cambridge and Oxford Universities would all make a welcome return to Rodney Parade.

Before the season could get under way it was usual to hold a series of trial matches, which would give a chance to those players wanting to join the club to showcase their talent, and on 2 September Ken Jones took to the field for his first rugby outing at Rodney Parade.

Such was the interest shown by local players wanting to join the club, together with those returning from the previous season, that two matches were played on that Monday evening with another to follow on Wednesday, by which time many of the hopefuls would have been eliminated. Trial teams came in many guises, particularly at international level, where a final trial would see the Probables and Possibles test each other after the Reds and Whites had lined up in a match played earlier in the season. Nothing so sophisticated was seen around the clubs and the four teams that took to the field for the first round of trial matches at Newport were simply called A, B, C and D. In the first match Ken scored three tries in the A team's comprehensive 19-3 victory over B. The four sides were selected at random so it was no surprise when D beat C 14-3, leaving the selectors the task of picking 30 players from those on show and giving a polite thanks but no thanks to the others who would not be required two days later. On Wednesday, Ken took his place in the Probables, scoring a try in the 22-11 victory over the Possibles, but try scoring aside, over the two matches he had shown enough all-round ability to convince the selectors he should be given a chance. When the team to play in the season's opening match was announced, Ken Jones was one of 13 players selected who had featured in the Probables XV. After sitting out the trial matches, club captain Jack Bale and wing forward RT Evans joined them in the starting line-up and it was the visit of Penarth to Rodney Parade that got the season under way on 7 September.

Newport played six matches in 22 days and were unbeaten come the end of the month. These are impressive statistics but unfortunately ones that don't stand close inspection. Games against Llanelly, Abertilley and Pontypool all ended scoreless, disappointing results for Newport after comfortable home and away victories the previous season. Swansea were also beaten twice in 1945–46, but with the early season visit to Swansea ending in a 14-14 draw, Newport's unbeaten record showed only Penarth and Bristol were defeated in that opening month. Perhaps this unconvincing start to the season could be put down to the jerseys? Newport's colours were recognised wherever the game was played; jerseys with black and amber hoops, black shorts and black stockings with two amber hoops at the top. The 1946–47 season saw the first team play in unfamiliar amber tops, suppliers still struggling to get materials and production lines back to normal after the war and those used in previous seasons showing much wear and tear. It would be 12 months and 24 matches into his career with the club before Ken Jones would get his hands on the real thing.

Ten matches were played through October and November, seven won with another 0-0 draw with Llanelly. Any perceived progress these results may suggest was spoilt by the two defeats that came at the hands of Cardiff, the club which had been Newport's greatest rivals since time immemorial. Such local derbies were major events on the club calendar and both were watched with interest by those men who would select the first Welsh team to take the field for eight years. International selection is rarely an easy task but that which faced the Welsh selectors in 1946 was particularly difficult following the extended break in fixtures. The only consolation was that the other home nations were in a similar position, but there was every likelihood that Wales would be represented by 15 uncapped players when the team to play England ran out at Cardiff Arms Park in January. This placed even greater emphasis on the trial matches and three were scheduled, the last due to take place in Cardiff on 4 January, two weeks before the resumption of international rugby in Wales.

The first was held on 2 November at a wet and windswept Ynysangharad Park in Pontypridd. Thirty hopefuls were in attendance with only Cardiff forward Les Manfield having previous experience of an international trial. Haydn Tanner, the Swansea scrum-half, was another familiar with the trial system but although selected he was unable to travel. Both men had represented Wales before the war, Manfield playing in the last two internationals while Tanner won his first cap in 1935 and had featured in every match since. The scrum-half was probably the selectors' preferred choice to be Wales' first post-war captain but his appearance in a trial would have to wait for another day. There was much swapping and changing at Pontypridd, players asked to mix and match as the selectors watched on in the hope that part of the puzzle would be solved but with very little to cheer. Newport had six representatives on show; club captain Jack Bale, RT Evans, Ken Jones and Hedley Rowland in the Probables with DR Morgan and George Parsons lining up for the Possibles. The selectors may have been disappointed with much of the talent on show at Pontypridd but time would see six of the Probables team selected to face England. Early days for sure but the jigsaw was starting to come together.

Ken Jones was approaching his 25th birthday but in truth he had relatively little experience of rugby football beyond his school and college days. There had been appearances for Talywain, Blaenavon and Pontypool but his first-class career had barely got under way with only a handful of matches for Newport to his name. Now he was not only taking the field in select company but also had a serious chance of winning a first Welsh cap. There are the well-documented circumstances that led to Ken and many other new faces lining up at Pontypridd and eight years on from Wales' last match the selectors were faced with a blank sheet of paper on which the future would be drafted.

Would Ken have represented Wales earlier if the international calendar had not been interrupted? This is an issue purely for conjecture but suffice to say that before the outbreak of war the right-wing berth was certainly up for grabs. In the six championship matches played in 1938 and 1939 WH Clement of Llanelly, Swansea's J Idwal Rees, FJV Ford from the Welsh Regiment, another Llanelly representative in Elvet L Jones and Bridgend's Chris Matthews were all selected on the right wing. Furthermore, in the uncapped match against the New Zealand Kiwis played in 1946 it was Newport's WE Williams who got the chance to impress. Six players selected on the right wing in the seven matches played over an eight-year period. At nineteen years of age Ken may have been considered too young in 1940 but his chance would surely have come earlier than January 1947.

Come December it was the turn of Newport to host the second trial match. The teams were much changed from the earlier selections with the home club's representation now reduced to five. Ken and George Parsons were chosen in the Probables with Hedley Rowland, Reg Blakemore and RT Evans in a Possibles team led by Rowland. Ken scored a try at Pontypridd in the Probables' 9-0 victory but failed to get on the scoreboard in front of his home crowd in what was another win for the 'senior' team, this time by 10-3. Did the selectors go home happier after this second trial match? Probably, as they would go with 11 of the players on show when convening to pick the team to face England. But there was still much work to be done.

While Ken and his club colleagues were playing in the second trial, Newport had travelled to Bristol and returned empty-handed, losing a close match 6-3, the third defeat of the season. Then followed a run of eight consecutive victories, the club benefiting from a delivery of straw which was used to cover the pitch during a particularly cold snap of weather. When Swansea visited Newport on 21 December the match was able to go ahead despite the freezing conditions, the only game played in Wales that day. The Welsh selectors had little option but to turn out in force at Rodney Parade before announcing the teams for the final trial from which it was expected the Welsh XV would be chosen.

The final Welsh trial took place at Cardiff on 4 January. Representing Newport, DR Morgan, RT Evans and Ken lined up for the Probables with Reg Blakemore and George

Parsons included in the Possibles pack, with the promising Newport and Cambridge University centre Ken Spray given a chance to show what he could do at this level following a run of good performances, in particular in Newport's recent 14-5 home win against Swansea. A disappointing match saw the teams score two unconverted tries apiece and while the backs were starting to fall into place the same could hardly be said about the forwards. It is doubtful if the selectors were in unanimous agreement about any of the eight positions at this late stage, and the England match was now only two weeks away. They made no secret of the fact they would attend the Monmouthshire–Glamorgan county match at Newport the following Thursday and the press began writing that encounter up as an unofficial trial. The county sides had met earlier in the season at the Gnoll, Neath with Monmouthshire winning an exciting match 19-13. Ken Jones caught the eye that day with a try scored from fully 60 yards out and at Rodney Parade a similar effort was the only score in a match from which the selectors would have gleaned very little.

When the Welsh team was finally announced it included two men who had played before the war in Llanelly full-back C Howard Davies and Haydn Tanner, who would captain the side. The Cardiff midfield trio of Bleddyn Williams, Billy Cleaver and Jack Matthews got the nod with Cleaver in the centre and Williams at outside-half, a reversal of their future roles. Newport's Reg Blakemore and George Parsons were selected up front and Ken Jones was named on the right wing. Confirming the problems when selecting the forwards, now included was Neath second row JRG Stephens, who had not appeared in any of the trial matches. It was an unwritten law that players selected for a first cap should be excluded from their club sides the week before their international debut, which meant the Newport trio would miss the club's two-match tour of Devon with matches against Plymouth and Devonport Services. In being selected to represent his country it was somewhat ironic that Ken would pull on the red jersey of Wales before he donned the black and amber hoops of Newport – the two sets of colours in which he would set the rugby world alight.

When Ken Jones ran out with the Welsh team at Cardiff Arms Park on 18 January 1947 he was 25 years and 20 days old. He stood 5 feet 11 inches tall and weighed 12 stone. When Wales took to the field at Cardiff Arms Park on 19 January 1957 for another encounter with the old enemy, Ken was 35 years and 21 days old, stood 5 feet 11 inches tall and weighed 12 stone. There was one significant difference between the two occasions – in 1957 Ken Jones was not in the Welsh team. Perhaps that isn't surprising as ten years would have passed since his debut. Bleddyn Williams, Jack Matthews and Billy Cleaver among others were also absent in 1957 but the match does have some significance in that it was the first time Ken did not take his place in the side since his debut. For 43 consecutive matches (there would be one more) the man on the right wing was listed in the match programme as KJ Jones (Newport). By 1957 KJ Jones would have rewritten the history books but it is certain that the 43,000 spectators at the Arms Park in January 1947; the great Welsh rugby public who weren't in attendance; the various committee men, administrators and selectors; the players; and even Ken Jones himself would have viewed such a prospect as nigh on impossible. Ten years and 43 consecutive caps? You must be having a laugh!

And when Wales trooped off the beaten side the odds on such a record probably lengthened, although the finger of blame could not be pointed at Ken Jones. He received few chances, largely due to the lacklustre performance of the pack, who struggled throughout and even failed to gain any ascendancy with England reduced to seven forwards with Mickey Steele-Bodger moved to centre following the departure of the injured Keith Scott. Wales were leading 6-5 after scoring two tries to England's one, but a late dropped goal, then worth four points, saw the visitors secure victory. Three Welsh players – Llanelly's Griff Bevan together with Reg Blakemore and George Parsons of Newport – would never play for their country again. They were among the four forwards dropped for the trip to Edinburgh, which confirmed what had been all too apparent during the trial matches. Of the backs, only Jack Matthews found himself out of favour, Williams taking his place in the centre with a first cap awarded to Pontypridd's Glyn Davies at outside-half.

Davies and Billy Cleaver would contest the outside-half position over the next five seasons, the Big Five (the Welsh selectors) fortunate to have two players of outstanding ability at their disposal, but at Rodney Parade the hunt for a player to fill the position was proving to be a major problem. In a season that saw 58 players appear for Newport, ten were tried at stand-off, rarely was the same name included in two or three consecutive matches and at the end of the season the selectors were no nearer to solving the problem. The knock-on effect through the three-quarters saw Ken Jones reduced to scoring only ten tries in 24 appearances and as early as January there was growing concern that this prolific talent was not seeing enough of the ball. Come February, the problem had escalated to such an extent that when the team was named to travel to London to play the Harlequins there was another name added to the growing list of men selected at stand-off. But for the inclement weather which forced the cancellation of many club matches throughout England and Wales during the month, we would be able to comment on how Ken Jones fared in his new position but the match was called off.

Further north, a heavy covering of straw protected the Murrayfield pitch in Edinburgh and the Scotland–Wales match was able to go ahead as scheduled on 1 February. With Scotland having lost in Paris and Wales in Cardiff both teams were desperate to secure the victory that would get their season up and running. An opportunist interception try by

Bleddyn Willams and a Bill Tamplin penalty set the visitors on their way but by half-time Scotland had responded well to lead 8-6. The next 40 minutes saw Wales take control of the match, largely thanks to a supreme performance by the forwards. The pack had failed to ignite against England and as far back as the first trial it was evident that any quality among the forwards was seen in an individual capacity rather than as a collective. In the second half the forwards finally came together as a unit and laid the foundation for Wales to score 16 unanswered points including four tries. Billy Cleaver got the first, Ken Jones the second, Les Williams crossed on the left wing and Ken ran in another in the game's closing moments. Wales' victory by 22 points to 8 was her biggest at Murrayfield and it would be 50 years before the number of points scored and the margin of victory achieved was improved upon.

Ken Jones scored many tries for Wales, among which were outstanding individual efforts and those made memorable more for the occasion and the impact they had on the result, rather than the effort that went into scoring them. From the player's perspective a first try for one's country will always rank among those best remembered but when Ken crossed for his first at Murrayfield, many spectators were left wondering what had actually happened. From the press box high in the roof of the stand it was impossible to tell and reporters were at a loss as to what to send down the wire. When Billy Cleaver was stopped short of the line near the right corner flag a loose maul quickly developed from which a Welsh forward drove on. Bill Gore had nowhere to go but managed to offload the ball to Ken Jones, who had even less room at his disposal. Somehow he managed to conjure his way between the touchline, corner flag and Scottish full-back, a gap described in inches not feet, to score a try unlike any of those for which he is best remembered. This was no 50 or 60-yard dash. There was no sudden change of pace or devastating body swerve. And there was little room for a subtle side-step, just a step or two through the eye of a needle. But it was his first international try and Ken would never forget it.

It was six weeks before Wales' next match, Ireland's visit postponed due to a frozen pitch at St Helen's, Swansea. The club fixture list was also severely disrupted throughout February but Newport did manage to stage matches against Oxford University and Cardiff, both ending in 3-3 draws. Come March, fixtures were going ahead as planned but there had been sufficient disruption for the WRU to announce an extension to the season, which would now end on 10 May.

When the Welsh team to play France in Paris was announced there was much cause for celebration at Rodney Parade. Ken had kept his place and there was a first cap for RT 'Bob' Evans in the back row while second row George Parsons earned a recall after missing out on the trip to Murrayfield. When the team and officials met up at Cardiff station, WRU Secretary Walter Rees instructed Parsons to remove his luggage from the train as he would not be accompanying the party to France. It had been brought to the attention of the WRU that Parsons had been in talks with representatives of a rugby league club, which immediately disqualified him from taking any part in the amateur game. While Parsons protested his innocence, his appeal would have to wait for another day and the train left without him.

Since the introduction of professional rugby league in 1895 the northern clubs had combed South Wales looking for recruits. Many union players had signed on the dotted line and taken the money for reasons which could not be ignored, unemployment and poor working conditions uppermost among them, but in the eyes of those responsible for administering the game there was no greater sin. Long since resigned to the problem, Newport RFC had seen enough of its players sign professional papers in earlier days to fully appreciate the threat. In the current season wing three-quarter WE Williams, hooker Frank Osmond and full-back D Ralph Morgan had all signed for Swinton Rugby League

Football Club and worse was to follow in the close season when Reg Blakemore would join St Helens. George Parsons was not a player who could be easily replaced and his strong denial of the charges suggested that a mistake might have been made. Initially suspended, Parsons was reinstated after an appeal was upheld and he returned for two rescheduled matches in May. It all left a bitter taste and after a short time with Abertillery RFC, Parsons signed professional papers for St Helens RLFC.

Stade Colombes, Paris on 22 March was not a place for the faint-hearted. At the final whistle only a Bill Tamplin penalty goal separated the teams but it was the sheer intensity and physicality of a tremendously hard match that would stay long in the memory of the 50,000 who witnessed it. The Welsh pack continued where it had left off at Murrayfield, subduing a French eight of which much was expected. Elsewhere it was all about defence, with neither set of three-quarters able to break down the opposition. Ken Jones had an outstanding game, completely nullifying the dangerous threat posed by his opposite number Jean Lassègue, who was equally successful in marshalling his Welsh counterpart. Time and again the pair tackled each other into touch, which at Colombes meant onto the cinder running track that encircled the field. Despite rarely having played in such an abrasive battle, all members of the Welsh team remained in one piece, which gave the selectors the simple task of saying 'same again' for the visit of Ireland, that match now rescheduled for the following Saturday.

Already three weeks late in getting under way, the delay was further compounded when the bus bringing the Irish team from their Porthcawl hotel to Swansea was held up in traffic at Neath. The players changed in transit and after a warm-up behind the posts the match eventually got under way 40 minutes late. Heavy rain during the morning saw the playing surface rapidly deteriorate into a muddy tract and it was a credit to the 30 players that the match wasn't allowed to turn into a battle confined among the forwards. Both sides showed intent when in possession but it was the reliable boot of Bill Tamplin that opened the scoring with a penalty kick early in the second half. And it remained at 3-0 until the final minutes, when Bob Evans was up in support to take a scoring pass from Cleaver. Wales ended the season on a high. Three matches were won after the opening defeat by England and several players looked real stars in the making, not least among them the Newport right wing. Five days later, not only did his rugby season appear to be over but there were also concerns as to when he would be able to get the spikes out.

Ligaments are tough, fibrous tissues which link bones together. Those that support the complicated structure surrounding the knee are particularly susceptible to wear and tear and the problem is exacerbated when the joint is put under pressures beyond those experienced in normal, everyday life.

Still concerned that Ken Jones was not seeing enough of the ball, the selectors continued looking for options. Plans to experiment with him at outside-half apparently forgotten, Ken was named in the centre for the visit of Abertillery on the Thursday following the Ireland match. Immediately after falling awkwardly and badly twisting his left knee Ken knew he had a problem but rather than leave the field in what was a close match which Newport would win 3-0, he elected to play on and by doing so increased the likelihood of further damage. In the modern era he would be taken from the field, given immediate treatment and probably spend some weeks in a plaster cast but this was 1947, rugby was an amateur pursuit, sports science was somewhere in the future and players thought such injuries were nothing more than a minor inconvenience that could be 'run off'.

Newport had three fixtures over the Easter holiday weekend. Ken wisely decided to sit out the Devonport Services and London Welsh games but elected to play against the Barbarians on Tuesday. His first attempt to run flat out alerted him that all was not well and he was forced to play out the remainder of the match at half speed. Ken later admitted he had been rather foolish to entertain playing in the first place but that was just one of several crazy decisions he made, decisions which could have brought his blossoming rugby and athletics careers to premature ends. Firstly, he should have left the field when the injury occurred against Abertillery; secondly, he should never have declared his availability to play against the Barbarians; and thirdly, when he knew all was not well in that match he should have immediately left the field. Ken took a big risk with his career over the Easter weekend of 1947 but he got away with it. One reporter wrote how he had spoken with an unnamed specialist in the field of osteopathy who was adamant that if he received a heavy knock on the knee when playing against the Barbarians 'he'll be finished with football and track running for good...'.

Ken Jones didn't suffer many serious injuries during his career but on those occasions when he was sidelined it was usually because of a leg injury. He tore calf muscles, pulled hamstrings and over the years there would be further ligament problems. The injury picked up playing against Abertillery and the subsequent errors of judgement pointed to the fact that more care would need to be taken. All well and good but Ken Jones was a difficult man to tie down. At this early stage in his career he was reluctant to sit out matches and would never relax when forced to watch from the stands, so it will come as no surprise to learn that he made a rapid 'recovery' and was selected for the two postponed matches played in May. Neath won a thrilling encounter 12-11 at Rodney Parade and, in the final game, Cross Keys were comfortably beaten at home 21-0, Ken crossing for his tenth and last try of the campaign.

International honours aside, Ken Jones' first season of senior rugby was a little disappointing, mainly due to

Newport's inconsistent form. The final analysis showed nine of the 41 matches played were lost and eight drawn. Ken made 24 appearances, represented Monmouthshire twice and won four international caps. Including trial matches he played 35 games in that first season, more than enough when one considers that here was a man who would not get a break from competitive sport during the next eight years.

A taste of things to come saw Ken honoured by West Mon Old Boys at a function held in the Clarence Hotel, Pontypool, and a few days later by Blaenavon RFC at the town's Conservative Club following a friendly match in which a Ken Jones' XV were beaten 3-0 by the home side – 36 matches. All of a sudden it seemed that everybody wanted a piece of him. If he wasn't judging the performances at West Mon's school sports then he was casting his eye over the finalists at a local beauty competition. Life was tough! But there was a plus side. The committee of Blaenavon RFC presented Ken with a leather briefcase while bemoaning the fact that each Saturday he was in action at Newport upwards of 150 supporters left the town by train or road to cheer him on and in doing so deprived Blaenavon of much-needed support through the turnstiles at the Recreation Ground. The briefcase would certainly prove useful but the silver tea set he was presented with by the West Mon Old Boys was much more practical. Irene had started to fill a 'bottom drawer' and come 30 December Ken would have more than a 26th birthday to celebrate.

While Ken had been successful in securing a teaching post, albeit one based in Bath, things had not worked out quite so well for Irene. Unable to find a vacancy in the area, the start of the school year in September took her back to Birmingham, where she would continue to work but at the same time carry on looking for a suitable alternative, one that would cut out the weekend travelling which invariably ended up with her watching a rugby match. She didn't have to wait long and when a job became available it was at Swainswick Primary

School on the outskirts of Bath. Due to take up her new responsibilities in January, Irene fell in with an old college friend who was already teaching in Bath and for the next 12 months the pair shared a flat.

Ken settled in with Lew and his family at Saltford, from where he had an easy commute into Bath during the week and a fairly straightforward journey to Newport at weekends. A good bus service ran to the centre of Bristol, from where he could connect with the South Wales trains that departed regularly from Temple Meads station. An early Saturday morning train would complete the 45-minute journey to Newport in comfortable time for Ken to join the team coach before it set off to any away matches. If the club were playing at home time was very much on his side. Evening training sessions were another matter and Ken was limited in the number he could attend. Knowing that he was the fittest player in the squad and could be relied on to look after his own needs, the Newport committee were prepared to overlook what would normally be seen as a major transgression. It would be some years before Ken would pass a driving test but for the time being there was little inconvenience in his life. All things considered, everything had fallen nicely into place with a lot achieved in the short time since his return from India.

By the time he arrived home from the subcontinent, it had been confirmed that the 1948 Olympic Games would be hosted by London. Since the announcement, any track or field athlete worth their salt had realised that every appearance at the major meetings offered a chance to stake a claim for selection and there was little margin for error with competition for places fierce. Ken knew he was capable of times that would see him in the mix for a place in both sprints but his performances in India would need to be repeated at British tracks. Sorting the wheat from the chaff over measured distances sounds a fairly straightforward exercise but many of the recognised meetings held during the summer introduced various factors that made comparing like for like difficult. There were different surfaces to take into consideration and some tracks were better equipped than others. A perfect example would be Taunton, which was famous for fast times in the sprints but this could be attributed to the track being 'downhill'. Throw into the mix that timekeeping was not the sophisticated tool it is today and it would be easy to read too much into performances recorded at the Somerset venue. And there were the many handicap races in which lesser competitors were given a number of yards' start depending on ability, another factor to help muddy the waters. All of which meant that Ken would have to perform well at meetings of some secondary importance but, more importantly, take that form into the Welsh Championships and the AAA Championships at the White City in London. It was there that he would meet the best British athletes and he needed to beat them.

Living in Bristol had not disrupted Ken's club rugby but his sprinting required that he train most days and, as we know, doing this in Newport was not at all practical. Still retaining his membership of Newport Athletic Club, he also joined Bristol AC, which not only enabled him to have a local training base but also made him eligible to compete for both Somerset and the Southern Counties. Ken Jones soon became a firm favourite at athletics meetings throughout the West Country. Running at Taunton in the Somerset Police Sports he won the 220yds handicap with a performance that local correspondent Bill Hawkins described as 'the fastest bit of sprinting I have ever witnessed... the fastest seen in Bristol [sic] for many years...'; and that after conceding up to 14 yards.

Classed as an official Olympic trial, the meeting between the Midland and Southern Counties at the St George Grammar School ground in Bristol attracted a big crowd, who saw Ken confirm his form with another impressive victory in the 220yds timed at 22.1. The Wiltshire Police Sports at Trowbridge on 25 June saw the handicapper get the better of

Jones, who failed to make up a generous four yards on Brian Shenton, a future European 200m champion who hung on for victory by the smallest of margins.

The Welsh Championships had been a moveable feast since the first meeting was held at Newport in 1907. Abercarn Welfare Ground, Barry Cricket Ground, Cardiff Arms Park, Crumlyn Burrows, Penarth Recreation Ground, Taff Vale Park, Pontypridd and St Helen's, Swansea had all hosted the meeting, as had Pontypool Park, and it was there that the 1947 championships were held on 28 June and where Ken Jones would defend his titles. The weather may have been unfavourable, with heavy rain falling in the morning, but this didn't prevent the folk of Blaenavon heading the short distance south to give vocal encouragement to the local hero. The wet surface ensured that no track records would be threatened but it did not prevent Ken from repeating his sprint double. Times of 10.2 and 24.1 may have been good enough at Pontypool Park on a wet Saturday afternoon but when news came through that E McDonald Bailey had broken the British 100yds record at the Southern Championships with a time of 9.6, the goalposts had been moved. Even making allowances for the conditions, 10.2 looked positively slow.

Regardless of results elsewhere, the AAA Championships were the biggest of the season and rarely would the Great Britain selectors look beyond them in their search for international competitors. Performing well at the White City was a prerequisite and while underachievement at the venue didn't automatically mean an athlete was excluded from the deliberations it certainly made life difficult. Spread over two days, the meeting saw the heats and semi-finals of the 220yds held on Friday with the final and all rounds of the 100yds taking place on Saturday. Ken won his 220yds heat in 22.5, the second fastest time of the round with only McDonald Bailey in 22.1 ahead of him on paper. The two lined up in the first semi-final with the first three qualifying for the final but realistically, five athletes were running for two places.

McDonald Bailey was supreme, winning in 21.6 with Ken second fully six yards behind. A long way in a sprint but he would have slept well knowing that his time was faster than the winner of the second semi-final.

A pulled muscle put paid to any heroics the Welshman may have been contemplating. The damage was done in the 100yds heat, ruling Ken out of the remainder of that competition although, as was his wont, he took his place in the line-up at the start of the 220yds final but was out of contention by the time the runners hit the straight. The championships may have ended in disappointment, but Ken had done enough to impress the selectors and later in the season he was selected to run for the AAA against the Combined Services and named as reserve for the international meeting against France in Paris on 7 September. He was also among a group of British athletes invited to compete in a two-day meeting in Dublin at the end of the season. The first day of the Clonliffe Harriers International meeting was held at College Park, but the grass track was in poor condition and the second day saw the athletes relocate to nearby Terenure. Not that this helped in any way, with the leading athletes heavily penalised by some overenthusiastic handicapping that ruled out any chance of the large crowds seeing them at their best. Ken was at the point in his hectic schedule where, figuratively speaking, he was putting a running shoe on one foot and a rugby boot on the other. Aware that Newport's season had already got under way, the visit to Dublin may have been difficult to justify but it had given him the chance to watch the Irish 220yds champion in action. The following year, Jack Gregory and Ken Jones would join forces in the quest for gold, little suspecting where that journey would take them.

There must have been a huge collective sigh of relief when Ken Jones took to the field at Rodney Parade on 27 September for his first match of the season and his first in the famous black and amber jersey, the club now supplied with its proper colours. A month earlier the local press revealed that representatives of Leeds Rugby League Football Club had offered Ken the chance to sign professional papers. Flattered he may well have been, but in truth the whole concept of playing rugby for money was totally alien to him, a belief he strongly maintained throughout his involvement in the sport. The departure of Reg Blakemore and the others who had left Newport in recent months for pastures new in the north of England was still hurting. If one of the club's star players were to follow it would have a devastating effect, not just locally, but throughout Wales.

At the time, the £1,500 offer was almost certainly the biggest yet made to a rugby union player, but despite the large sum and the future earning potential Ken gracefully declined. 'It was a very tempting offer and I would no doubt have been able to arrange a transfer to a Leeds school ... I had no hesitation, however, in turning the offer down.' Ken had never given a thought to playing professional rugby and as a final comment on the affair added: '...and I never shall!'

Newport went into the home match against Swansea on the back of three successive defeats. Newbridge, Cross Keys and Bristol had all beaten the Black and Ambers and there was little to enthuse over in the victories against Penarth and Abertillery at the start of the month. Ken's return to the team coincided with one of those days when everything goes to plan, the ball bounces in your favour and the opposition can do little to stem the tide. Newport scored nine tries against Swansea in a thrilling 33-16 victory and the indifferent form of recent weeks was immediately forgotten. At no time was it suggested that the return to duty of one of the club's star players kick-started its season and in such a free-flowing match the wing was limited to one try, wing-forward Bob Evans stealing the headlines with a well-deserved hat-trick.

While Newport were rattling up the points at Rodney Parade, 15 miles away Cardiff were playing the Australian tourists at the Arms Park. As both these teams would be met in the coming weeks there was particular interest in the outcome which produced a home victory, Cardiff thoroughly deserving the 11-3 win after outplaying the Wallabies in every department. 'Bring them on' must have been the feeling in the Newport changing room after the team's thrilling performance but from looking world beaters, the players were soon brought back to earth with a bang. Working in Bath made travelling for midweek matches difficult and Monday saw the team that had routed Swansea head to Pontypool Park without Ken. Rather than build on the momentum of 48 hours earlier the players returned to the dismal form of previous weeks by losing by 7 points to 3 and in doing so bringing to an end the worst September in Newport's long history, four of the seven matches lost. With the worst start to a season confirmed, Newport next headed for Cardiff and the first of the season's four fixtures against their great rivals. If the players had paused to consider what their Swansea counterparts were feeling when Newport ran in nine tries they may have been prepared for the onslaught Cardiff subjected them to seven days later. There were only six tries to count but as the visitors failed to get on the scoreboard in many ways this was an even more comprehensive defeat than that suffered by Swansea. Bleddyn Williams was the main protagonist, scoring four tries in a 29-0 victory.

By the end of the season, just how good a team Cardiff were would be put beyond doubt, the club losing only two of 41 matches played. The victories over Australia and Newport came on the back of a surprise defeat at Pontypool and only an equally unexpected result at Penarth in April prevented an invincible record. Licking their wounds back at Rodney Parade, the Newport players would have needed no reminding that with the Australians arriving later in the month it was essential the games at Blackheath and Leicester were won if the team was to be mentally prepared to face a major touring team, particularly one that reports suggested was improving with each match.

It can bring down the fittest of individuals and in the second week of October it brought down Ken Jones – flu! Not a common or garden cold, not man's flu but the real thing; the bug that confines its victim to bed with a high fever and brings unremitting aches and pains to every part of the body. That's what Ken had and it made him unavailable for the trip to Blackheath; and he should have stayed at home rather than travel to Leicester but, as we have seen previously, here was a man who would not be told. Newport won without him in London and with him at Leicester, where his absence would not have changed the result, but after that run out he was deemed fit to face the Wallabies five days later. Fit to face the man many saw as the best wing in world rugby – Charles 'Chugger' Eastes.

'What is Ken Jones like?' This was the question asked continually by the Australians on their arrival in Newport. 'What is he like?' Suggestions that Eastes would be moved to the right wing to avoid a clash with the Welsh flyer gathered momentum when he was listed in that position in the matchday programme but when the teams lined up for the kick-off 'Chugger' took up his normal position on the left. Previous form counted for nothing as the Newport pack swept all before them. The Australians scored an early try but a smart drop-goal by Rowland saw the home team take the lead shortly before the interval, which was how it remained until ten minutes from time when a second Australian try and conversion proved decisive in the tourists' 8-4 victory. At this point in the game the visitors were reduced to 14 men, Eastes forced from the field midway through the second half. His much-anticipated duel with Ken Jones was very much a one-sided affair. Eastes regularly beat his man and was more than equal to the task when called upon to defend, and it was when making what appeared to be an innocuous tackle on his opposite number that the damage was done. Eastes executed a copybook tackle to bring Jones to ground but the players landed awkwardly and his forearm became the meat in the sandwich between Ken's lower body and a hard patch of turf. Eastes' tour ended at Rodney Parade, the broken arm needing a metal plate to correct the damage. But he returned to Australia knowing he had comfortably got the better of his much-lauded opponent.

There is little doubt that when Ken took the field against Australia he was not fully fit. He had lost half a stone since his recent illness and did not fully appreciate how debilitating an effect this would have on his body.

Interviewed after the match he readily admitted that he probably shouldn't have played and owned up to the fact that he thought it was his worst performance for the club, an opinion shared by many onlookers. This huge disappointment was tempered with the news that he was included in an extensive list of 196 athletes from which the Great Britain team for the 1948 Olympics would be chosen. All options were certainly covered, with the selectors naming 14 athletes in the 100m and 16 in the 200m, but at least Ken was in the mix. His initial reaction to the news was to play rugby until the end of January, from when he would concentrate all his efforts on training for the athletics season. This was later amended to take in February and March, allowing him to play throughout the Five Nations if selected.

Resigned to losing their man before the end of the season, the Newport selectors also had to look elsewhere when picking the team for the next two matches. After missing the club's short tour to Devon earlier in the year when selected for his first cap, Ken was now unavailable for the visit of Devonport Services to Rodney Parade and the away match at Plymouth a week later.

The reasons were twofold. Firstly, his relocation to the West Country had already seen him run for the Southern Counties in the summer and now he was selected to represent Somerset in a County Championship match against Gloucestershire; and secondly, the following Saturday would see the first Welsh trial at Bridgend.

At Taunton, Somerset put up a spirited performance against a strong Gloucestershire team before going down 9-10. The visitors were unbeaten in the Divisional matches before losing to the Eastern Counties in the semi-final of the highly regarded tournament. English county rugby was a new experience for the Welsh wing but seven days later he was back on familiar territory when taking his place in the Probables at the Brewery Field. Newport's poor start to the season was highlighted with only Ken and Bob Evans selected for the senior team and left wing Maurice Baker chosen out of position in the centre for the Possibles. Very little was learned in an entertaining match that ended 18-18 with the Possibles proving the more enterprising combination, scoring five tries to three. Ken and Bob Evans both got their names on the score sheet.

A look at his diary would have revealed four important dates in the final two months of the year; Cardiff at Rodney Parade on 8 November; the final Welsh trial on 6 December; Wales would play Australia on 20 December; with the most important arriving ten days later. A match in Blaenavon, but one of a very different kind. Ken and Irene were due to tie the knot on 30 December.

As the season began to unfold Cardiff were clearly the dominant Welsh club, playing a brand of rugby that was both entertaining and successful. They were irrepressible and Newport could do nothing to prevent another defeat, this by twelve points to nil, and another four tries; two matches played, two matches lost, ten tries conceded, no points scored. Painful to play, painful to watch.

The final Welsh trial produced nothing unexpected and it was clear the selectors were going to have to look little further than Cardiff when picking the side to face the Wallabies. When it was announced, the team included nine players from the in-form club, two from Llanelly with Aberavon, Cambridge University, Pontypridd and Newport each providing one. Ken Jones was one of five players selected to make a fifth consecutive appearance alongside the Cardiff quartet of Billy Cleaver, Bleddyn Williams, Les Williams and Gwyn Evans. Over five matches and 11 months the make-up of the Welsh XV had been transformed.

The Wallabies arrived in Cardiff in good spirits. Only two of their 25 matches played had ended in defeat, a combined Lancashire–Cheshire XV causing an upset in winning 9-8 to emulate Cardiff. The internationals in Scotland and Ireland were both won with some ease and the tourists now had the chance to make up for the earlier defeat at the Arms Park. It was a game dominated by outstanding defences with the outcome decided by penalties – two converted by Bill Tamplin and five missed by the visitors. Wales won 6-0 but failed to score a try and when England were beaten 11-0 two weeks later the Australians could make the proud boast that their line was not crossed in any of the internationals.

Ken and Irene may well have chosen their wedding day to coincide with his twenty-sixth birthday. Then again, the date may have been determined by the fact that on Saturday 27 December Newport had a home match against the Wasps and a week later on 3 January, Richmond were due at Rodney Parade. Needless to say, Ken played against both but the important match of the week took place at St Peter's Church, Blaenavon, on Tuesday 30 December. Built in 1804, St Peter's is found at the bottom end of the town, a short distance from the railway station where the bride and groom had first met 15 years earlier. Much had happened since those early encounters, events that had taken Ken to Cheltenham, India and now Bristol and Bath, with Irene following along the road to Cheltenham before joining Ken in the West Country via Birmingham. At Blaenavon, as the lights were about to be put out on 1947, the confirmation of what the people of the town had seen coming long before the happy couple may have entertained the idea was about to take place and the Blaenavon folk were not going to miss it.

Forty invited guests took their places in the pews but the church was quickly filled to overflowing by those keen to be a part of the day. With the church unable to accommodate any more, people settled for vantage points outside, from which they were happy to watch on as the proceedings unfolded. The bride wore a turquoise two-piece suit with a brown felt hat, matching accessories and shoulder spray of pink carnations, the groom looking equally splendid in his dark, two-piece suit. Attending the bride was Ken's younger sister Phyllis, now 16 years old, and the best man's duties fell on the capable shoulders of Hedley Rowland. Following the reception at the nearby Workmen's Hall, the wedding party headed for Newport and the train to London where the couple would spend four nights before returning to Newport on Saturday morning, giving Ken plenty of time to take his place against Richmond in the afternoon. That would have seemed a long way off on Tuesday night as the Joneses went about setting the town alight. The days were spent doing the things that tourists do when in the capital; walking up The Mall to Buckingham Palace; taking in the busy focal points at Piccadilly Circus and Trafalgar Square; and looking through the windows of the famous Knightsbridge shops. Restaurants were visited and there was time to take in two West End shows: the year's big successes, Irving Berlin's *Annie Get Your Gun* and the Rodgers and Hammerstein triumph *Oklahoma*. On Wednesday night the couple joined thousands of others at a packed Trafalgar Square to see in the new year, a unique experience to add to the honeymoon diary before Saturday morning announced itself and the newlyweds made their way to Paddington Station for the journey home.

Newport could have managed without Ken Jones in the two matches that sandwiched the big day in Blaenavon. Wasps were comfortably beaten 25-0, Ken scoring a simple try after taking a perfect pass from Ken Spray, who had carved out a grand opening in midfield. And Richmond were despatched in similar style, Newport winning 22-0 with Ken finding the crowd somewhat sympathetic when, the line at his mercy, he knocked on a perfect pass from Spray after the centre had again worked his magic in the middle of the field. The wing may well have been surplus to requirements against the London teams but how he would have enjoyed watching the debutant at outside-half playing his first two matches for the club. Roy Burnett announced his arrival at Newport RFC in some style and the long-standing problems that had been prevalent in the key position were finally solved.

Ken's announcement earlier in the season that he would not play any rugby after January came up for review in the new year. His late try at Twickenham had salvaged a 3-3 draw in a match that saw Wales dominate every area of play but to no avail as England, the referee and their own ineptness conspired to deny the men in red. Critical of the overall style of play adopted by Wales, writing in the following day's *News of the World*, former Welsh wing Willie Llewellyn bemoaned the fact that despite a glut of possession '...the fastest man on the field did not get a single pass from his centre throughout the game... Ken Jones' score was the result of a pass from a forward. This is not good enough. Fast wings are put in a side to score and should be given the chances...'. Llewellyn scored four tries on his international debut against England, and attributed his success totally to the men inside him who had created the opportunities.

Heedless of such comment, the Big Five made only one change in the team for the visit of Scotland, with Stan Williams recalled to the second row in place of Des Jones. Three tries by Welsh backs in a 14-0 win suggest they may have been right and it was same again two weeks later when France arrived at Swansea. A first French victory in Wales by 11-3 did lead to some changes but among the backs, only the unfortunate Jack Matthews, playing out of position on the left wing, was dropped for the last match of the season. Ireland were yet to win a Grand Slam but after beating France, England and

Scotland the stage was set for a great afternoon of rugby football at Ravenhill, Belfast, Irish rugby's Ulster base.

Led by recently appointed captain and hooker Karl Mullen, and guided by the mercurial Jack Kyle at outside-half, Ireland scored two tries to Wales' one and the party could begin – and it was a long one! No one would have believed it at the time, but it was to be fully 61 years before Ireland would claim a second Grand Slam.

The match against the Barbarians on Easter Tuesday was Ken's self-imposed but oft-revised deadline and would be his last before concentrating all his efforts toward gaining Olympic selection. Newport had enjoyed better form since the turn of the year but a third defeat by Cardiff on 6 March set the scene for a showdown at the Arms Park in April, a game in which the club would be desperate to avoid defeat. On his return from international rugby Ken appeared at Cross Keys and in the home match against Bath before lining up against a star-studded Barbarians for his season's swansong. Newport won a thrilling match 5-3, the seventh consecutive victory in the month, and they extended the run when beating Gloucester on the first Saturday in April. A week later Ken could only look on from the stands as Cardiff completed a highly sought but rarely achieved four wins in a season over Newport. Next season couldn't come quick enough but in the meantime...

On their return from honeymoon Ken and Irene set up home in Bath. The training facilities at Newport and Bristol may have been better but there was the travelling to consider, leading Ken to look for a suitable alternative nearer home. Following school he would spend most evenings at the Recreation Ground, home of Bath and City Athletic Club, and it was there that he came under the guidance of fellow Welshman WO Williams of Westbury Harriers, who had competed against Ken in the past, most notably when coming third in the 100yds final at the Welsh Championships in 1947.

If Ken had a chink in his armour, one area where there was definite room for improvement, it was in his start, a skill that Williams had long since mastered. Time after time the pair would settle down in their 'holes' (starting blocks were not yet in common use) and on a given signal make that all-important break. Ken gained a lot from these regular sessions but starting would never be his strong point and most of the races he won saw him come from behind.

There was the usual round of early season meetings but come the middle of June the leading contenders for Olympic selection headed for Uxbridge and the Southern Counties Championships where there was much more than a title to be won. The heats of the 100yds all went to form with Ken, Alastair McCorquodale and McDonald Bailey each winning in even time and Alan Grieve taking the fourth a tenth slower; but it was in the semi-finals that thoughts of an upset began to make waves. In clocking 9.8, Ken Jones recorded the fastest time of the year and in doing so equalled the English native record – no mean achievement for a man born in Wales! In commentary, Harold Abrahams alluded to the fact that he didn't know if Newport was in England or Wales and whether or not Ken could lay claim to the record. All of which was irrelevant, Ken hailing from Blaenavon as he was all too keen to point out. But this wasn't a day about records and in winning the final in 9.9 ahead of McCorquodale and Bailey, Ken Jones proved he was the form sprinter in the country. A week later the Welsh Championships took place at Port Talbot. Ken retained both sprint titles, running another 9.9 in the 100yds and 23.1 in the 220yds. His 100yds title earned him the unanimous praise of the committee and he received the Fellowship Cup for the outstanding performance of the championships, the first time the cup had been presented since the war.

No one was covering more miles in his search for Olympic athletes than team manager Jack Crump. He travelled the length and breadth of the country in search of the men who would compete for Great Britain. Earlier in the year he had spoken at a gathering of leading Monmouthshire athletes held at Newport Athletic Club during which he confirmed that Ken Jones was a real 'possible' for Olympic selection. Meetings at Abertillery, Chesterfield, Oxford and Chiswick saw leading contenders blow hot and cold but always there or thereabouts was the Welshman. That is until the White City and the AAA Championships. Ken rarely produced his best form at the championships and in 1948, when all eyes were on the Olympic hopefuls, he could do no better than fifth in the final of the 100yds. The race may have been won by the Australian John Treloar but with McCorquodale, McDonald Bailey and Jack Archer also ahead of him, he was behind three men, each of whom was eligible to run for Great Britain.

One major meeting remained before Crump and his fellow selectors would announce the Great Britain team. A triangular competition between a combined England/Wales team v Scotland and Ireland was to be held at Fallowfield in Manchester and as a final preparation for the Games, all events would be measured using the metric system favoured by the Olympic Committee. McCorquodale was first across the line with Jones and McDonald Bailey only inches behind. Throughout the season these three had consistently proved themselves to be the best over the shorter sprint; all that was needed was the rubber stamp confirming their selection. They would be put out of their misery the following day.

CHAPTER FOUR

GOLD TO SILVER

The first Olympic Games of the modern era were held in Athens in 1896. This was at the instigation of Baron Pierre de Coubertin, a French philanthropist who firmly believed that a revival of the ancient Greek games held in honour of Zeus between 776 BC and AD 393 would be to the betterment of mankind. De Coubertin was of the opinion that the bringing together of athletes from around the world to compete against each other in a variety of sporting events would reach beyond boundaries and could only enhance international relationships. With the financial assistance of a Greek millionaire, de Coubertin's vision became reality in 1896, and in four yearly cycles thereafter, some of the world's major cities played host to the Olympic Games.

Following Athens, it was the turn of Paris in 1900 and St Louis in 1904 before the cycle was broken, the Games returning to Athens in 1906 to celebrate the tenth anniversary of the first competition. This was an attempt to appease those who thought the Games should have a permanent home in Greece. The original intention was that every ten years an Olympiad would be held in Athens in addition to those falling within the four-year cycle, but the concept was not repeated after 1906. When Italy advised the Olympic Committee it would not be able to back the 1908 Games, the recently formed British Olympic Association agreed to step in and the Olympics headed to London for the first time, with the White City the major venue. Stockholm, in 1912, hosted the last games before the First World War and it was Antwerp where the Olympic flame next appeared in 1920. A return to Paris in 1924 was followed by Amsterdam in 1928, Los Angeles in 1932 and, four years later, it was the turn of Berlin.

The 1936 Olympics were undoubtedly a great success when measured by the performances of the athletes, with 18 new Games records set in the track and field events alone, but it was the performances of the American sprinter Jesse Owens that would for ever be associated with Berlin's defining moments. Owens won the 100m, 200m and the long jump and was a member of the USA 4x100m relay team that also struck gold. Jesse Owens was a superstar, but he was a black superstar and, as such, a great embarrassment to the governing Nazi party and its leader Adolf Hitler. The Olympics were awarded to Berlin before Hitler came into power but his policies regarding race and colour soon led to countries threatening to boycott the event. This did not materialise but it was Hitler's refusal to acknowledge Owens' supremacy on the track that made the headlines, the leader showing a total disregard for all that the Olympic movement stands for.

Helsinki, London and Tokyo were shortlisted for the 1940 Games. But for the outbreak of the Second World War the Olympics would have arrived in Asia for the first time and four years later would have returned to London. The cancellation of this programme led to a 12-year break, but as the war entered its final months so the International Olympic Committee (IOC) could begin to focus on 1948. Los Angeles had its backers but it was the invitation from London that met with most support, swayed perhaps by the fact that the city had missed out in 1944. On 14 March 1946, the mayor of

London received confirmation from the IOC that the Games of the XIVth Olympiad would take place in a little over two years' time and that it had been awarded to London.

Why the 14th? Since the revival of the Olympics in 1896, ten cities had hosted the Games but the interim event in 1906 and those cancelled in 1940 and 1944 were included in the totting-up process, meaning London would welcome the XIVth Olympiad. Feelings were mixed. The city had been devastated by heavy bombing during the war and there was much rebuilding and restoration to be done. A major financial crisis had led to industrial strikes, there were fuel shortages and the food rationing which had prevailed during the war was still in place. Was this the time to think about bringing the Olympic Games and all that it entailed to London? The answer was yes.

With little money available there would be no new facilities. Fortunately, there were several existing venues that could be utilised. Wembley Stadium was identified immediately as the venue for athletics and it would also be used for the football, hockey and equestrian finals. The nearby Empire Pool was brought up to Olympic standard and it was there that the swimming, diving and water polo medals would be contested.

In the city, Earls Court was chosen for the boxing, wrestling, weight-lifting and gymnastics competitions; Harringay Arena was allocated basketball; and the Victoria and Albert Museum was identified as the ideal location for the innovative Olympic Sport in Art competitions which ranged from art and sculpture through to literature and music. Elsewhere, Henley, already famous for rowing, would also be the venue for the canoeing events; yachting would be based at Torbay; cycling at Herne Hill and Windsor; with Aldershot able to provide all the necessary diversification required for the modern pentathlon.

By using established venues, the London Olympic Committee was able to keep costs to a minimum but Wembley Stadium would still need to be upgraded if 80,000 spectators were to be accommodated in comfort. It was anticipated that most would arrive by rail, highlighting the need for a thoroughfare linking Wembley Park station with the stadium. On completion this walkway was named Olympic Way, but in time it would become synonymous with another major sporting event and the Saturday in May when thousands of football fans descended on the stadium for the FA Cup final. This would lead to the approach becoming known simply as Wembley Way.

With the infrastructure of the Games mapped out, the next task was to invite countries to take part and sort out appropriate accommodation for what was expected to be a large number of athletes and administrators. A total of 65 countries were invited but there was to be no representation from Germany or Japan, both countries excluded from the invitation list. The final figure shows that 59 countries competed in London in 1948, a record number at the time, and collectively they brought more than 4,000 competitors and administrators. These would be billeted at RAF camps, schools, government buildings and other facilities which could be easily adapted for 'bed, breakfast and evening meal'. Not surprising then that the 1948 Games became known as the 'Austerity Olympics'.

The Triangular International Athletic Tournament held at Fallowfield, Manchester, on Saturday 17 July was the last chance for athletes to impress the selectors before the team to represent Great Britain in the track and field events was announced. The following day the selection committee spent seven hours deliberating over the pros and cons of the various candidates before announcing the 65 members of the men's team. Ken Jones was one of three named in the 100m and he was also included in an eight-man squad from which the 4x100m relay team would be chosen.

E McDonald Bailey was also included but there was some concern among officialdom that he should be running for

Trinidad, the place of his birth, rather than Great Britain. The sprinter qualified for Great Britain because he had been domiciled in England for some years, but not wishing to cause a diplomatic upset, it was considered only right and proper that the issue should be dealt with through the proper channels. A telegram was despatched to the Trinidadian authorities. When this remained unanswered, and despite that country's subsequent representation, McDonald Bailey took his place in the Great Britain team which he had previously confirmed as his preferred choice. Bailey's preparation had been hampered by injury and he was below his best in the weeks leading up to the Olympics. His under par performances saw him having to settle for minor places in the Southern Counties Championships, the AAA Championships and the Triangular International Match, and during the Games his problems were further compounded by a bout of laryngitis contracted during the two days of competition for the 100m crown. He is still rated as one of Great Britain's finest sprinters, but 1948 can only be looked upon as McDonald Bailey's annus horribilis as the record books confirm he was AAA champion over 100yds and 220yds in 1946, 1947 and every year from 1949 to 1953.

Joining Ken Jones and Bailey in the 100m was Scotsman Alastair McCorquodale, who had only been introduced to competitive athletics 12 months earlier while still serving with the Coldstream Guards. McCorquodale went to Harrow School where he excelled at cricket, the sport he would always favour above all others. There he proved himself to be a good all-round athlete, winning the victor ludorum at the annual sports day in 1944 and 1945. On joining the armed forces, his casual approach to athletics was given a much-needed impetus when he realised that being selected to represent the Army at meetings invariably included a weekend pass. McCorquodale soon became a recognised face on the circuit and in 1947 was clearly a candidate for Olympic selection. With no plans to forge a career in the Army, once discharged there was every chance that this talent may well have been lost to athletics. In a later interview McCorquodale admitted his first priority after leaving the Army in 1948 was to get fully fit. With the Olympics six months away he joined the London Athletic Club, where he came under the influence of quadruple Olympic medallist Guy Butler, at the time considered to be one of the best athletics coaches in the land. With a strict programme designed specifically for him and a new regime limiting his alcohol and cigarette consumption, an Olympic athlete started to rear his head.

Nothing short of absolute fitness would be good enough if competitors were to perform at their best in competition of the highest standard. Nobody wants to have to sacrifice their place in a team through injury and many sportsmen have undoubtedly competed knowing that they were not one hundred per cent fit, but preferring to keep the problem to themselves. When rumours began circulating to the effect that star sprinter Ken Jones was struggling with a pulled muscle they were quickly dispelled. Vernon Parfitt was as close to Ken as anybody at this time and he declared him perfectly fit on 24 July, but such conjecture could not be ignored. The Great Britain selectors requested that Ken travel to London, where he was given a complete examination before being allowed to join the rest of the squad in Uxbridge two days before the opening ceremony.

On 17 July, as the cream of British athletics were in Fallowfield making a final bid for places in the Great Britain team, a 17-year-old Greek girl set out from the old stadium in Olympia carrying an Olympic torch on the first leg of the 2,000-mile journey to London. More than 1,600 torch-bearers would be involved, each carrying their own torch with the symbolic flame passed on from one bearer to the next. Only once on its long journey was the Olympic flame extinguished, on its arrival at Dover. The start of the 12-day relay saw the runners make for the spot outside Olympia where, at his request, Baron de Coubertin's heart was buried. Then it was on to the coast and a meeting with a Greek ship for the sea voyage to Corfu, from where a British vessel took over and the flame continued its way across the Adriatic Sea to Bari in southern Italy. Through Italy and into Switzerland, where a diversion was made, this time to de Coubertin's grave in Lausanne, then it was on to France. Luxembourg was followed by Belgium where a ceremony was held at the Tomb of the Unknown Soldier in Brussels before the relay continued on the final stage of its journey through mainland Europe, eventually arriving in Calais on 27 July. There it became the responsibility of the host nation, beginning with the crew of the destroyer HMS *Bicester* which transported it to Dover. With the flame not due to arrive at Wembley Stadium until 29 July, the opportunity to take it on an extended route through the towns and villages of the south-east and Home Counties was not passed up. This allowed thousands of people to witness what is a unique experience in sport, and for the remainder of the journey the roads were lined with those anxious for a glimpse of the flame as it was carried to its final destination.

London was enjoying a heatwave, with temperatures reaching well into the eighties, and Wembley Stadium was bathed in sunshine on that July afternoon. There were 80,000 spectators present for the opening ceremony and at 4.00pm precisely, His Majesty King George VI, Patron of the British Olympic Association, declared 'I proclaim open the Olympic Games of London celebrating the XIVth Olympiad of the modern era.' Seven thousand pigeons were released before all eyes focused on the tunnel, from where the final torch-bearer would emerge. His identity had been a well-kept secret and when the runner entered the stadium he was not one of the leading athletes of the day but a Cambridge University-educated medical student. John Mark stood over six feet tall, had dashing looks and a sweep of blond hair – the epitome of a healthy young man. Sydney Wooderson had been the original choice but the Oxbridge-dominated British Olympic Committee decided that Mark was a better physical specimen. Mark collected the final torch in the dressing rooms hidden away under the stands and after completing a lap of the track, he ascended the ramp to the bowl and lit the Olympic Flame. John Mark's 15 minutes of fame were over but the flame would continue to burn for the duration of London's Olympics.

It took one and a half hours for the athletes to parade before the king. Tradition dictated that the Greek team would lead the parade, with the host nation the final team to enter the stadium. Smartly kitted out in blue blazers with white slacks or skirts, the Great Britain squad not surprisingly raised the biggest cheer from the capacity crowd. The British athletes were required to wear berets that had been donated by Kangol, a leading manufacturer; blue for the men and white for the women. The headwear incorporated a badge depicting the Olympic symbol of five rings, the Union Jack and the number 1948. There were strict instructions regarding the wearing of the berets; firm on the head with the badge to the front and the brim an inch above the eye-line. Hardly the preferred choice of headwear in a heatwave!

Part of the ceremony saw 59 boy scouts lined up in front of the Royal Box. Each stood in front of one of the teams, holding a placard announcing the name of the competing nation. In the extreme heat the scout holding aloft the name of Chile was the first to fall, a replacement quickly called up before the same misfortune befell the boy holding the board, presumably a much bigger one, announcing the presence of the representatives of Liechtenstein. Then it was the turn of the unfortunate lad designated Denmark, who was thankfully the last to succumb to the heat. The athletes spent more than four hours in line before being allowed to disperse. An uncomfortable afternoon in such extreme temperatures, not helped when expected to wear some form of uniform and certainly not ideal preparation for what would follow. Knowing that the opening ceremony was likely to be of interminable duration, athletes involved on the first day of competition were excused from attending the formalities. For Ken Jones, McDonald Bailey and Alastair McCorquodale, who would contest the 100m the following day, this allowed time to relax and familiarise themselves with their base for the coming week – the camp of RAF Bomber Command in Uxbridge.

Uxbridge lies some ten miles to the west of Wembley. The RAF camp was built around ten barrack blocks and it was these that would serve as sleeping quarters for many of the athletes, including the Great Britain and USA teams. The blocks were fitted out to accommodate 150 athletes, who each had an individual cubicle with an iron bedstead, easy chair and reading lamp. Communal areas included the baths and showers, canteens and dining rooms and the landscaped gardens. Beyond these basic requirements the camp also offered a range of shops, banking and post office facilities, dry cleaning, shoe repairers and cinemas. Dental and medical staff were also on hand if required.

The billets may have been adapted from existing facilities but with all the basic needs well catered for, athletes could focus on the job in hand. The nearby RAF Stadium was made available for training and when their date with destiny arrived athletes were transferred from Uxbridge to Wembley courtesy of a fleet of double-decker buses. The morning of Friday 30 July saw the British sprinters step aboard a red London bus before setting off on their quest for Olympic gold.

The men's 100m is the blue riband event of the Olympic Games. The excitement generated by the search to find the fastest man on earth is hugely disproportionate to the time it takes for the matter to be resolved. In 1948, the measurement was a little over ten seconds. Ten seconds in which 80,000 spectators would hold their collective breath as the athletes settled down for the start. The sound of the starter's pistol would herald a cheer that would grow in volume as the runners made their way to the finish where the new champion would be hailed by a deafening roar. It would all be over in not much longer than the blinking of an eye.

For the British competitors, who would normally compete over the shorter 100yds, this was unfamiliar territory. They were now going to have to travel a little bit further, the metric 100m translating to approximately 109yds and one foot. The problem was diluted somewhat when 220yds and 440yds were adjusted to 200m and 400m but the shorter sprint highlighted the difference. To help athletes prepare for the new distances the Great Britain selectors had arranged that six meetings staged in the build-up to the Games would use metric measurements. The recent triangular competition was the last of these and the first three home in the 100m, McCorquodale, Jones and Bailey, had been clocked at 10.8, 10.9 and 11.0. There were some doubts about the accuracy of these times as the distances between the athletes was negligible to the naked eye and at such speed the clock suggests there should have been a metre between first and second and another separating second and third. Suffice to say, however, that on these performances Jesse Owens' world record, which stood at 10.2, was unlikely to be threatened by the British trio.

McDonald Bailey and McCorquodale had no previous experience of performing in front of so many people. It is also extremely unlikely that any of the other athletes taking part would have seen such numbers as those sitting in the stands and on the terraces eagerly waiting for events to unfold. As the previous Olympiad had taken place 12 years earlier a reappearance at the Games was unlikely, meaning that to have witnessed such large numbers of paying customers an athlete needed to have competed on another sporting stage. But Ken Jones had enjoyed success elsewhere on the international stage and was no stranger to appearing in front of many thousands of spectators. And he wasn't the first rugby player to do so; there was a precedent.

At the Games of the VIIIth Olympiad held in Paris in 1924, Scotsman Eric Liddell was another who had successfully transferred his skills from the rugby field to the athletics track or, as seems more likely, from the athletics track to the rugby field. Liddell won seven caps playing on the wing for Scotland, his great pace seeing him cross for three tries. Although entered to compete in the 100m in Paris, subsequent events dictated otherwise. Liddell held strong religious beliefs and these prevented him competing on a Sunday. With the heats of the 100m scheduled to take place on the sabbath, Eric Liddell was invited to compete in the 400m as an alternative. Harold Abrahams duly won the sprint gold medal and Liddell justified his stance and the change to the longer distance by also striking gold, breaking the Olympic record in the process. By the summer of 1948, Ken Jones had bettered the Scotsman's haul of international caps; now he needed a medal to go with them.

When the athletes arrived at the stadium they were greeted by another glorious day. Temperatures threatened to exceed those enjoyed during the opening ceremony and by early afternoon the thermometer was registering in the high eighties. Thirty-five countries were represented in the 100m with a total of 68 athletes involved. To accommodate such numbers the day's programme included 12 preliminary heats and four second-round heats, following which the 12 men who would contest the semi-finals the following day could be confirmed.

Sprinting is an exact science. Everything must be right; the finely tuned athlete has to be mentally and physically prepared, after which his performance depends on other factors beyond his control. Wembley Stadium not only attracted crowds to watch football matches but it was also recognised as one of the country's leading greyhound racing venues. To accommodate the Games the track that ran around the outside of the pitch had been dug up and replaced by a six-lane running track, one that met the standards demanded by such a high-profile event. The developers set about their task and after digging up the existing facility precise measurements were taken before the 400m circuit could be laid using 800 tons of cinders. The new surface was raked and steam-rollered until the inspectors were satisfied there were no irregularities that would hamper an athlete's progress. Only then could the artwork begin: the accurate white lines that separated the six lanes; the cross markings where hurdles and steeplechase barriers would be sited; the all-important finish line; and those boxes within which competitors in the relays had to ensure the baton exchange was completed. In August 1948 members of the British Olympic Association could look on proudly at the near perfect running surface which had been produced. But the track was found wanting in one small detail. As a consequence of the intense compression impacted when laying the cinders there was no give in the surface and the sprinters who had come prepared with a trowel to dig out their feet marks found the track uncooperative. Starting blocks were a relatively new innovation but they came into their own at Wembley as the speed merchants looked for alternative ways of getting that all-important start.

When the group of six athletes went through their final preparations before the first heat it was in the knowledge that only two of them would progress to the next round. The draw made on Wednesday had put Alastair McCorquodale in the first heat. Lining up alongside him was Barney Ewell of the USA, one of the favourites for the gold medal, and athletes from Cuba, Jamaica, Malta and Poland. The British team were in high spirits after the Scot finished second to the American, both being awarded 10.5. This was a good benchmark which only one athlete would improve on over the remaining 11 heats. Ken Jones was included in heat four and as he spent time in the warm-up area, firstly Mel Patton joined his fellow American in the second round by winning heat 2 in 10.6 and the Panamanian Lloyd LaBeach laid down his mark of intent, matching Ewell's time when winning the third heat.

Performing in front of such a large number of spectators did not concern Ken. Attendances at matches may not have reached those seen before the war but Wales regularly played in front of crowds in excess of 40,000 and at Twickenham earlier in the year 73,000 had seen him score the try that salvaged a 3-3 draw for the visitors. But even this could not have prepared him for the reception that greeted the athletes as they entered the stadium for the fourth heat of the 100m. He knew his father and Irene were somewhere among the 60,000 spectators but for the first time in front of such numbers, Ken Jones was on his own. He was not accompanied by 14 other like-minded individuals with whom he could exchange a knowing nod or give or take a quick word of encouragement. He could only take encouragement from the adrenalin pumping through him and the excitement prevailing all around. Now he had to focus like never before, run his race and hope he was good enough.

The line-up included sprinters from Greece, Iceland, the Netherlands and Peru, with the biggest threat likely to come from the Uruguayan Juan Lopez. And so it proved. Lopez got the perfect start and was a stride up on the rest of the field at the halfway mark. Ken knew second place would see him into the next round but he stuck his chest out and made a mighty effort to catch the South American in the final strides. At the tape little separated them, Lopez winning in 10.5 and Ken runner-up in a respectable 10.6. Harrison Dillard scorched to victory in the fifth heat in 10.4, the fastest time of the first round, and in the next McDonald Bailey defied all the below par performances he brought into the Games, winning in 10.5. The Australian star John Treloar was the fifth sprinter to run 10.5 when winning heat 7 but thereafter the pace eased up, heat 12 producing the slowest figures when Mario Fayos from Uruguay and Rajamicka Phillips, representing India, both clocked 11.0 flat.

The line-up for the second round included the three British runners, three Americans, three Australians and two Uruguayans who, together with runners from Cuba and Panama, looked the likely contenders for a place in the final. The British and USA qualifiers were matched head to head: Jones would meet Dillard in the first heat; Bailey was included alongside Ewell in the second; and McCorquodale found himself up against Patton in the third. This time the first three in each of the four heats would return for the semi-finals the following day with British hopes of a finalist looking good.

With no respite from the high temperatures the afternoon was warming up and reports filtered through from the high jump that some of the competitors had been overcome by the unrelenting heat. There was nowhere to hide in the outfield and the medical staff in attendance were justifying their presence with many spectators in the 'bleachers' also finding the going tough as the second round of the 100m became the focus of attention. As the six runners in the first heat prepared to take their marks, Ken got his first close look at Harrison Dillard and a second at the Uruguayan Lopez. Completing the line-up were competitors from Brazil, Canada and Portugal and Ken knew he had to show a clean pair of heels to these three if he was to remain in contention.

As expected, Dillard was quickest out of the blocks and wasn't headed during the race. Lopez again got the better of the Welshman, but knowing the remainder were beaten, Jones eased up over the final 15 metres to finish third in 10.7 but assured of his place in the semi-finals. McDonald Bailey found Barney Ewell too quick in the second heat but his runner-up spot ensured he would also be on the bus to Wembley on Saturday. And when McCorquodale recorded another 10.5 performance in finishing second to Mel Patton, Great Britain could boast three of the 12 fastest men in the world. Nothing had been seen to suggest the expected American supremacy in the event was under serious threat but tomorrow was another day and there was a lot to run for. Ken's comment on the day's proceedings was: 'It was fun.'

The Olympic Games rarely passes without one or more of the competitors arriving on the world stage and becoming household names. In the three Games held during the 1920s, the Finn Paavo Nurmi won a glut of medals – nine gold and three silver – in the middle- and long-distance events. In 1932, much to the delight of the home crowd, Eddie Tolan won the sprint double in Los Angeles, creating two new games records, and the name Jesse Owens will forever be associated with Berlin in 1936. In 1948 it was a Czechoslovakian army lieutenant and a Dutch housewife who would be added to the unofficial hall of fame.

With the first day's programme of events almost complete, at 6.00pm 27 competitors lined up for the start of the 10,000m. Viljo Heino of Finland was the current world record holder but his time had come under serious threat a few weeks earlier when the Czech Emil Zátopek ran within two seconds of it. Despite British success elsewhere on the opening day it was for Zátopek that the crowd reserved their greatest applause. Few of the runners avoided the ignominy of being lapped. Heino withdrew after 15 laps and Zátopek went on to win in a new Olympic record of 29mins 59.6, breaking the previous best by almost 12 seconds with silver medallist, Alain Mimoun of France, a distant 48 seconds behind.

The women's athletics was restricted to only nine events in 1948 but this would soon change, thanks in no small part to the exploits of Francina 'Fanny' Blankers-Koen. The current holder of the high jump and long jump world records, the 30-year-old decided against competing in either event, preferring to test herself against the best in the world on the track. Gold medals in the 100m, 200m, 80m hurdles and 4x100m relay confirm what a fine athlete she was and during the eight days of track and field competition she made an indelible mark on all those who watched her. By the end of the week her name would roll off the tongue with similar ease to a Smith, Jones or Williams.

The second day of competition got under way with the temperatures once again threatening to reach the high eighties. This being the start of the August bank holiday weekend the crowds descended on Wembley in their thousands. An estimated 83,000 packed the stadium and they were treated to some outstanding performances. Zátopek reappeared in the heats of the 5,000m but British interest was firmly focused on the 100m with the two semi-finals scheduled for the morning session and the final to take place in the afternoon.

Again the mathematics was simple. The first three over the line in each of the semi-finals would go forward to the final. Alastair McCorquodale ran brilliantly in the first, chasing home Dillard and Ewell to secure his place, and McDonald Bailey joined him when coming third behind the improving Patton and the consistent LaBeach in the second. Sadly, Ken Jones brought up the rear of what was a highly competitive field, finishing in a disappointing 10.7. To this day there are those who remain convinced he appeared to ease up at what would have been the 100yds mark and fell back to sixth from a promising second place at that late stage of the race. Whatever the reason, he would not be lining up in the 100m final, which was won by Harrison Dillard, with Barney Ewell taking silver and LaBeach bronze. Alastair McCorquodale ran well for fourth place with McDonald Bailey finishing sixth.

Unlike Paris in 1924 there were no events held on Sunday, which allowed Ken time to reflect on his performances in the 100m. There could be no doubt that the three fastest British sprinters had been selected and that in the build-up to the Games there was very little to choose between them. McDonald Bailey had carried a muscle injury from the previous season and his performances in the competitions leading into the Olympics were mixed. Jones had beaten him at Uxbridge in the Southern Counties Championship and again at Manchester, with Bailey getting the better of the Welshman in the AAA final. McCorquodale's late arrival on the athletics scene had thrown a new name into the mix at the start of the season and his performances suggested he would be the pick of the British trio, as indeed proved to be the case. Second at Uxbridge, he was runner-up behind Treloar in the AAA before winning in Manchester over the metric distance, and in recording 10.4 at Wembley he bettered Ken's all-time career best of 10.6. With his chance of individual success dashed, Ken now started to focus on the 4x100m relay due to take place over the final two days of competition.

McCorquodale was the only British athlete entered for both the 100m and 200m. He was a late inclusion in the 4x100m relay, joining Ken Jones, Jack Archer and Jack Gregory, with McDonald Bailey clearly not one hundred per cent fit. With three 100m semi-finalists in the quartet there was justifiable cause for optimism that the team would not only reach the final, but were in with a real chance of a medal.

McCorquodale progressed through the 200m heats on Monday and his involvement in the later stages of the event on Tuesday, which saw him eliminated at the semi-final stage, meant he could take no part in the relay squad's early training sessions. The heats of the relay were scheduled for Friday, giving the team only two days to fine-tune the passing of the baton through the three exchanges. This was an essential part of the relay as the transfer not only had to be completed with the runners flat out but also within a designated 20m box, something that would be highlighted come Saturday's final.

It was pure coincidence that McCorquodale, the youngest member of the quartet at 22, was chosen to run the first leg before passing the baton to the 25-year-old Jack Gregory. Ken Jones, clocking in at 26, would run the bend on the third leg and it was Jack Archer, due to celebrate his 27th birthday three days after the final, who would hopefully bring the team home in a medal position. Despite the little time available to them, the squad mastered the all-important baton exchanges and produced several sub-42.0 runs on the training ground. The current world and Olympic records had been set by the USA at Berlin in 1936 and stood at 39.8. This was not expected to be improved upon at Wembley, but if the squad could continue breaking the 42.0 mark, then the medals were within reach. There may have been a dearth of medals from the track and field events in 1948 but the 4x100m relay was one in which Great Britain had a pedigree. At Stockholm in 1912 the team had struck gold and they took the silver in Paris 12 years later. This was followed by bronze in Amsterdam in 1928 and now the class of 1948 were strongly fancied to add to this haul.

The heatwave experienced over the holiday weekend had long gone by the second Friday, the seventh day of competition on the track. In its place was a mix of intermittent rain and clear skies, but overall temperatures were much lower. A burst of heavy rain fell during the early part of the afternoon, and come the start of the relay competition, the wet track looked anything but inviting to a finely tuned relay team. Fifteen countries had entered and these would contest three heats to decide the six finalists. Rather than five countries in each heat there was an imbalance that saw the USA, Italy, Brazil and Turkey take part in the first; Great Britain up against Hungary, Australia, Belgium, Uruguay, and Bermuda in the second; and the Netherlands, Canada, Argentina, Iceland and France in a third. Any arguments about the division of labour fell on deaf ears and, fairly or otherwise, the first two in each heat would contest the final.

The favourites were the American quartet, which included Ewell, Dillard and Patton, three 100m finalists, and Lorenzo Wright, who had just missed out on the medals when coming fourth in the long jump. This impressive line-up won the first heat in 41.1, with the Italians next home to secure their place in the final. Although run in a slower time, the second heat produced a much closer finish. Drawn in the inside lane, Great

Britain did not get the best of starts. McCorquodale, clearly at odds with the bend and the wet surface, struggled to make any impression on the stagger, if anything conceding ground to some of those outside him. This was compensated for by a smooth exchange with Gregory, who ran a fine second leg down the back straight, making up any lost ground before concentrating on Ken Jones' open hand as the Welshman got into his stride. It was the exchange between Gregory and Jones that stole a march on their rivals and after running a perfect bend Ken gave the baton to Archer with what was described as 'the finest thing of the day in the relays'.

Practice makes perfect, and with the Hungarians and Australians in such close attendance the British quartet would look back on the heat and fully appreciate how the time spent on the training ground had helped win the race. They were in the final, but the time of 41.4 suggested they would need to be equally efficient the next day and dig much deeper into the tank if they were to trouble the Americans.

In 1934 a young German film director was invited to make a documentary account of the Nuremberg rally. Despite its contentious subject matter, *Triumph of the Will* received worldwide acclaim and two years later Leni Riefenstahl was asked to repeat the exercise, this time with the Berlin Olympic Games as the subject of her directorial skills. The end result, *Olympia*, also met with critical acclaim. Riefenstahl focussed her barrage of cameras on the athletes and spectators with such effect that she was able to transfer the excitement, tension and emotion of the Games to the screen, enabling cinemagoers to experience the drama from a better perspective than enjoyed by those in attendance. From the outset, the organising committee had decided the 1948 Olympics would receive similar fly-on-the-wall attention and that cameras would be prominently positioned at all events to enable a lasting account of the Olympics to be made. Little did the competing athletes in the men's 4x100m relay final realise that their every action over the next 40-plus seconds would be subjected to such scrutiny as they lined up at 3.30pm on Saturday.

Great Britain were drawn in lane four with the favourites one lane inside them. Lanes one and two were occupied by Hungary and the Netherlands with Italy and Canada in five and six. Barney Ewell had been forced to settle for the silver medal in both the 100m and 200m sprints but this was a final chance for gold and he was out of the blocks and away, making great inroads into the stagger before handing over to Lorenzo Wright. McCorquodale ran a good first leg and his smooth exchange with Gregory ensured that Britain were in second place down the back straight, but it was the USA who were clear leaders with the stagger still in their favour. The exchange between Gregory and Jones was another perfect example of how the complex manoeuvre should be done but that between Wright and Dillard was also well executed and Ken had his work cut out trying to maintain what little remained of the stagger ahead of the pursuing Dillard. At the final changeover Jones and Archer completed another excellent transfer but Mel Patton was long gone. Jack Archer did well not to allow the American to increase the lead but there could be no doubting the winners, the USA crossing the finish line some six, seven or even eight metres ahead, depending on which report of the race is to be believed. The winning time was 40.6 with Great Britain claiming second place in 41.3, suggesting the longer version of the winning distance may be the more accurate. Italy ran into third, 0.2 seconds behind Great Britain, with Hungary having to settle for the so near yet so far fourth spot.

While the Great Britain team congratulated each other on a job well done, the Americans made their way over to the winners' area in preparation for the medal ceremony scheduled to follow immediately. Then the announcement came over the loudspeaker system. Due to a faulty baton change between the first and second runners, Ewell and

Wright, the USA team was disqualified and the gold medal would be awarded to Great Britain, Italy receiving the silver with Hungary elevated to bronze. The judge assessing the legitimacy of the first changeover reported that the Americans had not completed it within the allocated 20m box and as such were in contravention of the rules. Great Britain had won on a disqualification and each member of the team felt a certain dissatisfaction in being awarded gold on a technical discrepancy after being so comprehensively beaten. Following the announcement, the stadium was hushed, 85,000 spectators not really sure what was happening. Then the word started to spread and with it the realisation that the disqualification heralded a British victory. Pandemonium broke out and shortly afterwards 'God Save the King' was heard in the stadium for the first time since the opening ceremony.

Within an hour of the race finishing, American officials had lodged an appeal. Team manager Dean Cromwell told press reporters that 'I have been wrong one million times before and maybe I shall be wrong one million and one times but I think I am right about this incident... we knew we were going to win this race and the boys were instructed to make sure each passing of the baton was safe. The team are particularly hurt and chagrined by this outcome. Both boys – Ewell and Wright – stake their lives on the legitimacy of the handover.' It was clear that the dispute was not going to go away and regardless of the fact that the British newspapers reported a gold medal in the Sunday and Monday editions the matter was still unresolved 48 hours after the final.

The decision to make a documentary film of the London Olympics was justified long before the Games closed. On Monday, at a film studio in the city, Castleton Knight, producer of the documentary, viewed all the available footage of the race together with a selection of stills capturing the moment when the baton was transferred from Ewell to Wright. He watched the footage many times over and finally came to the conclusion that the exchange had been legitimate and the USA were not guilty of any infringement. On the basis of this evidence a screening was arranged for Tuesday. Held at 8.00am, it was attended by members of the Olympic Committee, and after viewing the evidence a simple statement was issued to the waiting press who were later shown the film. 'The jury of the IAAF having seen the film and photographs of the 400m relay of the Olympic Games are satisfied that an error was made and the placings have been revised as follows – 1 USA, 2 Great Britain, 3 Italy.'

Castleton Knight concurred, 'I definitely agree with the decision. I did have some doubts yesterday but after studying a number of enlargements and watching the film over, a third line was identified and this confirmed that the baton change was legal.' Running tracks have many lines and marks crossing the lanes. Some identify the boxes within which baton transfers must be completed and there are others which mark where hurdles are to be positioned and it appears one such line may have caused the confusion. The final decision confirmed Ewell and Wright had completed the transfer of the baton at least a metre within the box.

The Americans were obviously delighted with the ruling but there would be no presentation ceremony. Instead it fell to Lord Burghley, chairman of the Council of the British Olympic Association, to hand the gold medals to Dan Ferris, secretary of the Amateur Athletic Union of the USA. This took place on Wednesday in front of a very sparse gathering at the stadium, there for the latter stages of the men's hockey tournament. Lord Burghley commented there was 'no doubt about it. The Americans were inside the line and we are only too happy to have the opportunity to put the error right.' Ferris was equally magnanimous stating that 'the whole affair was conducted with the same high level of sportsmanship which prevailed throughout the games... sorry for Great Britain but full of admiration for her great sportsmen'.

Ken Jones would later describe the Olympic Games as the greatest single experience of his sporting career. Considering those he enjoyed elsewhere during his ten years as a world-class athlete and rugby player this says much about the standing and prestige of Baron de Coubertin's reincarnation of the ancient Greek module. The Olympic Games are now the biggest sporting event in the world and to compete in them is often reward enough for the dedication and commitment demanded. To win a medal is the dream come true, and even if gold has to eventually become silver, once the inevitable disappointment has passed the recipient can always look back on a job well done. Ken Jones, Olympic silver medallist, has a great ring to it and forgetting the drama surrounding the relay final it is little surprise that this should have topped his personal list of sporting moments to treasure.

CHAPTER FIVE

DECISIONS, DECISIONS

W hen Ken Jones collected his Olympic medal he joined a very short list of Welsh athletes similarly recognised. At Stockholm in 1912, Cardiff-born David Jacobs won a gold medal in the 4x100m relay and in 1920 at Antwerp there was double Welsh success when Neath's Cecil Griffiths and John Ainsworth-Davis from Aberystwyth helped the Great Britain 4x400m relay team to another gold medal-winning performance. The 1948 Olympics not only saw a relay team win silver but it also produced the first individual medal won by a Welshman when Cwmbran's Tom Richards came second in the marathon. The passage of time would see many outstanding Welsh athletes add their names to the list but by 1948, only five men had brought an Olympic medal home to Wales.

Blaenavon had certainly celebrated in style when Ken became the first rugby player born in the town to represent Wales and now there was reason to party again. The council had already discussed ways of recognising Ken's exploits on the rugby field and running track but any decision as to what form this should take was held back until the end of the Games. With the strict attitudes regarding amateurism observed by both the WRU and the AAA, it was essential that any presentation could not be construed as being in breach of either organisation's code of conduct. There was much to discuss, and while the town's New Imperial Club beat the council out of the traps when announcing similar intent, Councillor TH Walthen JP was charged with the responsibility of organising an official fund and subscriptions were invited from local businesses and individuals which could be paid into the local branch of the Midland Bank. The target set was £500.

The track and field events at the Olympics were completed on 7 August and the Games officially closed a week later. Any hopes of an immediate return to normality were soon forgotten when the invitations started coming thick and fast. There were invitations to celebratory dinners; invitations to meet local dignitaries at official luncheons; invitations to compete at various track meetings; and invitations to just come and watch events unfold as a guest of honour. Olympic medallists were thin on the ground and the demands for their time were high but while some invitations had to be returned with a polite 'thank you but no', there was one meeting that Ken would not miss and he was prepared to put his reputation on the line by competing in two handicaps.

The Blaenavon Workmen's Hall Grand Athletics and Cycling Meeting was held at the Recreation Ground on Saturday 21 August. Its preliminaries included a civic welcome given by Councillor Walthen in which he confirmed the opening of the fund to commemorate Ken's sporting achievements. Responding, Ken was his usual modest and reserved self but he did take this opportunity to air some thoughts on the lack of certain amenities in Blaenavon. He suggested that nothing would give him greater pleasure than knowing the town had an athletic club to complement the well-established rugby and cricket clubs, both of which encouraged the involvement of the young men of the town. Throughout his sporting career and beyond, Ken Jones was a firm believer that if the facilities were available young talent would find its way through the system. Every town and village had a rugby ground and the game in Wales thrived. Why couldn't budding athletes be given the same opportunity? How any monies collected would be spent was yet to be decided but Ken would never let the chance to promote sport at grass roots level pass when the people who could do something about it were a captive audience.

The formalities duly dispensed with, Ken delighted the large crowd to some quality sprinting to completely cancel out the handicap advantage enjoyed by the other competitors. Four times he scorched over the Recreation Ground when winning his heats and the finals of the 100yds and 220yds. Only fitting that the Olympian should return to Blaenavon and give his home town the first chance to see him in action following the Games, and only fitting that after attending the Blaenavon meeting his next appointment on the track was at Newport. On 26 August, Ken represented Monmouthshire against Glamorgan at Rodney Parade in a match featuring eight events. His participation in the 100yds created much interest as it was billed as an attempt on the Welsh record of 9.8, but a wet surface prevented a fast time and spectators had to settle for another winning performance. A week later at St Helen's, Swansea, the final of the 100yds handicap saw Ken, starting off scratch, once more make light of the competitors ahead of him in another bid for a new record. Again the conditions underfoot didn't help – neither did a stiff wind – but by setting a new track record of 9.9 he showed that in the right circumstances he was capable of breaking the Welsh record equalled at Uxbridge earlier in the season. Over the next six seasons Ken Jones would run 9.8 no fewer than five times but it would be down to another Jones to eventually improve on the time when Birchgrove Harrier Ron Jones clocked 9.7 at the White City in 1959.

After spending two enjoyable years at Bathwick Junior School Ken decided it was time for a change. He desperately wanted to move into the field of physical education, which meant a return to college if he was to gain the necessary qualification that would enable him to teach the subject at a higher level. He was accepted for a one-year course at Loughborough College in Leicestershire, a move that would limit his availability for Newport but at the same time open up new avenues in the rugby-playing world.

The basic standard of physical education courses that featured on the curriculum at colleges such as St Paul's, Cheltenham, before the Second World War had been addressed and Loughborough was now one of the leading destinations for students wishing to pursue this area of education. For Ken Jones and other students who were participating in sport at a high level, Loughborough was perfect. The college had a good rugby team and the Universities Athletic Union (UAU) drew together the cream of student talent for some highly competitive fixtures against leading clubs. There would also be plenty of top-class competition to enjoy come the athletics season and with the course work geared toward physical fitness, students could be expected to maintain high personal levels which they would find difficult to improve on. Even international rugby players and Olympic athletes would benefit from the day in, day out regime dedicated to creating the body beautiful and knowing what to do with it.

Shortly after Ken arrived at Loughborough, Newport travelled to London to play Blackheath. This set up the possibility of seeing two of Britain's Olympic medal-winning relay team face each other on a rugby field, with Jack Gregory Blackheath's first-choice left wing. Released from college, Ken made the 130-mile journey to south-east London where he met up with the rest of the Newport team at the Rectory Field, only to be told on arrival that Gregory had travelled to Dublin – the clash between the Olympians would have to wait for another day. Disappointment aside, Ken enjoyed the opportunity to pull on his club jersey, knowing that opportunities to do so would be few and far between in the coming months. Gregory may have been absent but the long journey south had its rewards as Ken scored the game's opening try and played a big part in Newport's impressive 25-0 victory before making his way back to Leicestershire.

Today, Ken Jones would be referred to as a mature student. He entered Loughborough as a 26-year-old married man who would celebrate his 27th birthday during his time at the college. Being separated from his wife within nine months of tying the knot would not have been easy but the couple had been parted for three years when the only contact was by letter, so this new separation was seen as nothing more than a minor inconvenience in a relationship now in its 14th year. The breaks between terms, Ken's involvement with international rugby and the matches that took the college rugby team west and, on occasion, into Wales, all played a part in helping to move the academic year along. Coupled with the knowledge that the end result would make the sacrifices seem well worthwhile, the couple remained firmly focused on the light at the end of the tunnel.

West Mon School, Talywain, Blaenavon, Pontypool, St Paul's College, Cheltenham, Somerset, Newport, Monmouthshire and Wales had all benefited from Ken Jones' rugby prowess. Now it was the turn of Loughborough College. Renowned for producing good rugby teams, in 1948–49 the college boasted one of the best. Only one of the 31 matches played was lost with two drawn, Loughborough scoring a massive 653 points and conceding only 83. The highlight of the season was the UAU Cup, a knock-out competition attracting teams from all the major universities and colleges. Loughborough had never won it, never even contested a final, but on 1 March they entertained Cardiff University in a semi-final played on the college playing fields in front of a big crowd. The quarter-final had brought Swansea University to Loughborough but the students from west Wales were sent back empty-handed, leaving Cardiff University the only Welsh representative still in the tournament.

There was little to choose between the teams, which were tied 0-0 at half-time. Early in the second half Loughborough's Stan Beaumont crossed for an unconverted try and that was how the score remained until the final minute when the same player added a second try that also went unconverted for a final score of 6-0. Loughborough College were in the final for the first time, where they would meet Manchester University, comfortable winners of the other semi-final in which they beat Hull University 29-0. The final was to be played at Cheltenham on 12 March. It would have given Ken enormous pleasure to return to one of his old stamping grounds for such an auspicious occasion but a quick look at the fixture list would have told him that with Wales scheduled to play Ireland in Swansea on the same day he would be unable to help Loughborough in the final. The college would have to make do without his services, not only on the field but also in his capacity as a tour guide off it following the match, when it was hoped there would be much cause for celebration.

It was unfortunate that the two matches clashed, as Ken desperately wanted to take his place in the college team for the biggest game in their history. No team should ever be measured on the strength of one player but there is every reason to think that if Ken Jones had played in the UAU final, Loughborough College might have had reason to celebrate. But it was not to be, with the final producing the only defeat of the season, Manchester University gaining a hard-earned victory by 8 points to 5. As events were unfolding at Cheltenham, Wales were faring little better in Swansea. The championship had started promisingly enough when England were beaten 9-3 at the Arms Park, Wales scoring three tries to a drop goal, now reduced to three points in value. It was in this match that Jack Gregory won his only England cap but he was selected on the right wing. The Olympic medallists stood on opposite sides of the field, denying the crowd the opportunity of seeing two of rugby football's fastest players go head to head. Scotland put an end to any Welsh thoughts of Triple Crowns and Grand Slams when winning 6-5 at Murrayfield, which left Ireland as the only team with its Triple Crown aspirations still alive. Building on the success of the previous season, the men in green defeated Wales 5-0 to record back-to-back Triple Crowns. Any chance of a second Irish Grand Slam had disappeared in Paris and it was to the 'city of love' that Wales headed for the final match of the championship, where victory would repair some of the damage inflicted in recent weeks by her Celtic cousins.

It is remarkable to think that in 1949 an estimated 3,000 supporters made their way across the English Channel in support of the Welsh team. One can only hope that they enjoyed the delights on offer in Paris because there was little to enthuse about at Stade Colombes as Wales lost for a third time in a disappointing championship. The match witnessed the last appearance in a Welsh jersey by Haydn Tanner and it saw the international debuts of the young Newport centre Malcolm Thomas and Swansea wing-forward Clem Thomas, both players destined for greatness in the annals of Welsh rugby. Two instances best sum up the match and they both involved Ken Jones. He scored a first-half try which went unconverted and in the second half made an uncharacteristic error when allowing his opposite number to take him on the inside and score a try that was converted to give France a 5-3 victory. Wales ended the campaign propping up the table, outright winners of the Wooden Spoon, and there was little consolation taken from the knowledge that the three defeats had all been closely contested. That Wales scored five tries while conceding four only rubbed more salt in the wound. But this was not a poor Welsh team, far from it. The calibre of player the selectors had at their disposal probably made their counterparts elsewhere extremely envious but in 1949 the best-laid plans came to nought. It would be very different next time.

During the 1948–49 season Ken Jones appeared for seven teams; eight if one includes his three outings for the Probables in Welsh trial matches. In addition to playing regularly for Loughborough he was also selected for the UAU in matches against Waterloo at Blundellsands and the Scottish Universities in Glasgow. If there were any doubts concerning the standard of rugby Ken was involved with for much of the season, that it was in any way inferior and perhaps not ideal preparation for international rugby, they were easily dispelled. The universities and colleges had strong fixture lists, the rugby was intensely competitive and many leading players either played their rugby in the colours of a seat of learning or lined up against the enthusiastic students. For example, Waterloo was able to call upon England internationals John Heaton, Dickie Guest, Gordon Rimmer and Dick Uren in a first-class back division. These were players who would keep any students with fanciful ideas firmly in their place, even if they were 26 and had been around the block a few times.

If anything, Ken's second stint at college would have kept him well tuned for the bigger stage and he was certainly seeing more of the ball than he enjoyed in his first two seasons with Newport. There was an appearance for Monmouthshire against Glamorgan at Pontypool Park over the Christmas break and a return to international duty in the new year. Loughborough College, the UAU, Newport, Monmouthshire and Wales were teams Ken Jones could be expected to appear for in the season but two other clubs extended invitations which were readily accepted.

On 27 November the first England trial was held at Northampton. Leicester were represented in the 'Colours' by two first-team wing three-quarters and with other regular players sidelined through injury the club was struggling to raise a side to play the Middlesex Hospitals at Welford Road on the same day. The search for a replacement led to Loughborough College and Ken Jones was invited to appear for the famous English club, fully playing his part in a 20-6 victory. News of this guest appearance could not have been well received in Newport, particularly as the Black and Ambers were playing Gloucester at Rodney Parade on the same day. Newport won that match 16-6 but knowing that one of the club's star players was in action elsewhere, not for his college or the UAU but for another club, must have raised questions among the hierarchy and on the terraces. Any concerns the committee members and supporters might have felt were unfounded. Hadn't Ken travelled home two weeks earlier to play against Cardiff? Made the journey to London to play at Blackheath earlier in the season?

If there were any doubts as to where Ken Jones would play club rugby after completing his year at Loughborough then they were held by people who clearly did not know the man. At no time was there any suggestion he would do anything other than seek employment in Wales and continue playing for Newport, but come the end of a glittering career there would always be the one game played for Leicester included in the curriculum vitae.

Ken Jones also made his first appearance for another famous club during the 1948–49 season. An invitation side without a home, the institution that is the Barbarians RFC had a short fixture list but one that was regularly played out in front of full houses. Season after season Leicester, the East Midlands, Penarth, Cardiff, Swansea and Newport provided the opposition, much to the chagrin of all others, envious of the lucrative huge public interest the visit of the Barbarians generated. This was largely down to the expansive and entertaining brand of rugby for which the club was famous; and to pull on the black and white hooped jersey and black shorts and complete the strip with your club stockings was seen as a huge honour by those players fortunate enough to be invited to join the club. Ken was selected to play against the East Midlands in the Edgar Mobbs Memorial Match at Bedford on 3 March. This was a fixture of long-standing importance in the rugby calendar and of special significance to those involved. Edgar Mobbs DSO was 32 when the First World War broke out but refused a commission because of his age. Undeterred, he raised his own corps, which attracted more than 400 volunteers and became known as Mobbs' Army. His many wartime deeds are properly recorded elsewhere but suffice to say that Edgar Mobbs lost his life in July 1917 in an action said to be one of the most heroic of the war. Mobbs played for Northampton, won seven England caps and served on the Barbarians committee and it was a fitting gesture by the club when in 1921 it elected to play a match in his honour against the East Midlands, a fixture that continues to this day.

Ken took his place alongside fellow Welsh internationals Bleddyn Williams, Glyn Davies, Haydn Tanner, John Gwilliam and Gwyn Evans in a star-studded XV that royally entertained the large crowd before running out winners by 24-11. Ken scored a characteristic try after a 40-yard dash for the line but for much of the match he was contained by his opposite number, an 18-year-old schoolboy named John Hyde. Time after time Ken was prevented from reaching top gear by the superb tackling of the youngster, who was in no way to blame when his illustrious opponent broke away to score. But for Hyde's efforts there could well have been many more tries on the right flank and he deserved every favourable comment written about him in the match reviews that followed.

Ken Jones certainly travelled the miles during that 1948–49 season and there were very few occasions when he did not give value for money. He was now seen as one of a select band of players who people would pay to see play, one whose inclusion in a team would actually put bums on seats. There weren't many seats in the small stand at the Athletic Ground, Penarth, but spectators were not deterred, the small terrace and open areas surrounding the pitch always ten-deep when a big club with star players visited the coastal town a short distance west of Cardiff. The Barbarians traditionally used the town's Esplanade Hotel as their base for the Easter tour which began against Penarth on Good Friday. In 1949 Newport travelled to Penarth for the penultimate match of the season. Still on his mid-term break, Ken was included on the right wing and within 12 minutes had used his blistering pace and explosive side-step to score a hat-trick of tries, setting Newport on the way to a comfortable 25-5 victory. The euphoria of scoring three tries was soon forgotten when early in the second half he attempted to stop a threatening foot rush by the Penarth forwards and suffered a broken wrist for his efforts, which brought his season to a premature end. The injury meant that he was unable to take his place in a Ken Jones' International XV against Hedley Rowland's Monmouthshire XV at Blaenavon the following Monday, a match arranged as part of the fund-raising activities being held in his name, and he had to pull out of Captain Geoffrey Crawshay's Rest of Wales XV against Cardiff in the Gwyn Nicholls Memorial match the following Thursday. And after accepting an invitation to appear at the tournament, Newport would have to travel to Twickenham for the prestigious Middlesex Sevens without their sprint champion. Sport is a bit like that, full of its ups and downs, ecstasy and abject misery, but the athletics season wasn't far off and a broken wrist wasn't going to spoil that.

Ken returned to Loughborough determined to end his year at the College on a high. The wrist had knitted together well and within a few weeks he was able to get down to some serious training. Running at pace does involve a lot of arm movement and the wrist is relied upon at those all-important starts but Ken was soon seen on the college track working through his well-rehearsed routines and would be ready come the competitive end of university athletics. The college rugby team was not short of talented players but it pales into comparison when one looks at those available for selection for the athletics squad. Jack Archer had also entered Loughborough to study for a physical education degree, as had two other men who competed at the London Olympics.

Running for Ceylon, Duncan White won a silver medal in the 400m hurdles, his time of 51.8 breaking the previous Olympic record, and New Zealand's Doug Harris had the misfortune to snap an Achilles tendon in the semi-final of the 800m, an event in which he recorded the world's fastest time in 1947.

In the Northern University Championships held at Loughborough, the universities of Nottingham, Hull, Sheffield, Leeds and Leicester were humbled by their hosts, Loughborough winning 12 of the 17 events. White took both the 120yds and 440yds hurdles titles and Harris won the 880yds but it was the 100yds sprint that attracted the most interest among spectators with Olympic medallists Ken Jones and Jack Archer lining up in the final. The timekeepers were unable to separate the pair on the clock, both credited with 9.9, but Ken got the verdict by a matter of inches and doubled up when winning the 220yds in 22.3. Ken Jones' final competitive appearance as a student came at the annual England–Scotland Universities meeting held at Aberdeen. Again his main rival was Archer and it was another first and second in both events for the Loughborough men, Ken leading the way with another 9.9 in the short sprint and an improved time of 22.1 in the extended version.

Ken may have played for Leicester during the season but when the expected interest was shown in acquiring his services for the following campaign it came not from Welford Road but from Coundon Road and the Reddings, homes to Coventry RFC and Moseley RFC, two of the biggest clubs in England. Ken was undoubtedly flattered to have his name linked with the leading Midland clubs but made no comment on the rumoured interest being shown by Hunslet RLFC, which came to nought.

College life over, Ken was appointed sports master at Newport High School for Boys, ensuring that he would stay in the town for the foreseeable future. With the school year not due to start until September there was ample time for

Ken and Irene to find accommodation in Newport and after much searching they finally settled into a first-floor flat. Summerhill Avenue was a stone's throw from Rodney Parade, a comfortable walk to the town across the river and little further to Newport High School, where Ken would spend the next seven years. Unable to find a teaching position, Irene settled into a clerical job with William Adams, a local company that worked a number of quarries in the area but had its head office in Newport. In time she would follow Ken to Newport High School when she joined the teaching staff at the girls' school before settling at Stow Hill Secondary School, another centre of learning located in the town. With all their immediate needs close to hand the Joneses could begin to think long term. It was time to settle down.

During the summer of 1949 Ken produced some of the best performances of his career. The serious part of the season began when he retained his Welsh AAA titles at Abertillery, a meeting that saw him clock another 9.8 in the 100yds. Familiar ground was also trodden at the White City when he was again upstaged by McDonald Bailey and Jack Archer and a new arrival on the British athletics scene, the Jamaican Les Laing. McDonald Bailey completed another championship double with Laing runner-up in both sprints. The minor places went to Archer, who edged the Welshman out of third place in the 100yds with Jones having to settle for third in the 220yds. It was another day of reckoning in London that had ended disappointingly, but elsewhere there was much to savour.

Ken won both sprints when representing the AAA against Devon and Cornwall in Falmouth and repeated the double in the Monmouthshire AAA Championships at Newport. He had to settle for second place in the 220yds behind Les Laing when the pair represented England and Wales against Scotland and Ireland in Belfast on 13 August but seven days later Ken had his day in a triangular match between the Midland Counties, Southern Counties and Wales held at St

George's Playing Fields, Bristol. In winning the 100yds in 9.8 he equalled the English native record with which statisticians had been happy to credit him, and he had the added satisfaction of beating Laing into second place, albeit by a matter of inches. The two renewed their rivalry later in the day in the final of the 220yds, this time with the roles reversed. With the season drawing to a close, an international meeting in Oslo saw Ken representing Great Britain against athletes from Norway, Sweden, Finland and the USA. Reverting once again to the metric system, he ran into second place in both the 100m and 200m behind Andy Stanfield of the USA.

Aware that elsewhere players were getting out the boots in preparation for another rugby season, Ken joined several other international stars and headed to Edinburgh from Oslo for the Highland Games which were held at Murrayfield. A fine performance saw him take the 100yds title to bring the season to a satisfactory conclusion. There were the usual highs and lows but overall, the Olympic medal winner of 12 months earlier had enhanced his reputation as one of the finest sprinters in the land. Now things were about to get physical again.

Another athletics season behind him and with a new rugby season already under way, Ken Jones was now faced with one of the biggest dilemmas of his sporting career. The Empire Games would be held in Auckland in February and the British Lions were due to leave for a tour of New Zealand and Australia in March. With a new job to consider, his involvement in either of these great sporting events would be subject to approval from above but, for certain, he would not be able to take part in both. With lack of funds, the British Empire Games Council for Wales was not going to be able to send a large representation to New Zealand but Ken and marathon runner Tom Richards were invited to compete together with the swimmer John Brockway and cyclist Malcolm Campbell. Should Ken run for his country or take the chance that he

(left) The earliest known photograph of Ken Jones taken circa 1923. (right) An 11-year-old Ken in a traditional pose for the photo album taken in 1933.
(Jones' Family Archive)

Ken Jones in the first of many team photographs. This is the Blaenavon Schools Junior XV in 1931. Ken is sitting second from the right. (Jones' Family Archive)

Bob Barwell was the first person to recognise the prodigious talent waiting to be unleashed. Ken would always name Barwell as his earliest influence, the man who pointed him in the right direction. (Jones' Family Archive)

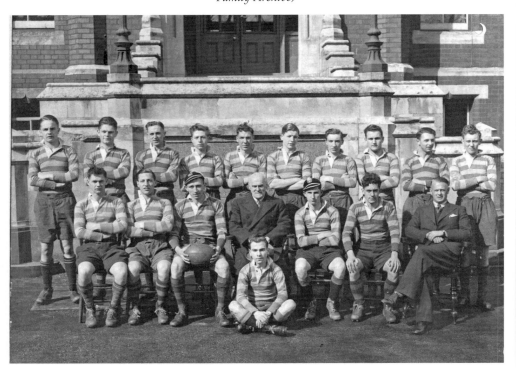

The first time Ken Jones captained a team was at West Mon. This was in 1939–40 when the First XV won 11 of the 13 matches played, scoring 212 points against 45 conceded.

The St Paul's First XV 1941–42. This was Ken's second year at the college and he was chosen to lead the team in what proved to be a successful season, Cheltenham RFC one of the many teams defeated. (Jones' Family Archive)

It ain't half hot! Ken and a group of mates cool down in the heat in Lucknow. The physique of a fine tuned athlete is starting to take shape but could that be a cigarette he is holding? (Jones' Family Archive)

Irene didn't recognise her fiancé when the couple met at Snow Hill Station. The sun-tanned man with the moustache may not have looked familiar but it is unlikely Ken would have forgotten his bride to be. (Jones' Family Archive)

Ken celebrated his 26th birthday in some style. The happy couple are oblivious to the snow on the ground as they pose for the photographer outside St Peter's Church, Blaenavon. Best man, Hedley Rowlands, and Matron of Honour, Phyllis, take centre stage alongside Mr and Mrs Ken Jones. (Jones Family Archive)

This picture of the 1946–47 Newport team shows the players in the famous black and amber hoops but sources confirm the team played in yellow jerseys throughout the season, suggesting this photograph was taken at a later date. Ken is seated first from the left.

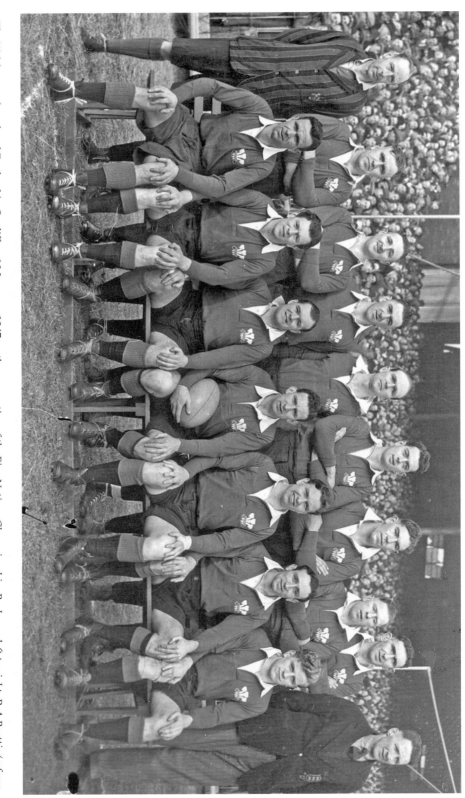

The Welsh team that played England in Cardiff on 18 January, 1947 on the resumption of the Five Nations Championship. Back row left to right: R A Beattie (referee SRU), Griff Bevan, Dai Jones, Ossie Williams, Gwyn Evans, Rees Stephens, George Parsons, Reg Blakemore, Stan Williams, Ivor Jones (touch-judge WRU), seated left to right Howard Davies, Les Williams, Jack Matthews, Haydn Tanner (capt), Bleddyn Williams, Ken Jones, Billy Cleaver.

The Great Britain Olympic squad in a photograph believed to have been taken at the athletes' camp in Uxbridge. Ken is fifth from the left in the back row.

Juan Lopez of Uruguay (72) wins heat 4 of the 100m with Ken (34) a close second. (Olympic Photo Association)

Ken Jones and John Archer complete a perfect exchange in the heat of the 4x100m relay. The squad qualified for the final where they were beaten by the USA before the bizarre circumstances that saw them presented with the gold medals only having to return them after an appeal by the USA was upheld.

The medal ceremony went ahead despite the pending appeal, allowing God save the King to be played at the stadium for the first time since the opening ceremony.

The 4x100m relay team. From left to right, John Archer, Ken Jones, Jack Gregory and Alastair McCorquodale.

After completing his course at Loughborough Ken Jones was appointed PE master at Newport High School for Boys where he would remain for the next seven years. Here he teaches a group of pupils the life-enhancing skill of being able to stand on one's head.

The 1950 British Lions. back row left to right Mick Lane, Noel Henderson, Rees Stephens, Roy John, Peter Kininmonth, Jimmy Nelson, Bob Evans, Bill McKay, Don Hayward, Gus Black, middle row left to right Jack Kyle, John Robins, Tom Clifford, George Norton, Dai Davies, Ranald McDonald, Doug Smith, Rex Willis, Ivor Preece, Vic Roberts, Gordon Rimmer, seated left to right Cliff Davies, Grahame Budge, Bleddyn Williams, Jack Matthews, Surgeon Captain (D) L B Osborne RN (hon. manager), Karl Mullen (captain), E L Savage (hon. secretary), Billy Cleaver, Ken Jones, Malcolm Thomas, Jim McCarthy.

After its long journey south the Ceramic arrived in Wellington on 2 May. The British Lions were a happy group but eager to get underway. Ken is sixth from the right on the bottom tier. In the same row are Bob Evans and Malcolm Thomas found second and fourth from the right respectively.

The Lions pay attention to Surgeon Captain Osborne as the manager responds to one of the many official welcomes received by the party on its journey through New Zealand.

One of the most exciting memories of the tour – Ken Jones on his way to the line, this time against Wellington.

And the tries kept coming. This was one of a brace scored against the combined Waikato–King Country–Thames Valley side in a 30-0 victory, the biggest winning margin recorded in New Zealand.

The Lions team that drew the first Test in Dunedin. Standing left to right, RT Evans, Roy John, Ivor Preece, Ranald McDonald, Billy Cleaver, Ken Jones, Peter Kininmonth, Don Hayward; in front, Tom Clifford, Bill Mckay, Jack Matthews, Gus Black, Karl Mullen, Jack Kyle, John Robins.

New Zealand scrum-half Vince Bevan makes his way around the blind side of a scrum in the first Test. John Robins and Ken Jones lie in wait.

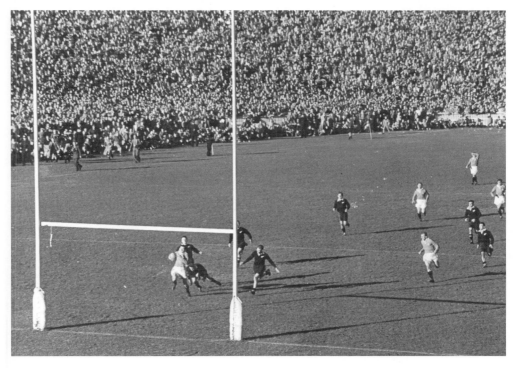

A full house at Eden Park looks on as Ken heads for the posts and the 'greatest try'. It wasn't enough to save the fourth Test but it secured the Welsh wing a place in New Zealand's rugby folklore. (New Zealand Herald)

When Ken was in New Zealand, Gareth Morgan of Bangor University claimed the Welsh AAA 100yds title. In 1951 normal service was resumed, Ken winning the sprint final in 10.3. Morgan (6) now had to settle for second place.

would be selected to tour with the British Lions? His inclusion in the Lions squad seemed a foregone conclusion but the threat of injury was never far away, making his decision to decline the invitation extended by the council something of a gamble. It also meant that if selected to tour with the Lions, he would be unable to defend his Welsh AAA titles and would also rule himself out of consideration for a place in the Great Britain team at the European Championships in Brussels later in the summer. Ken Jones would have held high hopes of running into the medal places in Auckland, which only made his decision harder, but in the end rugby won the day. Now all he had to do was avoid any serious injuries.

On Monday 5 September 1949 Ken Jones made his way up the steep drive that provided the main approach to Newport High School for Boys. On his right were cricket nets and tennis courts with more tennis courts and the markings of a hockey pitch to the left. Two large Victorian edifices dominated the landscape at the top of the drive – Newport High School for Boys to the right and Newport High School for Girls to the left. And never the twain shall meet! Ken would have been familiar with the walk between the two main buildings and the short flight of steps to the rear leading up to the rugby pitch and gymnasium which housed the changing rooms he would have used when visiting the school with teams from West Mon.

But this was now his domain; the gym, playing fields and demanding cross-country course that pupils either loved or hated were about to take over his working day and he couldn't wait to get started. In the well-equipped gym he would put the boys to work on the various pieces of apparatus and outside, come rain or shine, prepare pupils for rugby in the winter and athletics in the summer, ever on the lookout for lads to represent the school and the handful who might just be able to take their sporting skills to a higher level. Every morning started with the headmaster conducting assembly from the stage in the main hall and then it was each to his own as the boys dispersed to the various classrooms for the first of eight lessons that made up the day.

Discipline was rigid. Ken Jones could surely remember what it was like to be called up before the headmaster or a teacher to receive his just deserts for an infringement of the school code of conduct; now he would be the one dispensing any appropriate punishment; such is the difference between being 'Jones' or simply 'boy', and becoming 'Mr Jones' or 'Sir'. Boys found to have wandered off the straight and narrow would be summarily punished, either by the headmaster with his long cane, other masters using their preferred method of dishing out the sentence, or the school prefects, sixth-formers given the authority to deal with minor transgressions with a size-ten plimsoll aimed at a welcoming backside. All pretty civilised really! And the crimes that merited such punishment? Not wearing the school cap outside the grounds ranked high on the scale of criminal activity; running down corridors was equally frowned upon, particularly if a master had got out of bed on the wrong side; smoking behind the bicycle sheds was a no go; and heaven help any boy seen fraternising with the fairer sex! Some pupils treated being caught out and suitably punished with an element of pride, seeing it as a sort of totem in their progress toward manhood. Certainly there were masters who administered a lighter punishment with the cane than others, but not Mr Jones; boys did not want to get on the wrong side of the new PE master – no, Sir!

While other masters strode about the school in collar and tie with long black gowns sweeping all about them, Ken would be kitted out in a tracksuit, running vest and shorts, gym shoes or rugby boots. During his time at Newport High School, Ken Jones put hundreds of boys on the road to physical fitness, taught them the rudiments of rugby football and guided them in the pursuit of running faster, jumping higher and throwing further – life was good. The new sports master was an instant success, the boys were eager to please a sporting superstar, and there can be little doubt that many would have regularly made their way to Rodney Parade to watch 'Sir' practise what he preached.

By heading to Edinburgh from Oslo, Ken missed Newport's first match of the season, a resounding 28-8 home victory over Cross Keys, but he took his place in the team at Bristol the following Saturday. This was the first of 11 consecutive appearances, his longest run in the side to date, but something was missing. Reminiscent of two seasons earlier he wasn't seeing much of the ball and as a consequence rarely featured on the score sheet. The club's early-season form was not helping matters – four of the nine matches were lost with two drawn – but the selectors were once again pressing to get Ken more involved and were prepared to make the necessary changes to help the process along. November had arrived and with it the first Welsh trial. Senior players were not required to attend but Newport still provided five players and with five others struggling with injury, options were limited and the selectors asked the Welsh right wing to play in the centre against Plymouth Albion.

Centres do get to see more of the ball but they also have to put their bodies on the line with more regularity than the men out wide, making the threat of injury more likely. There was a fine juggling act in process and it was imperative that nobody dropped any of the balls. Three weeks into the season Ken had confirmed his decision not to compete in the Empire Games. All his eggs were now in one basket and perhaps this was not the time to be experimenting with a change of position.

Ken wasn't the only wing struggling to get on the scoreboard. Of the 17 tries scored by the club only three had come from the men out wide. When Ken Sergeant with two and one from John Lane doubled that figure in the first half against Plymouth much of the credit went to the new man in the centre, who time after time carved up the midfield to free his wings with devastating effect. Successful it may have been, but the introduction of Ken Jones to the centre was never going to be allowed to continue and he returned to the wing, where he lived off scraps for the rest of the campaign. In 22 appearances in 1949–50, the fastest man in world rugby scored a paltry five tries. The club's indifferent early-season form disappeared in November and from then to the end of April only four more matches were lost with a further three drawn. The results would have been well received on the terraces but all the while Ken watched and waited with the often forlorn hope that he would get his hands on the ball. He might just as well have joined his pupils on the terraces – what a waste.

A minor injury prevented him from lining up in the second Welsh trial held at Aberavon on 17 December but he played for Newport over the Christmas holiday and was included in the 'Wales' XV against the Rest in the final trial on 7 January. A crowd of 25,000 turned up at Cardiff Arms Park and saw the senior team win an exciting match 22-6, Ken looking particularly sharp. His two tries were a much-needed confidence booster and he looked assured of his place in the Welsh team that would travel to Twickenham in a fortnight's time. He was fully aware he could have been on his way to New Zealand and the Empire Games, and that the next few weeks would determine whether or not the right decision had been made. One of several Welsh players hoping to be selected for the Lions tour, Ken knew that a good performance against a much-fancied England team was essential to his cause. The committee of the four home unions reasoned that as the 30-strong squad would assemble in London at the end of March it was necessary to advise those selected as soon as possible. With the announcement of the party expected on 13 February, the Welsh players would only have the matches with England and Scotland in which to impress; any heroic deeds against Ireland and France would not be recognised, leaving little margin for error.

In 1950 spectators attending international rugby matches were still allowed to pay at the gate. On 21 January, an estimated 75,500 were allowed into Twickenham before the gates were closed one hour before kick-off with thousands of expectant supporters left stranded outside. Wales included six new caps and there was an 11th-hour change of captain when Bleddyn Williams was forced to withdraw from the team, number 8 John Gwilliam chosen to lead the side in his absence. Williams' withdrawal saw Malcolm Thomas move into the centre with Newport's Trevor Brewer called up for a first cap on the left wing. The added responsibility inspired Gwilliam, who led his forwards with great enthusiasm, the pack completely dominating the England eight. This proved to be the determining factor of the match and despite England taking an early five-point lead courtesy of an interception try by John Smith, Wales soon took control to confound those pundits who had predicted a comfortable England victory. Forwards Cliff Davies and Ray Cale scored the Welsh tries, one of which was converted, together with a penalty goal.

The next day the name Jones was splashed across the banner headlines of the newspapers, but not in reference to the Welsh right wing; it was the 18-years-and-nine-months-old debutant at full-back. Lewis Jones was a revelation. He was outstanding in broken play, causing chaos among the England ranks with his carefree counter-attacking. His innovative approach led to a spectacular move that finished with a try by Cliff Davies, but it was his ability to read a situation and react to it immediately that belied his tender age. With five points to his name from a conversion and penalty goal, the new full-back's contribution to Wales' 11-5 victory was significant but had probably come too late to influence the Lions selectors. This was only Wales' second victory at Twickenham in 15 visits dating back to 1910 when the famous ground was first used for international rugby. Two weeks later a Welsh team brimming with new-found confidence beat Scotland 12-0 at St Helen's, tries from Malcolm Thomas and Ken, his sixth for his country and fourth against Scotland, setting up the victory. For the Welsh and Scottish players the match was a final chance to shine in front of the Lions selectors. The next week they would be back at Twickenham watching England play Ireland before sitting down to finalise the squad to take on the mighty All Blacks in their own back yard.

Their task complete, the committee of the four home unions announced their selections on 13 February as promised. For the first time in its colourful history the British Lions squad was made up entirely of players with international experience. Included were nine from Ireland, five Scots and a disappointing three Englishmen; disappointing in that a few short weeks earlier much had been expected from an England team that had so far failed to live up to expectations and would end the season with only a 3-0 victory over Ireland to its credit. A quick calculation confirms that the squad included 13 players from Wales, which would certainly have been 14 but for John Gwilliam's decision not to leave his teaching post in Edinburgh for such an extended period. Cardiff were represented by Billy Cleaver, Cliff Davies, Jack Matthews, Bleddyn Williams and Rex Willis; Roy John and Rees Stephens were Neath's first British Lions although RK Green had toured with the Anglo-Welsh team in 1908; Don Hayward was certainly the first Newbridge player to be selected; and from English clubs came John Robins of Birkenhead Park and Dai Davies, who played for Somerset Police. Newport's Bob Evans and Malcolm Thomas were included, as was Ken Jones, who, despite all the preamble regarding a lack of tries in the season thus far was probably one of the first names on the list.

To be selected for the British Lions remains the highest honour attainable by a player from one of the four home unions. Once selected, the risk of injury is ever present until the date of departure and in 1950 there were Five Nations matches to be played alongside club rugby before any Lion elect could rest easy. When Ireland and Wales took to the field at Ravenhill on 11 March a quick glance at the matchday programme would confirm that 18 of those taking part had been selected to tour. Some of them were key players, including Irish captain Karl Mullen, the man chosen to lead the Lions, who would be particularly hard to replace. Every player was in on merit and would be missed if unable to tour, but together with Mullen, Jack Kyle, Jack Matthews, Bob Evans, Bill McKay and Ken Jones were all likely to be selected in the Tests and to lose any of these outstanding men would be most unfortunate. There may have been a lot at stake for many of the individuals on show but no quarter was asked and neither was any given in what was a full-on encounter from the start – to hell with the consequences.

Matches between the two countries were never less than wars of attrition up front and both sets of forwards spent the first half seeking to gain some sort of dominance in the tight and loose. They all but cancelled each other out and when the game's first score came early in the second half it was from a counter-attack following a speculative kick upfield. Jack Matthews caught the ball and immediately took play into the Irish 25 before releasing Ken on the wing, who had a clear run to the line. The conversion missed, Ireland were soon on level terms courtesy of a penalty from George Norton and that was how it remained until three minutes from time. Ireland were awarded a scrum on their 25 but what should have been a simple pass from scrum-half Carroll to Jack Kyle went terribly wrong and the stand-off had little chance, receiving both ball and Wales flanker Ray Cale at the same time. Cleaver gathered up the loose ball and linked with Lewis Jones, who made ground before releasing Malcolm Thomas on the left wing with 15 yards between him and the line. It appeared as if all 15 Irish players were converging on Thomas and the corner flag but the Welshman did enough to satisfy Irish touch judge Ossie Williams that he had grounded the ball correctly and Wales could celebrate a long-overdue Triple Crown.

The following day the winning of Triple Crowns and selection for the British Lions were put into perspective when a chartered aircraft that had taken Welsh supporters to Ireland crashed on the return journey at an airfield on the outskirts of Cardiff. The Llandow air disaster claimed 80 lives, leaving only three survivors, and at the time was the biggest civil air disaster on record. In the close-knit society that was Welsh rugby everybody knew either one of the victims or knew someone who did. For Ken, Bob Evans and Malcolm Thomas this immediacy was through Newport RFC when it was confirmed that one of the casualties was Doug Burnett, brother of outside-half Roy. Two weeks later at a sombre Cardiff Arms Park, five buglers sounded the Last Post before a minute's silence was observed by the 53,000 supporters in attendance for the final match of the championship. France were the visitors and they had no answer to a Welsh team on top of its game. Despite leading only 5-0 at the interval Wales ran out comfortable winners by 21-0, Ken Jones adding two more tries to his growing tally.

Following the French match Ken had five days to wait before he would set out on the greatest adventure of his sporting career. It should not be forgotten that the local education authority had played its part by allowing him to be involved in the tour. His absence would leave Newport High School a man short for the remainder of the academic year and the start of the next, with the Lions away for six months of which four would see the school open for business. Newport RFC would also have to do without the services of three of its star players for nine matches in April and five come the start of the next season. The club would win all 14 fixtures, part of a winning sequence that would extend well into the following year. Proof, if any were needed, that rugby football was a team game dependent on the ability of a group of players to come together and perform as a collective, something the 1950 British Lions were going to have to achieve if they were to be successful. Reputations were about to be put on the line in the toughest of arenas. Playing standards cranked up a notch or two. Would they be good enough? Only time would provide the answer.

CHAPTER SIX

A LION ROARS

The championship over, those selected for the Lions could now fully focus on the tour. The squad of 30 players together with the management team were due to meet in London on Thursday 30 March. There were those irritating last-minute purchases to be made before the bags could be packed, but at least there were no papers to be cancelled, nor would the milkman have to be asked to put deliveries on hold. Yet again Irene and Ken were about to be separated for an extended period, this time one lasting a little over six months, with the party not due to return home until 7 October. Future tours would gain the benefit of air travel, much reducing the period spent in transit, but the 1950 Lions travelled by sea, the outward journey taking them west through the Panama Canal with the return route via Ceylon and the Suez Canal. A complete circumnavigation of the world, but one that added two months to the time spent in New Zealand and Australia.

The Swansea–Paddington train picked up two strapping young men and their luggage at Neath on Thursday morning. Roy John and Rees Stephens climbed on board ready to welcome Cliff Davies, John Robins, Jack Matthews and

Bleddyn Williams when the train pulled into Cardiff, and 15 minutes later it was the turn of Don Hayward, Bob Evans, Malcolm Thomas and Ken Jones, who were waiting on Platform 3 at Newport station. Married members of the team were allowed to take their wives to London, where over the next 48 hours all final preparations would be completed.

After arriving at London's Paddington Station the party headed for the Mayfair Hotel to meet up with Dai Davies, Rex Willis and Billy Cleaver, who had travelled from other parts of the country, together with the representatives from England, Ireland and Scotland. Waiting at the hotel were tour manager, Surgeon-Captain (D)B 'Ginger' Osborne RN and tour secretary Edward 'Ted' Savage. Unknown to most of the squad they may have been, but the roles of these two men were as important to the success of the tour as that of any of the players. All the facets of touring and much else besides – official functions (of which there would be many), meetings with the press, local public relations exercises, and the important matter of team selection – would come within the remit of Ginger Osborne and Ted Savage. In the coming months both men would earn the unreserved respect and friendship of their younger charges.

The short time spent in London was barely long enough to complete all outstanding business. On Thursday evening the players and officials attended an official dinner hosted by the New Zealand Society, which presented a first opportunity for the all-important bonding process to begin. The large contingent of Welsh players were clearly comfortable in each other's company but they were going to have to integrate with the other members of the squad, the players from England, Ireland and Scotland, who would in turn also have to forget old rivalries and set upon the task of becoming a group of young men with a common purpose. The success or otherwise of a Lions tour depends greatly on such niceties being observed and in time the camaraderie enjoyed by the class of 1950 would not be found wanting, Anglos and Celts coming together as one in their search for rugby immortality. As their menfolk set about doing what men do in such circumstances, Irene and the other wives who had travelled to London were entertained at a restaurant 'up town' before taking in a West End show.

On the Friday morning a coach took the players and officials to Twickenham, where the players changed into the red jerseys, white shorts and blue stockings before taking their places for the official team photograph. And what a fine job the photographer did, all players snapped looking directly at the camera with their right arm folded over the left and lined up in perfect symmetrical formation; nine standing in the back row, ten in the second, six more seated alongside the management with skipper Mullen in pole position and four half-backs sitting cross-legged on the floor. While at HQ the players also collected their tour blazers which had been purchased locally and sent to London to have the Lions badge stitched onto the breast pocket. There was also a tour tie and a personal allocation of lapel badges to pick up but apart from these, the players had to provide all other items of clothing from their own wardrobes.

On returning to their hotel they were left to their own devices for the remainder of the day. Then it was Saturday morning, bringing with it a noticeable increase in the anticipation and excitement that was now prevalent. All that remained was to secure the locks on the cases, bid a final farewell to those who were to be left behind and climb aboard the coach that would deliver them to Euston Station in good time to meet the 10.30am Liverpool train. On arrival in Liverpool, the party was taken directly to the docks and a first sighting of the Shaw Savill line flagship vessel TSS *Ceramic*, which would be their home for the next month. When the *Ceramic* left her moorings a few hours later at 3.30pm on Saturday 1 April, the great adventure had truly begun.

That same afternoon Cardiff and Newport met at Cardiff Arms Park for the fourth and final encounter of the season.

Cardiff had won the first three and much improvement was needed if Newport were to avoid a second whitewash in three seasons. It is certain those Cardiff and Newport players among the Lions showed more than a passing interest in the outcome of this particular match. When or how the result was relayed to them is not known but when it did come through it confirmed that Newport had won by 8 points to nil. Ken Jones would surely have felt more than a little irony in this pleasing news. Since he had joined Newport in September 1946 the two clubs had met on no fewer than 15 occasions before that last encounter of the current season, with Cardiff winning 13 matches and two drawn. Ken had appeared in all but two of them, missing one when he was playing for the UAU and a second that took place after he had called a premature end to his season to concentrate on athletics prior to the Olympic Games. This was a pretty grim statistic which we can be sure Ken wasn't about to advertise to Bleddyn and co. who, one hopes, remained blissfully unaware of the fact that the world's fastest rugby player had yet to taste victory over the Blue and Blacks of Cardiff – 'Man overboard' may well have been the order of the day.

Life aboard a cruise ship is such that many people are prepared to spend not insignificant sums of money to sample a few weeks of the luxury on offer. Tales of the catering available on such journeys were legendary and for young men heading for New Zealand and a Test series against the mighty All Blacks the temptation to overindulge had to be tempered. 'Eat what you are used to' was the general instruction; easier said than done. There was the real threat of boredom creeping in for this was no ordinary cruise in as much as there were very few ports of call to provide a welcome opportunity to get the feel of dry land. Then there was the need to work off any excess baggage that may have been picked up along the way. With his physical education degree, who better then than Ken Jones to keep the players in shape during the weeks at sea? It fell to him together with John Robins to put together a fitness programme and every morning the Lions could be seen on deck stretching and bending, doing sit-ups and press-ups, jogging and sprinting and generally keeping a level of fitness that would not find them wanting come the first match scheduled a week after arrival in Wellington. DR 'Dai' Gent, an alumnus of St Paul's, Cheltenham and now rugby correspondent for *The Times*, travelling with the team, described the daily workouts as 'mighty tough going... I have never seen such rigorous training'. And it was needed to counter the three meals a day, meals offering a choice of dishes far too tempting for even the most dedicated of players to resist. Then there were the cocktail parties – Captain AV Richardson Requests the Pleasure...; The Rt Hon. WJ Jordan (New Zealand High Commissioner to London) Requests the Pleasure...; The Manager and Committee of the British Isles Rugby Union Team Request the Pleasure.... An endless round of social events was on offer but the Lions, while not abstemious, had a great reputation for moderation while aboard the *Ceramic*. Who with is another matter!

In a letter home Ken wrote: 'Entertainment was limited on board at first but under the able guidance of Bill Cleaver our evenings soon became filled with whist drives and race meetings, brains trusts and quizzes, cinema shows and the old Army game of housie, housie....' The race meetings were held in the Smoke Room. Five 'horses' together with jockeys riding piggyback contested each race, with their progress up the track decided by the throw of a dice. Several of the players entered horses with varying degrees of success. Dr Jack Matthews' Injection, a filly by Needle out of Bottle, was never going to be as popular a selection as Ivor Preece's chestnut Exposed by Broken Strap out of Brassiere, but the nights passed by with the help of such amusement.

With few opportunities to get ashore, those on offer presented welcome diversions: '...the approximate half-way mark on our trip was reached at the oil refining island of Curacao at which we spent a very pleasant day ashore... a day later we passed through the Panama Canal. A wonderful experience this and a magnificent sight too. The journey from east to west through the many locks and lakes was so smooth that it was very difficult at times to decide whether the ship was being lifted or lowered or just sailing straight ahead. A most enjoyable evening was spent ashore at Balbo, Panama City, and gave to many of us our first sample of the American way of life with its bright lights and nightclubs. The long last lap was almost over and as the Pacific in places didn't behave as its name suggests, much to the annoyance of quite a few of our team, we were more than glad to arise very early one morning to witness our arrival at Wellington – a most impressive sight.'

This was on Tuesday 2 May. When he stepped ashore 34 days after joining the Paddington train at Newport all Ken wanted was to get into his training kit, feel the ground underneath him as he went through his enormous repertoire of gear changes and see some action. With 29 other players in similar mood the 1950 British Lions were ready for action.

The itinerary showed 23 matches were to be played in New Zealand and six in Australia with an 'unofficial' match in Ceylon on the way home also included. A total of 30 matches that would push the Lions' playing resources to the limit. There were no easy matches in New Zealand; each of the provinces and the various combined teams were keen to lower the Lions' colours and it went without saying that the mighty All Blacks would conduct their own searching examination of the visitors when it came to the biggest stage. Such a long tour does have its advantages in that it makes it possible for all players to stake a claim for a Test place, but from the outset one suspects Ken was pencilled in on the right wing. If he could produce his usual high standard of performance on the field, stay fit and avoid any untimely injuries he was seemingly guaranteed to experience rugby football at this highest of levels.

The New Zealand sector of the tour was split into two halves. The welcoming party over, the Lions travelled from Wellington across the Cook Straits to South Island where the first ten matches would be played. Then it was back to Wellington and a journey around North Island that would take in the remaining 13 fixtures. Chosen to give the Lions their first taste of New Zealand rugby was a combined team drawn from the Nelson, Marlborough, Golden Bay and Motueka regions that dot the north-west coast of South Island, the match held at Trafalgar Park, Nelson on Wednesday 10 May. Not selected for the tour opener, Ken joined the other Lions not on duty in the stand and saw the visitors make fairly light work of the combined team, running out 24-3 winners. With the management keen to get the players involved again after the long lay-off there were ten changes in the team selected to play Buller on Saturday, Ken Jones among those named to make a first appearance in the famous jersey.

The 1950 British Lions were the first to wear the red jersey that has become known throughout the rugby-playing world. Previous tourists had worn a selection of hooped jerseys in various colours and in the 1930s the tourists favoured a navy blue jersey with white shorts and red stockings. The change to the red top, white shorts and navy stockings was at the instigation of the four home unions committee and to this a further refinement was made aboard the *Ceramic*, as *Times* correspondent Dai Gent reported. Discussing the matter of a dress code he wrote that Ginger Osborne and the then President of the RFU, Eric Watts Moses, agreed that 'players should take the field tidily dressed and endeavour to remain so for the whole of the game. This includes stockings and garters, for like so many of us, they dislike seeing players going about with their stockings over their ankles. Ginger Osborne was talking to his party about this the other day when he had an inspiration. Not only were they to wear garters, but they were to wear green flashes to the garters, thus reminding one another and all spectators of the fellowship in the composition of the British Isles team which already had red jerseys, white pants and blue stockings. The whole party was enthusiastic in its support of the idea and Karl Mullen and his fellow Irishmen were obviously touched.' When the Lions next toured the green flashes would be incorporated into the stocking as the turnover, and the colours of the four home countries would thereafter be included in the strip.

The New Zealand rugby public got its first look at the flying Welshman on Saturday 13 May at Victoria Square, Westport. The estimated 4,500 spectators saw the Lions win 24-9 and Ken Jones cross for one of the tourists' five tries. With the ball moved across to the left of the field, Jack Kyle cleverly cross kicked to the right into the welcoming arms of Jones, who ran unopposed to the line. This was a small indication of what was to come and in the following weeks the names Kyle and Jones would be mentioned wherever rugby was discussed. What started as a quiet rumour reached a crescendo three months later, by which time both men would be recognised in New Zealand as all-time greats.

And it wasn't just the public who began enthusing about the pair. The rugby press also realised the threats posed by the outside-half and right wing. Former selector and administrator CC Gibbons wrote of Kyle: '...he pulled enough tricks from his rugby magical box to indicate he is going to delight crowds as the tour proceeds... fast off the mark, beautifully balanced in his running, has safe hands... his cross kick when Jones scored was masterly.' And of Jones: '...the Welsh winger and Olympic sprinter is going to make some of our wingers wish he hadn't turned down the Empire Games trip for this tour... Jones is very fast and has football ability above the ordinary. For a fast man he handles exceptionally well and is bound to score a lot of tries before the tour is over.'

Three days later on a rain-soaked pitch at Greymouth, Ken Jones confirmed Gibbons' prediction when scoring a brace of tries against West Coast as the Lions notched up their third win, this by 32 points to 3.

Writing home, Ken confirmed there was much he could relate to during these early days in New Zealand; '…we visited farms, orchards and at Westport the coal mines where our boys from Wales felt very much at home amongst the many Welsh people living there. The mines were much different from ours and we were more than surprised to find seams of coal in places 40ft thick and in immense quantities. The main difficulty they experienced there was in transporting the coal from the mines since without exception they were situated at the top of mountains 3–4,000ft high. In addition, the west coast is one of the wettest parts of New Zealand and we had evidence of this in our third game at Greymouth…'

The honeymoon was over. The Lions would not know this yet but lying in wait on the eastern coast of South Island was Otago, one of the country's leading provinces who had not lost at home since 1946: four years in which the province also defeated 18 consecutive challengers in its defence of the Ranfurly Shield, New Zealand's major domestic competition. All eight forwards had played international rugby and included among the backs was current All Black skipper Ron Elvidge. While the Lions backs had quickly made their mark, scoring 12 of the 14 tries recorded, the forwards were still trying to come to terms with the abrasive New Zealand approach and it was up front that the next match would be won and lost. Ken Jones was selected for a third consecutive appearance but on this occasion opportunities were few and far between and much of his time was spent in defence, where some try-saving tackles helped to keep the home side in check. Not impressed, Ken wrote: 'Otago played a type of football very different from our idea of the New Zealand type of play. It was tough, dour football and their main idea was to win no matter how dull the game might be…' Otago duly inflicted the first defeat on the tourists, winning 23-9, but with the first Test a week away it was an ever-growing list of casualties that was giving most cause for concern. With only four matches played, nine of the tourists were struggling with injury and of them only Irish loose forward Bill McKay would be available for selection when the time came to pick the team for the all-important first Test. With another tough midweek fixture to be negotiated before that important date it was very much a case of mix and match as several players found themselves selected in unfamiliar positions. Ideally, the match before any Test sees the major players rested but the long injury list prevented this and when he may reasonably have expected an afternoon off after featuring in the previous three matches, Ken found himself selected for his fourth consecutive appearance. At Invercargill, New Zealand's southernmost city, Southland took no prisoners, the Lions sent packing with their tails between their legs, beaten 11-0 in the only provincial match in which they would fail to get on the scoreboard.

Test matches in New Zealand bring the country to a standstill – always have, always will. While 35,000 lucky spectators filled Carisbrook Park, Dunedin the rest of the nation huddled around radios listening to the commentary of Winston McCarthy, which vividly brought to life the afternoon's events. Carisbrook Park had seen the Lions overcome by an inspired Otago XV and long before the final whistle the partisan crowd were calling for the All Blacks to be replaced by the home province team. An uncharacteristic error by full-back Bob Scott allowed Ken Jones to swoop on the loose ball and score a try which put the Lions 9-3 ahead midway through the second half, but New Zealand got out of jail courtesy of a Scott penalty and a late try by skipper Elvidge – 9-9. Following on from two defeats this provided a welcome boost for the tourists, who had been forced to field a team far removed from that which would have taken the field had all the squad been fit. That they failed to close down the first Test would come back to haunt the Lions as the tour unfolded. It was very much a case of could have won and should have won, but for New Zealand the result brought to an end a run of six defeats that stretched back three years. In fact, by managing to secure only a draw, the All Blacks had not won on home soil since defeating Australia 14-6 at Eden Park, Auckland, on 28 September 1946 – the public were getting impatient.

For the sixth time of asking, Ken Jones was included on the right wing for the next midweek fixture against South Canterbury. The Lions interrupted their journey north from Dunedin to Christchurch to entertain the locals at Timaru. Some 10,000 spectators turned out to see the tourists and were not disappointed. Following the encouraging performance in the Test the Lions ran in six tries in a comfortable 27-8 victory. After several close calls that had the crowd cheering his progress down the flank, Jones duly delivered with his fifth try in New Zealand. With the tour now well under way, the knowledgeable local rugby followers had become familiar with the tourists and got to know and appreciate their strengths and weaknesses, with none impressing more than the Welsh wing.

The sports editor of the *Otago Daily Times* reported: 'I am becoming convinced that Jones, the Welsh winger, may be one of the greatest sources of danger to New Zealand in the remaining Tests. He ran with great speed today, often slipped into the attack to make an extra man, and proved remarkably quick at seizing an opening in the defence.'

After what must have seemed a whistle-stop tour of South Island it was with some relief that the party arrived in Christchurch knowing that they could unpack their bags for a 12-night stay at one hotel. This was the longest term of residence since they had embarked at Wellington a month earlier and most welcome, but it didn't come without its problems. Writing home, Ken reported that 'the trams proved a source of annoyance for they focussed on the main square in which our hotel was situated, running till late at night and commencing very, very early in the morning by our present standards'. Such letters home were the only realistic way of maintaining contact but on occasion a chance meeting could make the 12,000 miles seem a lot less.

Mrs E Reece was walking home in suburban Christchurch when she heard the sound of Welsh voices singing. Blaenavon-born Mrs Reece had emigrated to New Zealand with her husband Ted some years earlier and recognising the once all-too-familiar incantations she decided to seek out the source. A motor convoy was taking some of the Lions back to their hotel and with ever-increasing interest, the intrepid lady followed her prey. A regular reader of the *Free Press*, Pontypool's local newspaper which was sent to her by relatives in Blaenavon, she was aware that local hero Ken Jones was among the party and after being given the necessary prompt, proceeded to seek him out. Equally delighted to meet someone from his home town, Ken invited Mrs Reece to bring her husband to the hotel the following day, where he introduced them to the Lions squad. Not to be outdone the invitation was reciprocated, Ken spending the next day at home with the Reeces reminiscing about Blaenavon and many familiar names. In a letter to her brother William White, Mrs Reece described how much of a joy it had been to meet Ken and that '...we were given grandstand tickets for the match against Christchurch and sat with officials of the British team. We heard and were fired anew with the strains of Cwm Rhondda and my thoughts went back to the once familiar scenes of the Eastern Valley. What a match it was! I don't suppose there was a Welshman on the seat he was supposed to occupy and the crowning moment of the game from our point of view was Ken's dash to score.'

What a match indeed. By registering a 16 points to 5 victory the Lions put the tour firmly back on track. The log now showed five wins and a draw from the eight matches played and with a midweek match against relatively weak opponents next up, the Lions could now begin to focus on the second Test, which would be played at Lancaster Park a week later.

After appearing in seven consecutive matches Ken was happy to step down when players returning from injury allowed the selectors to give him a long overdue rest. Ireland's Michael Lane had played on the right wing in the first match and after recovering from injury he took over from Ken against Ashburton County–North Otago, scoring two tries in a 29-6 win. Injured against Otago, Bleddyn Williams had been included in the team that defeated Canterbury and kept his place in the centre for the midweek match, which also saw the return to duty of Malcolm Thomas who had been out of action since damaging ribs in Dunedin. Both players came through unscathed and the selectors now had a much bigger player base to choose from.

After unarguably getting the better of the All Blacks in the first Test, the Lions team for the second showed only two changes: Williams and Thomas replacing Ivor Preece and Ranald Macdonald in the centre and on the left wing. The New Zealand team also showed two changes. Otago first five-eighth (stand-off) Laurie Haig was included alongside his province second five-eighth (inside centre) Ron Elvidge, and there was a change on the left wing. If Ken Jones had opted to run for Wales in the Empire Games held earlier in the year it is likely he would have come across the New Zealand sprinter Peter Henderson. Henderson had qualified for the 100yds final in Auckland, recording times of 9.9 and evens in the earlier rounds. Ken regularly broke even time over the distance and a meeting between the two rugby stars on the track would have satisfied a lot of unanswered questions. But unanswered they would have to remain because the fastest rugby player in the southern hemisphere and the fastest in the northern hemisphere were destined only to face each other on a rugby pitch.

The second Test did little for the game of rugby other than break the All Blacks' dismal run of seven matches without a win. Statistics rarely lie; however, one has to question how a reported 108 line-outs can be accommodated in 80 minutes' play. But with both teams content to kick for position, play moved up and down the touchlines with monotonous regularity. Midway through the first half New Zealand broke the pattern by scoring two tries, one of which was converted, for an eight-point lead. During this period the Lions lost Bill McKay, forced to leave the field with concussion, and to their credit the remaining 14 players did not concede any further points. The personal duel between the two wings ended in a stalemate and it would have to wait for another day, but with New Zealand now one up in the four-match series the Lions left South Island knowing there was much work to be done if they were to mount a serious challenge in the remaining two matches.

The first leg of the tour complete, the Lions record showed that six of the ten matches played on South Island were won; Otago, Southland and New Zealand, in the second Test, had defeated them and the first Test was drawn. At the official function following the second Test it was announced that George Norton, the Irish full-back who had broken his arm against Southland, would be allowed to stay with the team as the guest of the New Zealand Rugby Football Union and a similar courtesy had been extended by their Australian counterparts. It was also confirmed that a replacement would join the party, allowing Welsh full-back Lewis Jones to enter the record books as the first British Lion to travel to the southern hemisphere by air.

No such luck for the rest of the party, who went by ship from Christchurch to Wellington, once again crossing the notoriously inclement Cook Strait. The hospitality afforded the Lions by the people of South Island had made a huge impression on the visitors and they were particularly sad to leave this beautiful island, as Ken wrote in a letter to the headmaster and staff at Newport High School. 'It was from Christchurch that we finally sailed for the North Island again for the second phase of our tour. It was with much regret for we had had a wonderful time and many wonderful experiences. The people themselves could never do too much for us, we were entertained royally and on many of the rugby grounds it was often hard to discover whether the spectators were more for us or their own local side. We spent many evenings at the homes of people and they took us in more as members of the family than as visitors. Everywhere we found that, though people were born out here, their real home was Britain and they were proud of the fact.'

The first of the 13 matches played in North Island was against Wairarapa–Bush at Masterton. Only five players who featured in the second Test were included, Ken among those given the day off. The Lions ran riot in the first 30 minutes scoring six tries without reply, but failed to maintain the scoring spree, eventually running out winners by 27-13. Malcolm Thomas had been the Lions' top points scorer in South Island with 45 – three tries, eight penalties and six conversions – and he added to the total with a hat-trick of tries and two conversions in Masterton. The Newport club would have been particularly proud of their players' performances in the Lions jersey as Ken Jones' six tries made him the tourists' second-highest points scorer to date. And if Bob Evans was yet to get on the score sheet, the popular police officer was making his name as one of the Lions' outstanding forwards.

Napier was New Zealand's newest city. Situated on the east coast, it had been devastated by an earthquake in 1931, with large areas reduced to rubble, but the city that welcomed the 1950 Lions laid testament to the commitment the New Zealand government had given to the rebuild. Although there were still two weeks and another three matches to be played before the third Test, the Lions team selected to meet Hawke's Bay had the look of a shadow Test fifteen and 11 of the players would eventually face the All Blacks in Wellington. An impressive 20-0 victory saw the backs entertain the crowd with their enterprising approach, Jack Kyle earning more praise from the local critics as he continued to control and vary the tactics. Ken Jones waited patiently on his wing but on this occasion saw little of the ball and the Napier crowd of 12,000 were unfortunate not to have seen the wing cross the line in full stride – the Welshman would play in a further seven matches in New Zealand and score in each of them.

Sunday, 18 June, 3.57am. The Lions were enjoying a good night's sleep after the match and post-match festivities when, along with the rest of the residents in the Hawke's Bay area, they were woken by an unfamiliar and quite alarming sound. For 45 seconds the deep rumble continued, leaving the tourists mystified as to its source. Any local who had been around in 1931 could have enlightened them immediately to the fact that they were experiencing an earthquake. Thankfully it was nothing like the strength of the one that had destroyed Napier 19 years earlier, but was strong enough to register between four and five on the Modified Mercalli and Richter scales. As Ken wrote: '...sufficient to make the lights sway to and fro.'

There was much to discuss at breakfast on Sunday but any free day was to be enjoyed and as there didn't appear to be any damage caused by the night's events, the Lions set about some serious R&R. For some this meant going to Taupo to see the geysers; others chose to join a wild boar hunt, skipper Karl Mullen claiming two kills; and for others it was the local golf course that provided the main attraction. Ken Jones was a most accomplished sportsman but his pursuit of the little white ball never attracted much attention, with Mark Twain's description of golf as being nothing more than 'a good walk spoiled' perhaps best describing Ken's efforts. 'Since golf is a popular pastime amongst many of our team I too have attempted to complete 18 holes, unsuccessfully up to the time of writing since my stock of golf balls has generally disappeared long before the favourite 19th hole has come into sight.'

The road now led back to Wellington via Gisborne, a small town north of Napier, where a combined Poverty Bay–East

Coast–Bay of Plenty XV was comfortably beaten by a Lions team captained by Jack Matthews on the occasion of his 30th birthday, the centre celebrating with two tries in what was another comprehensive win for the tourists by 27 points to 3. The Lions had passed through Wellington twice on their travels but now they would get the opportunity to have a good look at the capital city; a Saturday encounter with the local province followed by the third Test a week later meant the bags could stay unpacked for a while.

The Saturday match before the Test usually gives an indication of the selectors' preference and the Lions backs were the same as had played against Hawke's Bay with the forwards showing two changes from that line-up, John Robins and Rees Stephens replacing Cliff Davies and Jimmy Nelson. Wellington had not been a happy hunting ground for British teams. If the Lions had checked the record books they would have learnt that Wellington had earned a hard-fought 3-3 draw against RL Seddon's 1888 side; beaten AF Harding's 1908 tourists 19-13; and repeated the feat when overcoming FD Prentice's Lions 12-8 in 1930. Neither had the Lions won a Test in the capital where, despite managing a 3-3 draw in 1908, they were defeated 22-8 in 1930.

All the statistics may have been in their favour but at half-time Wellington found themselves trailing by 12 points to nil and, more tellingly, the Lions had run in four tries, all of which went unconverted. An early effort by Bleddyn Williams and a second from Jim McCarthy meant the Lions had now scored 49 tries on tour. The landmark 50th came courtesy of some deft footwork by Williams in midfield before the centre passed to Ken Jones for the wing to race over in the corner. Williams' second followed some elaborate handling between himself, Matthews and Jones which brought the 30,000 spectators to their feet. The Lions were flying. Surprisingly, the visitors failed to add to their score in the second half, Wellington scoring a try and a penalty goal for a final score of 12-6, but the Lions left the field with that feeling of a job well done after winning a match later hailed as one of the best of the tour. So much for the statistics.

With no midweek match to consider, the Lions selectors decided to announce the Test team at a press conference held at the team hotel on Monday morning. In normal circumstances it is not always prudent to declare one's hand unnecessarily early but with their New Zealand counterparts likely to show faith in the team that won the second Test, the Lions selection committee were comfortable in giving the team the week to prepare for Saturday's match. Three changes from the side that was beaten at Christchurch saw Gordon Rimmer replace Angus Black at scrum-half and Roy John drop back to number 8 at the expense of Peter Kininmonth with Jim Nelson replacing John in the second row. But the best laid plans etc. were ripped apart when over the course of the next few days the Lions would lose both their skipper and their top try scorer. Shortly after the team was announced Karl Mullen pulled a leg muscle during the afternoon's training session and Ken Jones aggravated an ankle he had badly turned in Saturday's match. Both were given as long as possible to recover but by Wednesday Mullen had accepted his fate and on Friday Jones knew that he would watch the match from a seat in the grandstand. They were replaced by Dai Davies and Noel Henderson, with the captaincy passing to the capable hands of Bleddyn Williams.

The outcome of the series was at stake at Athletic Park. A New Zealand victory would see them take an unassailable 2-0 lead while a Lions win would restore the balance at 1-1, leaving everything to play for in the fourth Test in Auckland. Despite holding a slender half-time lead courtesy of a John Robins penalty, the Lions had failed to capitalise on the All Blacks being reduced to 14 players after 15 minutes when prop John Simpson was led from the field with what proved to be a career-ending knee injury. Later in the half New Zealand were down to 13 with captain Ron Elvidge forced off following a crunching tackle by Jack Matthews. Even with such a numerical advantage, the Lions were unable to assert any authority on proceedings, failing to add to their slender lead which was never likely to be enough if the All Blacks were returned to full strength.

Simpson sat out the remainder of the match but the New Zealand captain returned to the field early in the second half. The numbers may still have been in their favour but the Lions wasted their advantage and when Elvidge crashed over for a try to level the scores the writing was on the wall. Bob Scott kicked what proved to be the winning penalty with 15 minutes remaining on the clock and for the second time in the series the Lions were left to ponder on what might have been. With the All Blacks forced to contest the set pieces with six forwards for much of the game, Peter Johnstone called upon to cover for the clearly out-of-sorts captain, the Lions decided to take them on up front when the better option may well have been to try to exploit the disrupted New Zealand three-quarter line. It wasn't to be. Six All Black forwards and an inspired Ron Elvidge proved more than equal to the tasks asked of them.

The third Test marked the halfway point of the tour but there were only eight matches to be played in New Zealand before the party moved on to Australia. That journey across the Tasman Sea would see the Lions return once more to Wellington, from where they would set sail, but in the meantime the trek through North Island continued with a match against Wanganui, a coastal town some 100 miles north of the capital. Ken Jones was provisionally selected for the midweek fixture but wisely decided that a few more days' rest would be the better option, his place taken by the versatile Malcolm Thomas. Lewis Jones had played at Gisborne but it was against Wanganui that the Lions management and players realised the many options the young Welshman introduced to the game. His 16 points scored with the boot helped the Lions rack up the points in a 31-3 victory and it was clear that here was a superstar in the making, but it would be in rugby league that Lewis Jones would reach the heights.

Ken returned to the team against Taranaki, entering the fray with great intent and a brace of tries in a confidence-boosting 25-3 win. The two matches since the Test had seen the Lions score 11 tries and as they entered the final stage of their New Zealand tour their reputation for engaging, open rugby meant increasing numbers of spectators were keen to see them play. And if a couple of Lions returned the compliment in person there was even greater excitement.

School visits were a big part of the off-field activities in which the Lions engaged. At Taranaki, Ken and Malcolm Thomas were invited to Westown Primary School which had long-standing links with Devonport High School in Plymouth. In the 1930s the schools exchanged trees for planting in their respective grounds and now Ken and Malcolm, who was stationed with the Royal Navy near Plymouth, were invited to plant two trees alongside those received earlier which were reportedly doing 'very well'. It was a different story back home where Devonport High School had suffered bomb damage during the war and the trees had been lost. Replacements were sent and, after being nurtured at Kew Gardens, were planted at Plymouth High School for Girls. Speaking to the gathering of local dignitaries, teaching staff and pupils Ken acknowledged that 'while I have visited others schools in New Zealand this is the first time I have been called upon to plant a tree. As you see these trees growing think that the bonds of friendship between New Zealand and Britain are growing closer and closer.' Malcolm Thomas confirmed he would visit the girls' school in Plymouth on his return and 'monitor progress'.

With Ken given another match day off it was Thomas who once again replaced him on the wing against Manawatu–Horowhenua at Palmerston North. Bad refereeing nearly cost the Lions the match after the home side were awarded a dubious try following some confusion in the Lions' dead ball area. Cleaver judged the ball to have crossed the dead ball line and that a drop-out 25 would follow, but the referee saw things differently. When a home forward got his hands on the ball as Cleaver punted it to Preece for the restart, he was allowed to touch down under the posts unopposed for a try that when converted left the Lions trailing 8-3. A poor game, arguably the worst of the tour, saw the tourists stage the necessary comeback to recover and take the spoils 13-8, with Thomas converting two tries and a penalty to bring his personal points tally to 73 and maintain his position as leading points scorer.

Three days later, the Lions scored 30 unanswered points against a combined Waikato–King Country–Thames Valley side at Hamilton for their biggest victory in New Zealand. Ken scored two of the seven tries to bring his total to nine, strengthening his position at the top of the try-scoring table.

From their most convincing win the Lions' next performance saw them scrape home in the closest. The party got its first look at Auckland from the coach, the city bypassed for the time being as they headed further north to Whangarei in Northland and a midweek match with North Auckland. The team were welcomed onto the ground by a record number of spectators basking in the glorious sunshine that is more prevalent in the northern reaches of the country. The sun on their backs and an expectant crowd would normally have seen the Lions in flamboyant mood, but not on this particular day. North Auckland may not have been the most fashionable of the provinces in 1950 but they lost only one match during the season, that against the Lions, who were happy to hear the final whistle with the scoreboard confirming they had edged the tight encounter 8-6, Ken's fifth try in his last three appearances helping to save the day.

With only Saturday's match against Auckland remaining before the final Test it provided a last chance for those selected to stake a claim for inclusion a week later. Lewis

Jones, Michael Lane, Rex Willis, Grahame Budge and Jimmy Nelson each rose to the occasion and would be chosen to win their first British Lions caps, but for one of New Zealand's proudest provinces it was a desperately long and disappointing afternoon. Saturday 22 July 1950 went down as one of the blackest days in the history of Auckland. The Lions' 32-9 victory saw any dreams the province may have had of emulating Otago and Southland firmly laid to rest, the Lions running in five tries and Lewis Jones adding 17 points with the boot. Ken's scoring record continued with another brace – the log now read 14 tries in 14 appearances – and the Welshman headed for the fourth Test in probably the best form of his career thus far. What would he produce against the All Blacks in seven days' time?

Writing in the *Weekly News* during the British Lions' return to New Zealand in 1959, TP McLean, New Zealand's most respected rugby correspondent, recalled what he heralded as the 'Greatest Try of All'. It would be impossible to improve on his narrative and although footage of the try exists, McLean's words provide a vivid account of events. Rugby football journalism of the highest order which has rarely been equalled.

> *...the All Blacks led 11 to 3, only a dozen minutes of play remained and the Lions, it was plain to see, were done for. 'And then the ball came to Willis and from him to Kyle and thence to Lewis Jones. Rugby lore commanded that Jones should kick for touch. A whimsical rugby genius commanded that he should feint and dummy and start to run. With the dummy and the burst of speed he was past Tanner. Every other All Black was minding his man and for once the cover defenders were far away. Perhaps they were still resting on the side of the scrum. What lay in front of Lewis Jones was not a tangled mass of All Black jerseys but a green field and, far away, Scott, the lone sentinel.*

Lewis Jones ran, lord how he ran! At halfway, or thereabouts, Scott loomed in his path. He was perhaps conscious too, that Henderson, in an extremity of excitement, had been lured from his post on the wing and was coming in toward him. Almost certainly, with the divine instinct of genius, Lewis Jones knew that Kenneth Jones, the red panther of Wales, was striding smoothly to his right, perfectly positioned and only awaiting the signal and the ball to begin his effort.

And here, now, was Scott. Neither sooner nor later, but only at the perfect moment, Lewis flung the ball toward Kenneth. Henderson was almost in the path and with a blinding brilliance Lewis, recognising the danger, threw the pass a little high so that the All Black could not reach it. The ball reached Kenneth at chest height. He ran at all times with the sinuous grace of a greyhound and now his long legs stretched forth, flashing over the green and driving onward toward the goal.

As Jones swooped onward, so did the All Blacks run as never before. It is quite certain that none of them knew that 58,000 people were now shouting, if not actually screaming, with the excitement of the chase. All that Jones could see was the goalpost and all that his pursuers could see were those flying heels. With one tremendous effort, Roper half dived, half tumbled and as he fell his right hand forked out like the fangs of a snake, seeking to clip Jones' heels. An instant later Jones himself dived. With a great spring he leaped forward. The goal line was beneath him as he flew through the air. And then, partly in ecstasy and partly in uncontrollable flight, he tumbled over and over three or four times before at last his flight was stilled and he could gaze about him.

What a sight! Modest maidens, stout matrons, gawking schoolboys, the long and the short and the tall, were jumping, throwing paper and hats and bags, waving scarves and programmes and yelling, bellowing, making

*any kind of noise that seemed proper as an expression of
total joy.'*

Lewis Jones' conversion brought the Lions to within a score
at 11-8 but it was not to be. The 'greatest try' did not secure a
memorable victory and the final whistle heralded an end to
the four-match series, won by New Zealand 3-0 with only the
drawn first Test offering any solace to the shattered British
Lions. But it had been much closer than that, as all those who
attended one or more of the Tests would agree. Sport can be
very generous and it can also be very cruel. In New Zealand
in 1950, it chose to be the latter.

One fixture remained and it would take place back in
Wellington before the tourists set sail for Australia. This was
against the New Zealand Maoris, a combination team maybe,
but one with a huge amount of national pride and identity.
The Lions selectors made ten changes from the Test side, with
Ken one of the five players asked to play. This was his 16th
appearance and he celebrated by scoring his 16th try in a
close match in which the Lions eventually held on to win 14-9.
During the three months in New Zealand 23 matches were
played; 17 were won with one drawn and five lost.

If a British Lions tour is measured by results alone then the
1950 visit to New Zealand cannot be hailed an outstanding
success. But by the type of rugby produced, the wonderful
tries scored and the huge crowds that turned out to see them,
Karl Mullen's Lions will always be remembered favourably.
When the 15th edition of *The Rugby Almanack of New Zealand*
was published in 1951, it continued a long-standing tradition
in naming the five players of the year. The editors point
out that in addition to playing ability, leadership, conduct,
sportsmanship and service to the game in general are taken
into consideration when making the nominations. Joining All
Black forwards Patrick Murphy, Lester Harvey and Richard
White were Irish outside-half Jack Kyle and the flying wing
from Blaenavon, Kenneth Jeffrey Jones. His citation reported

that 'Ken Jones may be an Olympic runner, but he brings far more than mere speed to the rugby field. His determination, grand handling whilst going at top, ability to make the best of every opportunity and general all-round aptitude, made him a class rugby winger. Well built and strong, Jones thrilled the crowds with his pace and beautiful style.'

What the editors didn't know was that New Zealand rugby hadn't heard the last of Kenneth Jeffrey Jones – his day against the mighty All Blacks was still to come.

Four months after setting sail from Liverpool, the Lions were on their way home. The journey would be a long and protracted one but at least they were heading in the right direction. Arrival in Sydney on Sunday 6 August followed a particularly rough voyage across the Tasman Sea and the party were clearly delighted to set foot on terra firma once again. The Australian sector of the tour took in six fixtures, including two Tests, although the intensity of the matches was not expected to equal that seen in New Zealand.

A Combined Country XV provided the opposition in the first match, played at Canberra. The Lions ran out 47-3 winners with Malcolm Thomas replicating his performance in the opening match in New Zealand with another 21-point haul. Selected for the second match against a much stronger New South Wales at Sydney Cricket Ground, Ken Jones was forced to withdraw after pulling a leg muscle in training. The Lions continued to rattle up the points with a 22-6 victory and so satisfied were the selectors that the team announced to meet Australia in the first Test in Brisbane showed only one change, with Ken included on the wing in place of Thomas, his replacement in Sydney. Once again Jones was denied, forced to withdraw after the final training session, giving Malcolm Thomas the opportunity of another Test appearance.

Australia had toured New Zealand in 1949, winning 11 of 12 matches played including the two Tests. This gave local

154

supporters a certain degree of optimism but it should have been tempered by the fact that while the Wallabies were in New Zealand, the All Blacks were touring South Africa with a 30-man squad made up of the leading players. Bizarrely, the records show that on 3 September 1949 the Springboks defeated New Zealand 9-3 in Durban and Australia beat them 11-6 in Wellington! This counted for nothing in Brisbane, where the Lions won 19-6, Lewis Jones attracting the attention of the rugby league fraternity with a 16-point haul made up of a try, two conversions, two penalties and a drop goal – a full house. One local commentator suggested Jones' signature would be worth £5,000 – a serious amount of money in 1950 when the average weekly pay in the UK was approximately £5. Seven days later in Sydney, the Lions once again put Australia to the sword, scoring five tries in a resounding 24-3 victory, the Wallabies' worst result against the British Isles since fixtures began in 1899.

Ken was not selected for the second Test, and neither did he play against Metropolitan on the following Tuesday. With the Lions registering a fifth win in Australia by 26-17, it was beginning to look as if the public were not going to get a chance to see the Welshman in action. Not so. When the Lions took the field against a New South Wales XV at Newcastle in the last official match of the tour Ken took his place on the right wing and 7,000 spectators saw him wear the red number 4 jersey for the last time. It was a match too far. The Lions struggled to overcome the soaring temperatures and the rock hard pitch while for Ken Jones, his final appearance in a Lions jersey was far from memorable, the tourists beaten 17-12 with the Welshman rarely getting into the game.

The month-long journey home included several ports of call and at Colombo, Ceylon (modern day Sri Lanka) the 30th and final match of the marathon was played. Although it was classified as an 'unofficial' fixture, the 1950 British Lions showed much intent and purpose in scoring eight tries in a comprehensive 44-6 victory. Ceylon may not have offered the strongest opposition but the Lions certainly brought the curtain down on the great adventure with some style.

After stops at Bombay, Aden, Port Said and Marseilles, on Saturday, 7 October the *Strathnavar* docked at Tilbury, London and the Lions once again stood on home soil. They had come together at the Mayfair Hotel on 30 March, and 192 days later the time had come to bid each other farewell. For most, the next time they would meet would be on a rugby field, either as teammates or in opposition, but either way, in the true tradition that is the institution known as the British Lions, many friendships that would last a lifetime had been forged. During their absence the sports calendar had seen 'Budge' Patty win the men's singles final at Wimbledon; Bobby Locke retain the Open Golf Championship with a record aggregate score of 279; the USA beat England 1-0 in Brazil in the World Cup; and most importantly, the BBC had reached an agreement with leading sporting bodies to televise 100 major events during a calendar year. This was a sign of things to come and in the near future the likes of Ken Jones would be finding their way into homes around the country. There was much to look forward to.

CHAPTER SEVEN

DOWN BUT NOT OUT

The Saturday arrival gave those players expected back at work on Monday time to complete their individual journeys and prepare themselves for a return to the weekly routine; difficult `enough after a two-week holiday let alone a six-month leave of absence. Seven of the Welsh players returned to South Wales on Sunday. The 5.15pm departure from Paddington was expected in Newport at 8.30pm, an arrival time that had been well publicised, and when Malcolm Thomas and Don Hayward stepped down from the train there was a big reception committee waiting to greet them. For others, the homecoming would have to wait. A party had been arranged at the Mayfair Hotel on Sunday night and among those who remained in London were Ken Jones and Bob Evans. As a consequence, their arrival in Newport the following day would be very low key.

When the Lions were sorting out their baggage at Tilbury, the players at Newport RFC were preparing for the short journey to Cardiff for what would be the sixth match of the new season. Ken Jones had been elected club captain while in New Zealand with Bob Evans confirmed as vice-captain. In the absence of these leading players, outside-half Roy Burnett led the club and his tenure was proving to be a highly successful one. Undefeated during September, Newport had started the season in style with victories against Penarth, Bristol, Neath, Swansea and Gloucester. Now it was the turn of Cardiff to try and down the Black and Ambers. Ken's last match for his club had been against Cardiff on 4 March, Newport losing at home 11-8. The remaining 12 matches of the 1949–50 season were all won excepting a 3-3 draw at Gloucester and with five victories already recorded in the new season, Newport's unbeaten record extended to 17 matches and became 18 when Cardiff were defeated 8-3 at the Arms Park. Newport were on a roll, the team displaying a most exciting brand of rugby, one that Ken would readily associate with on his return. Under Burnett's guidance, 19 tries were scored in the six matches, Newport not afraid to run the ball at any given opportunity regardless of field position. Not only were the tries and victories mounting up but attendances were growing as the word spread that Rodney Parade was the place to be on a Saturday afternoon. Newport continued the rich vein of form with an away victory at Blackheath and then it was the turn of Leicester to visit Rodney Parade.

When the team to play the Tigers was announced it included Newport's three British Lions. This guaranteed a bumper crowd and an estimated 15,000 turned out to welcome the players home on what proved to be a day of mixed emotions. There were some brief formalities as the players lined up to hear welcome home addresses from the mayor, Councillor AE Willis, along with RS Snelling, chairman of Newport Athletic Club and Jack Wetter, chairman of Newport Rugby Club. Then it was down to business. There were no 'hangovers' evident among the returning Lions, who quickly adapted to the pace and vigour of club football, comfortably fitting in alongside their teammates in what was a well-oiled machine. Newport had much the better of the first half, scoring two tries to lead 13-6 at the interval. Midway through the second period and with no change on the scoreboard, Leicester mounted a series of attacks to stretch the home defence, which somehow managed to deny the visitors a try. The proud unbeaten record was under threat as wave after wave of red, green and white jerseys stormed into the 25 and when Nicholson on the Leicester left wing broke clear, a score seemed inevitable. Some of those in the crowd may have forgotten how quick Ken Jones was as he recovered well and tackled his opposite number into touch at the corner flag. Earlier in the match he had damaged his left hand but after having it strapped up and happy the knock was not serious, he returned to the field. In tackling the Leicester wing, Jones took a second knock on the hand and was clearly in a lot of pain.

Had Ray Lewis, Newport's physiotherapist, not been so insistent that the discomfort suggested something was broken Ken may well have continued and aggravated the problem further. Common sense prevailed and he was reluctantly led from the field and taken to the Royal Gwent Hospital for an X-ray that revealed a broken bone. The prognosis was not good; a period of up to six weeks during which the hand would be in a plaster cast followed by a further three to four weeks' rest before Ken could realistically expect a return to action. This was an altogether new and sobering experience. A turned ankle proved to be a nuisance in the latter part of the Lions tour and there had been short periods when Ken was sidelined from his athletics preparations by a variety of hamstring and muscle tears, but these were rare setbacks. Now, the prospect of having to spend the next nine or ten weeks sitting in the grandstand was particularly unwelcome news. Not only would he be unable to assume his role as club captain but the two months' lay-off would also rule him out of contention for both the first and second Welsh trials. Recent form suggested Newport would cope in his absence but there was concern that the lack of game time would count against him in the eyes of the national selectors. Ken had played against the Maoris on 2 August, New South Wales a month later and reappeared for Newport on 21 October. It seemed unlikely that he would return to competitive rugby before December, meaning he would have played barely 200 minutes' rugby in four months.

Ken Jones faced a challenge that he was determined to win. Nine to ten weeks out of action may have been the collective opinion of the medical practitioners he consulted but this was too long a period to contemplate. We are talking about a naturally fit individual and a broken hand couldn't stop him running and exercising the rest of his body as he waited to have the plaster removed. Five weeks later the support was taken off and after another two weeks, Ken declared himself available for selection. His return to club duty would be exactly seven weeks after breaking his hand, giving him more than enough time to convince the Welsh selectors of his return to full fitness and they would eventually select him for the final trial on 6 January.

While the club captain was viewing proceedings from the sidelines, Newport continued in their winning ways. Another five matches were won before Ken returned, notably a second victory of the season over Cardiff by 8-6. The match was played at Rodney Parade in front of 23,500 spectators who witnessed yet another confident performance by the home team and an 11th consecutive win of the season. A week later Abertillery became the 12th team to succumb to the all-conquering Black and Ambers and then on 25 November Newport travelled to London for the 13th match of the season – or was it?

In 1950, London Welsh played their home matches at Herne Hill in south London. When Newport arrived at the ground a great fog had descended but the referee and both captains decided the match should go ahead. Such was the density of the fog, those spectators who had arrived at the ground were admitted free of charge, leading the club to declare an estimated loss of £200 in gate receipts. Reports regarding the validity of the match differ but do agree that at half-time the match was scoreless and was abandoned early in the second half. Under the Laws of the game at the time, if a match was abandoned after half-time the result should stand but the result is not included in the 1950–51 statistics of either Newport RFC or London Welsh. Writing for the *South Wales Argus*, Jack Davis, who attended the match, commented: 'It was a pity that Newport's 100 per cent record went today in such farcical circumstances, but the second half was started, so the game counts as a match with a definite result.' Elsewhere in his report he notes that the referee blew for half-time after 25 minutes, later bringing an end to proceedings 11 minutes into the second period. It would appear that the short first half must have invalidated the match's standing. Suffice to say it doesn't exist in the records and how important that is would be revealed as the season unfolded.

Following the debacle at Herne Hill, Newport's next match also took them across the border, but this time only as far as Bristol. The visitors won 12-0, right wing Graham Ross scoring one of four tries in what Jack Davis described as 'the finest display Newport had given this season'. He was also impressed with some individual performances: 'Ross and Lane (left wing) revelled in their active employment. Neither had played better before.'

The Newport selectors were going to have the sort of problem selectors welcome when Ken Jones was declared fit to play – who to leave out. And the decision would be made sooner than expected when Ken confirmed his availability for the next match.

There were Newport supporters who held the opinion that the team should remain unchanged after the fine performance at Bristol. An exchange of letters published in the *South Wales Argus* highlighted the issue, with one signed off by 'an ex Newport player' who went to great lengths to convince readers that Ken should not gain automatic selection after the outstanding performances of the team to date. 'How can he possibly be selected over Ross and Lane... Newport have men far superior to home in attack...' Such was the strength of opinion, ridiculous as it seems, the demands for him to 'take his place in the United and win his spurs' might have carried the day. It was even suggested that his success in New Zealand was largely due to being part of a star-studded side. Graham Ross and John Lane certainly had a faithful following, with Lane in particular not seen to be receiving the recognition due to him. His opposite number at Bristol was Jack Gregory, Ken's teammate in the relay at the Olympics, and Lane clearly got the better of him on the day but it was Graham Ross who the selectors would have to pick if Ken was to be demoted to the second team. It was never going to happen and once the talisman right wing and club captain was passed fit he was immediately selected.

Cambridge University were the opponents and Jones' return apart, the match generated particular interest as it gave the Welsh selectors a chance to cast an eye over Roy Burnett and the Cambridge outside-half, Glyn Davies. These were the leading contenders for the position vacated by Billy Cleaver, who had announced his retirement from international rugby following the Lions tour, and four members of the 'Big Five' made their way to Rodney Parade. A few hours later they left the ground none the wiser as neither outside-half produced his best form and the selectors would have to wait until after the second Welsh trial before continuing their deliberations. However, any doubts that may have existed regarding the right-wing position were quickly dispelled when Ken scored a typical try in the opening minutes to announce his return. He continued to impress with several scything runs and good defensive work while for many commentators he appeared to have developed a 'very fine swerve'. This probably first saw the light of day in New Zealand but with his limited game time against Leicester the home crowd had not been introduced to it. Needless to say, Newport continued in winning ways, beating the students 16-6.

What might have been? What would have happened if the weather hadn't intervened and Swansea's visit to Rodney

Parade had not been postponed until later in the season? The match clashed with the Welsh trial at Maesteg, which would see Burnett and Davies go head to head for the second time in a week, and with Bobby Owen, Newport's other choice at stand-off, injured the selectors had a problem. When Ken volunteered his services at outside-half the offer was quickly taken up, a repeat of 1947 when Ken was selected at outside-half for the visit to the Harlequins. He would be partnered by scrum-half Billy Williams with centres Hedley Rowland and Bryn Williams primed to take over if the experiment failed but, again, bad weather prevented the match from being played. So Ken Jones never did play at outside-half in a senior rugby match but with his recently introduced 'very fine swerve' who knows what may have happened.

The second Welsh trial also fell victim to the bad weather and was rescheduled for a week later. Many familiar names would be missing from the Probables and Possibles as the selectors had previously given special dispensation for nine of Wales' Lions to travel to Dublin to play for a Karl Mullen XV against Old Belvedere on 23 December. It would have been difficult to withdraw so many players at the 11th hour and Ken, together with Malcolm Thomas, Don Hayward, John Robins, Rex Willis, Bleddyn Williams, Cliff Davies, Lewis Jones and Jack Matthews set off across the Irish Sea for a festive reunion with their tour captain. For the record, Mullen's XV won the match 23-6 with Willis, Matthews and Thomas among the try scorers and Lewis Jones contributing with four conversions – it was a blank afternoon for the right wing.

The first Saturday of the new year saw Newport visit Devonport Services on the same day the final Welsh trial was staged in Cardiff. Ken and Bob Evans were involved in the trial, together with naval officers Lewis Jones and Malcolm Thomas, who spent much of the season playing for the Services. Newport were hard pushed to maintain their unbeaten record, two late tries enough to claim the spoils 6-0. A week later it was the turn of Newbridge to visit Rodney Parade in a match that held some significance. In 1892–93, under the captaincy of Tom Graham, Newport won the first 19 matches played and that record would be equalled if Newbridge were defeated. It wasn't pretty. Newbridge adopted what was once called 'aggressive defence' as their modus operandi – modern parlance would be damage limitation – but even this destructive approach failed to contain Newport, the home side winning 8-0 to match the 57-year-old record.

Such was the multitude of talent at the Big Five's disposal that, despite being the form club in Wales with an unbeaten run that extended back to the previous March, Newport had only two representatives in the side chosen to play England – Ken and Bob Evans. Later in the championship Malcolm Thomas, primarily a Devonport Services player during the 1950–51 season, would have completed his time in the Royal Navy and represented Newport when he played against France. Throw the goal-kicking second row forward Ben Edwards, who won his only cap against Ireland, into the mix and that was the sum total of Newport's international representation in 1950–51, a season in which no Welsh club defeated the Black and Ambers. Quite extraordinary, especially when considering how Wales fared in the Five Nations.

The championship began well when England were overwhelmed 23-5 at Swansea. Wales crossed for five tries, two each from Jack Matthews and Malcolm Thomas (playing on the left wing) with Ken adding a fifth to kick start talk of another Grand Slam; such is the nature of the Welsh rugby supporter. For the Newport captain, the day got better when news came through that Newport had beaten Coventry to better the unbeaten record of the 1892–93 team. The significance of the 'cancelled' fixture with London Welsh was now fully understood.

Ken's season was finally starting to take shape. The injury and some discontent on the terraces might have disrupted the run-up to Christmas but at last everything appeared to be falling into place – what could go wrong? Before any thoughts of Murrayfield could take centre stage, Ken had two other dates to fulfil. Newport would travel to Richmond on the 27th of the month but it was a very different engagement from the routine match listings that stood out from the pages of his diary.

Ivor Williams was born in London on 15 March 1908. The son of Christopher Williams RA, Ivor would follow in his father's footsteps and become a distinguished artist, exhibiting at the Royal Academy and the Royal Society of Portrait Painters in addition to the National Eisteddfod of Wales. Relocated to Llandaff, a leafy suburb to the north of Cardiff, Williams' most recognised work was *Field-Marshal Montgomery Receiving the Freedom of the City of Newport*, which he completed in 1945 and which hung in the council chambers at Newport Civic Centre. His latest commission was a portrait of one of Wales' leading sportsmen. Many mornings the artist would arrive at Summerhill Avenue to find his subject still in bed, but Williams persisted in the commissioned task and on Wednesday 24 January 1951 the result of his endeavours was unveiled at Blaenavon Workmen's Hall. An estimated 1,000 people attended the evening which was a celebration in song, including contributions from the newly formed Blaenavon Ladies' Choir, the Avon Male Singers and soloists, Mrs L Roberts (soprano), Miss Barbara Thomas (contralto) and Mr Jack Giles (baritone), who were accompanied on piano by Mrs B Parry and Mr Bryn Thomas.

In unveiling the portrait which, although presented to Ken Jones, would hang at the Workmen's Hall, Captain Geoffrey Crawshay commented, 'No one has more regard for the local boy than Wales and Monmouthshire. When we hear of a local boy's success in any sphere, in any part of the world, we give full credit to his native town or village. Overnight, a local boy can become the high priest of one of the oldest religions in the world – hero-worship... If Ken Jones were to make it known that he consumed 12 dozen eggs before a big event I venture to suggest that every hen house in Blaenavon would be in peril...'

Responding, Ken observed that he had derived a lot of pleasure from his achievements 'and even more pleasure from the knowledge that Blaenavon has had thereby a certain amount of good publicity'. Recounting how he was deemed too small to get in the Church School rugby team he offered words of encouragement to all aspiring young athletes, suggesting that 'I know there are boys in the valleys who can do as much as I have done. All that is necessary is that they should grit their teeth and have a real go. Get down to it and put Wales in the forefront of the athletic world.' These last words undoubtedly registered with Bob Barwell, Ken's first coach, who was present among the seated audience. Now 74 years of age it was Barwell, of course, who was the first to identify the prodigious talent that lay within the slight ten-year-old frame and who helped develop it into the fine all-round sportsman Ken Jones had become.

Ken was joined by Irene and his parents, together with Bill Everson, Hedley Rowland, Bob Evans and Vernon Parfitt of Newport RFC and W Fisher representing the AAA. This was rather appropriate as the portrait, done in oils, showed Ken in his Great Britain athletics vest with a tracksuit top casually draped over one shoulder. A bureau-bookcase was also presented, both items inscribed with the words 'Presented by the townspeople of Blaenavon to commemorate the outstanding prowess of Kenneth J Jones as a member of the British team in the Olympic Games of 1948, a Welsh rugby international and a member of the British touring team of 1950.' Sixty years later the portrait still hangs in Blaenavon Workmen's Hall, a constant reminder of the town's most famous son. The monies collected by the fund set up to recognise Ken Jones' many sporting achievements could not have been spent more wisely.

There must have been a degree of satisfaction enjoyed by those who earlier in the season were critical of Ken's selection for Newport based on reputation alone. When the team to travel to Richmond was announced, John Lane and Graham Ross were on the wings with the captain included alongside Bryn Williams at centre. So the selectors finally appeased everybody, even if injuries had played a part in their deliberations, but they weren't exactly setting a precedent. Ken Jones had ventured infield before with some success and realistically this was a selection that was never likely to fail. In addition to his great pace, Ken had long since been recognised as a solid defensive player and with the 'new found swerve' it was the opinion of many onlookers that he was more suited to centre three-quarter play in 1950–51 than at any other time in his career.

Every season saw Newport play one or more matches away to one of the leading London-based clubs. Be it London Welsh, Blackheath, Richmond or Wasps, the fixtures had added appeal because they allowed the players and travelling committee members the opportunity to enjoy a night at a hotel in the city. Saturday would begin with the party meeting at Newport station in time to pile aboard the 8.20am Paddington express. As the train pulled out of the station, so the players headed for the dining car where one of the famous British Rail breakfasts could be enjoyed. The club were happy to pick up the tab for this right royal platter of eggs, bacon, fried bread, sausages, tomatoes and mushrooms together with coffee and toast, but only if a player had travelled a distance deemed far enough to have meant leaving home too early to enjoy breakfast. And there the problems began. Every ruse imaginable was introduced in an attempt to justify taking one's seat for the feast. Inevitably there were some who would be disappointed but not Ken Jones. Living in Blaenavon he obviously qualified for the allowance but on moving to Newport such dispensation no longer applied; but Ken Jones was nothing if not a wily individual and come hell or high

Ken Jones

water he always managed to take his place in the dining car as the train pulled out of the station.

At Paddington the party joined a Wallace Arnold coach that ferried them across the city to the Imperial Hotel on Russell Square from where the team would later be transferred to the afternoon's game. Following the match, the coach would return to London where the players could either take in a show or spend the evening enjoying the variety of nightlife on offer. No records exist to confirm what proved to be the more popular option.

Big breakfast or not, for the 21st consecutive time that season, Newport delivered. Richmond could not handle the adventurous backs and abrasive forwards and the visitors scored six tries in the 24-6 win, Ken touching down for the first when he collected a long throw-in at a line-out and fended off the full-back to cross under the posts. Leading Richmond was no. 8 Peter Kininmonth, who had toured with the Lions the previous year. Seven days later he would captain Scotland at Murrayfield against a Welsh team that showed only one change from the side that trounced England, Pontypool's Allen Forward replacing Llanelly's Peter Evans in the back row.

Work commitments prevented Ken from taking part in the final training session before the Welsh team departed for Edinburgh but he was ready and waiting when the train carrying the team and officials pulled into Newport station on its journey north. An estimated 20,000 Welsh supporters also made the pilgrimage but how many got into Murrayfield is not known, the ground coming under siege in the hours leading up to the 2.45pm kick-off. With the Scottish Rugby Union still operating a pay at the gate policy for the vast terraces, this led to contrasting reports regarding the number of spectators in attendance with the general consensus pointing to a figure in excess of 80,000, a world record at the time. Certainly thousands gave up trying to find a way into the stadium and headed back to the city, but

168

those who succeeded saw a match that would live long in the memory.

With Scotland leading by a penalty goal to nil at half-time the outcome was far from decided but the Scottish forwards were proving the dominant force with Wales rather lucky to still be within a score. It didn't last long. A monumental drop goal by Kininmonth led to a period of total domination during which the home team ran in three tries and at the final whistle Wales were a well-beaten side and the debates as to why would carry on well into the night and beyond. Indeed, Scotland's 19-0 victory in 1951 is still discussed whenever the two teams meet. There could be no excuses after such a resounding defeat, neither were any offered and the Welsh team headed home knowing the knives would be out and that there was much soul searching to be done before Ireland arrived in Cardiff in a month's time.

Also to consider were the 20,000 travelling supporters, most of whom would have witnessed the match and have their own version of the horror story that unfolded to relate. Reports suggest Ken had a miserable afternoon and in all his appearances for Wales, rarely could he have seen so little of the ball. A cartoon in a local paper headed 'The Bigger the Leek the Bigger the Fall' depicted a leek planted on the pitch clearly wilting with each Scottish score. The final drawing shows Ken scratching his head with the caption 'Ken Jones must have wondered why he came north for he never got a run'.

If things had come off the rails big time for Wales there were no such problems on the club front, with Newport recording their biggest win of the season when defeating Bath 39-9 at Rodney Parade. That result brought the total number of points scored in the 22 matches played to date to 350 and the nine points registered by Bath were the most Newport would concede during the season. Ken made a second appearance in the centre against Oxford University the following Thursday but he was back on the wing for the trip to Leicester on Saturday. Both matches were comfortably won and the club could now focus on the away trip to Cardiff a week later, the outcome of which would be the defining moment of the season thus far.

Newport and Cardiff first met on a rugby field on 22 January 1875, Newport winning by two goals to one try. The years that followed saw an intense rivalry develop between the clubs and since 1897 they had normally met four times a season. On three occasions Cardiff had won all four matches, most recently in 1947–48. This was something that had eluded Newport but surely the club would never have a better chance than that offered in 1950–51? The third of the season's meetings would take place at Cardiff Arms Park with the expectation that the 55,000 capacity stadium would be hard pressed to contain the number of spectators wanting to see the match. The final reckoning indicated that 48,000 packed the Arms Park on Saturday, 17 February, a world record attendance for a club match, and they were royally entertained.

Both teams were at full strength. Ken took his place on the right wing, the Newport selectors clearly not willing to take any risks against the Cardiff pairing of Jack Matthews and Bleddyn Williams. They opted for the more experienced Bryn Williams and Bobby Owen to contain the Lions stars while half-backs Billy Williams and Roy Burnett would oppose Rex Willis and Cliff Morgan, Billy Cleaver's successor as club outside-half. Among the forwards there were equally mouth-watering clashes to savour, particularly in the back row which would see the Newport trio of Doug Ackerman, Peter Davies and Bob Evans contest everything on and above the ground with John Nelson, CD Williams and Irish international wing forward Des O'Brien. The stage was set.

Few club matches would attract the attention of all the Welsh selectors at this point in the season but the Big Five were at Cardiff for what was seen as an unofficial trial match. In his book *One Hundred Years of Newport Rugby*, Jack Davis selected this particular encounter as the outstanding club match of the century. Few who were there would disagree but it took a mighty second-half effort from the visitors to secure the spoils after trailing 3-0 at the interval. Two tries by Tom Sterry and John Lane, the second converted by Ben Edwards, saw Newport home 8-3 and while there is much to remember from the game, it was a torrential hailstorm that fell after Newport had taken the lead which almost stole the show. Such was the intensity of the downpour that play was stopped while it spent its force, with the players looking for some sort of cover which clearly did not exist, except for Jack Matthews, who seemed to think that the posts would protect his large frame. Newport recorded a 25th consecutive victory of the season in front of a crowd greater than that in attendance at any Football League match that day.

Ken was forced to miss Newport's next match, the visit of Blackheath to Rodney Parade. Officially it was a sore throat that ruled him out but he was also carrying a leg injury picked up against Cardiff following a collision with Bleddyn Williams. The Black and Ambers continued in winning ways and a week later the sore throat may have cleared up but the leg was still causing problems and it was with great reluctance that the Newport captain sat in the stand for the fourth and final clash of the season against the Blue and Blacks.

This was the match for which Newport had waited more than 60 years; the match in which the club could finally lay to rest the albatross it had been reluctantly carrying; the match in which Cardiff could be beaten for the fourth time in the season. On police advice the ticket allocation had been limited to 27,000, a record for the ground excepting the visit of New Zealand in 1924 when 28,000 supporters reportedly filled Rodney Parade. An added incentive for the players was the presence of three members of the Big Five. The Welsh team to face Ireland had been announced in the week but with five places still undecided. Five 'AN Others', an unprecedented selection brought about by the disappointing performance at Murrayfield. Among the positions still to be filled were a berth in the second row and outside-half. Both problems would be solved during the course of the afternoon with Newport's Ben Edwards and Cardiff's Cliff Morgan doing enough to convince the selectors to award them first caps.

Newport didn't beat Cardiff, neither did they lose. The teams fought out a thrilling 3-3 draw which kept the supporters enthralled until referee Trevor Jones blew for full-time. A Ben Edwards penalty kick taken from wide out on the touchline and only a couple of yards inside the Cardiff half soared between the uprights in the third minute and the big second row man was on his way to that elusive first cap. When Bill Tamplin struck the upright with a straightforward penalty attempt in the 11th minute such was the surprise among the Newport players they made a terrible mess of clearing their line and immediately conceded another penalty. This time Tamplin made no mistake and that was how it remained. Both teams showed their great attacking flair but equally, both demonstrated sound defences and despite the home team's bitter disappointment at the final whistle, neither side deserved to lose on the day.

From his seat in the committee box, Ken could only ponder on what might have been, how important the drawn match would become in the annals of the club. Time would put even greater emphasis on the result because, although Newport repeated the task of winning the first three matches in a season, a fourth victory would always elude them.

Against Ireland at the Arms Park seven days later it was very much a case of *déjà vu*. Ben Edwards celebrated his first cap when converting a penalty from 45 yards, one not dissimilar to his effort a week earlier, but this time he had the assistance of firstly an upright then the crossbar to help the ball on its way. Ireland drew level courtesy of a Jack Kyle try 15 minutes later, following which neither team managed to break the deadlock. In the process of denying Ireland a Grand Slam and Triple Crown the Welsh players had restored some pride to the jersey but there would be much more tinkering before the season ended, some of it questionable. Despite favourable reports that went to some lengths in recognising a good all-round performance, Ben Edwards would never play for his country again.

What would sport be if not for the underdog? The little man who rises to the occasion and against all odds beats the champion; the club at the bottom of the table that makes little of its precarious position to conquer the team at the top. Certainly a lot less interesting. When Ken Jones led Newport onto the field at Teddington for a Saturday morning kick-off it is unlikely that defeat was uppermost in his mind. Modest man that Ken undoubtedly was, one unlikely ever to take winning as a matter of course, the odds were certainly stacked in his team's favour – Newport had lost only once to the Harlequins in the 17 matches played to date. Twickenham was hosting the England–Scotland Calcutta Cup match later in the day but it is doubtful that playing at the bigger venue would have helped the visitors' cause in any way because this was the match that would bring Newport's undefeated run to an end and there the matter should rest.

Ken took his place in the centre, allowing Ross and Lane to continue on the wings. They may have been without their international players and injured captain but the Harlequins called the shots and there was little Newport could do about it. Big Ben Edwards did miss a couple of straightforward kicks at goal but there were no complaints. No complaints even that the biggest thorn in the Newport armoury was 'Quins scrum-half Norman Fryer, who had played for the Welsh club in the seasons immediately following the war. His contribution on the day was immense, Jack Davis reporting that it 'sometimes looked like he was playing all Newport on his own...' . The only score of the match came courtesy of a 12th-minute penalty goal and the visitors were left experiencing the bitter taste of defeat for the first time since 4 March the previous year. The time scale extended beyond a year at 378 days and the unbeaten run had stretched to 40 matches. These are impressive statistics by any measure and that it all came to an end when least expected is the most surprising detail of all. It would be a long journey home and it is doubtful that either a West End show or a night on the town helped.

Easter fell early in 1951, bringing with it the traditional rugby festival that saw Newport play three matches in four days. Ken stood down for the first, Newport beating Devonport Services 12-3, but he resumed his place in the centre against London Welsh on Easter Monday and the Barbarians the following day. Two more victories entered the records and when Neath were despatched on the last day of the month it left seven outstanding fixtures in what would be a busy April.

The international season ended disappointingly in Paris, Wales defeated 8-3 despite leading at half-time through a Ken Jones try, his 11th in 21 appearances. It is not unusual for a particularly successful international season to be followed by a somewhat disappointing one. Neither is it unusual for a country, after having a large number of players selected for a British Lions tour, to be found wanting on their return. In 1951 Wales qualified on both these counts and all concerned were glad to see the Five Nations brought to an end in Paris. There was always next year to look forward to.

While Wales were being read the last rites at Stade Colombes, Newport fared a little better in beating Llanelly at Rodney Parade. Always nice to send the men from west Wales home with their tails between their legs and another chance to remind those beyond the Loughor that west is not always best came five days later with the arrival of Swansea in a rearranged fixture held over from December. Newport were one of the first clubs to install floodlights but during the 1950–51 season these were only called upon twice; against Oxford University in February and Swansea on a Thursday evening in mid-April when they were probably switched on only for the second half.

Another leg injury forced Ken to leave the field and kept him out of the team for Saturday's visit to Gloucester but Newport prevailed ,winning both matches and all the while improving the impressive season's stats which now read 36 matches played, 34 won, 1 drawn and 1 defeat with four fixtures remaining.

Newport RFC had strong connections with clubs in Devon and Cornwall and each season saw the club travel to the South West for a short tour on which two or three matches were played. The 1951 tour included matches against Plymouth Albion, Torquay Athletic and Exeter and a repeat of the Easter weekend with games played on Saturday, Monday and Tuesday. The three clubs were all familiar names on the Newport fixture list. Plymouth Albion had featured for many seasons, winning six of the 57 matches played to date; Torquay Athletic had won the first of four matches between the clubs; but Exeter had little to show for its endeavours over the years with only a draw to its credit after 13 meetings with the Welsh club.

A squad of 22 players set off for the West Country, fully aware they were there to be shot down, the three home teams having nothing to lose and everything to gain. What better way to bring the curtain down on the season than by defeating the best club in the land? Newport completed the double over Plymouth following the convincing 33-3 home win earlier in the season but this time it was much closer. Ken Jones and John Lane scored tries against a spirited home team that almost produced a shock result before finally going down by six points to five. It is worth noting that when the home side took a five-point lead it represented the biggest deficit by which Newport had trailed during the season. It was a little more convincing on Monday night when Newport ran in four tries in defeating Torquay 15-3, which left Exeter, where the team would stop on the homeward leg of the short tour. Records confirm that Exeter won only 19 of the 43 matches played in the 1950–51 season but among them the club claimed the scalp of the Black and Ambers. Unlike the season's only other defeat, which had been to a better side on the day, Newport's 3-0 loss at Exeter should never had happened. The visitors may have looked 30 points better than their opponents but the scoreboard never lies. End of season malaise? End of season festivities? Who knows? If anyone at Rodney Parade had been advised on 1 September that the club would only lose two matches in the forthcoming season they would have been delighted. Asked to identify the two defeats it is certain that Cardiff, Neath and the Barbarians, maybe Swansea and Gloucester, possibly Bristol and Llanelly, would all have been nominated. It is unlikely that the names Harlequins and Exeter would have been considered in such a hypothetical debate, but therein lies sport's enduring attraction and long may it continue.

The Newport players returned from the tour in low spirits but with one match still to be played there was an opportunity to ensure the season ended on a high. Cross Keys had requested the match scheduled to be played at Pandy Park be moved to Rodney Parade. The club hoped to build a stand on the riverside bank at its picturesque little ground and Newport agreed to the change of venue and confirmed all gate money would go toward the cost of the new stand. With the blessing of the WRU, the match went ahead in Newport and the £278 paid at the turnstiles was a big boost to Cross Keys' coffers. And so it was that the curtain came down on the season in front of a crowd numbering no more than 4,000, proof perhaps that it wasn't only the players who were looking forward to the summer break. Newport won this 40th and final match 8-3 but it was a lacklustre performance against a Cross Keys team that played its heart out.

With the rugby season rigidly contained within the period 1 September–30 April, two days remained for any outstanding matches to be played. Newport had accepted an invitation to play Pontypool as part of their golden jubilee celebrations. The clubs had not met for three seasons following a disagreement over fixtures and anticipation was high in the eastern valley. Newport may have ended their campaign with records aplenty but Pontypool had enjoyed no small amount of success themselves, Cardiff becoming the only team to win at the Park in the last official match of the season. The much-promoted season's finale took Ken back to his roots and without doubt the crowd that assembled on the huge popular bank on Monday evening would have included many from nearby Blaenavon. The kick-off was put back from the advertised 5.30pm to 6.00pm, allowing as many people as possible to get to the ground after work. The final figure put the gate at 10,000 and they were well entertained despite most of the match taking place in a downpour. When Pontypool centre Graham Dobbs broke his leg early in the first half, rather than play against 14 men, Ken sportingly invited the home side to field a replacement. Newport won the match 13-3 but regardless of the fact that both clubs took the field with great intent and purpose the result does not appear in any official records.

Ken Jones' first season as club captain was over. Of 40 matches played, 37 were won, one match was drawn and two were lost. Ken scored six tries in 18 matches, which looks slim pickings alongside the harvests reaped by John Lane with 27 tries in his 34 appearances and Graham Ross, who ran in 15 tries in two fewer. The reasons for this have been documented but there is more to captaincy than playing every match and scoring lots of points. Ken Jones had proved himself an exemplary captain both on and off the field and no one could ever criticise his total commitment to Newport RFC during what at times was a stressful and demanding campaign.

There was much to celebrate when 200 guests took their places in the gymnasium at Rodney Parade on 5 May for the end of season dinner. Newport ran several teams and if proof were needed that the club was in rude health the records of the United XV and the Extras confirmed it. The United won 26, drew one and lost one of the 28 matches played while the

Extras were unbeaten throughout the season, winning 18 times and drawing five. The combined results of the three senior teams at the club showed 81 out of a total of 91 matches had been won with seven drawn and three lost. Remarkable statistics by any standards. Club chairman in 1950–51 was Jack Wetter. He had captained the First XV in 1922–23 when Newport were invincible but readily admitted he was of the opinion that Ken Jones' team would have beaten his by a clear 15 points. And the local bank manager would also have been pleased – Newport's gate receipts for the season were £11,145, up from £6,704 in 1949–50.

Was the 1950–51 Newport team the best ever in the club's long and distinguished history? Many observers thought so but perhaps not. In its first four seasons the club remained unbeaten, but rugby football was in its infancy and few matches were played. The 1891–92 season saw Tom Graham lead an unbeaten team that won 29 matches and drew four. Then it was the turn of Jack Wetter, who led Newport to 35 victories and four drawn games in 1922–23. These were all outstanding achievements and but for two unexpected results against English clubs, the 1950–51 team would rank alongside them. However, when considering the crowds that flocked to Rodney Parade and elsewhere when Newport came to town, and the enterprising rugby the team always endeavoured to play, one can readily make a case that the team led by Ken Jones in 1950–51 ranks near the top of the list with a sequence of results that would never be improved on.

Ken had not competed in a major athletics championship for nearly two years. As the 1950–51 rugby season wound down so the time to focus on the track once more loomed on the horizon. With this in mind, Ken set himself a new target – he wanted to be in Helsinki on 3 August the following year for the opening ceremony of the Games of the XVth Olympiad and he did not want to be watching events unfold from the stands. Well aware that he would be well into his 31st year come the Games, he took encouragement from Don Finlay, who had won his final AAA 120 yards hurdles title at the ripe old age of 40. The age barrier held no fears for Ken, who was confident he could still produce times good enough for inclusion on any shortlist of British sprinters. Then it would be down to how he performed in the major championships the following year; he had to produce some personal bests in the current season and take that form forward.

Ken's best times for the 100yds and 100m were both recorded in 1948 when he clocked 9.8 and 10.6 and these were the yardsticks by which his performances over the coming months would be measured. McDonald Bailey won the 100yds at the AAA Championships in 1950 in 9.9 but had been clocked at 9.6 in the heats, equalling his own national record. Robin Pinnington and Jack Gregory both ran 9.8 over the same distance in 1950, and in 1951 no fewer than ten sprinters would break the 10.0 barrier – the time Ken would run in his first race of the new season but one which he would fail to improve on in the coming months.

That first meeting was a triangular tournament between Cardiff, Newport and Swansea. Organised by Penarth Harriers, the event was held at Penarth Grammar School on 9 June. An unlikely venue this may have been but with a precisely measured track, good running surface and accurate timekeeping it provided the necessary criteria for sprinting and Ken's even time performance was a promising start to the new season. In winning the 100yds in 10.0 he surprised many, not least himself, readily admitting after the race that with so little preparation he would have been satisfied with 10.3. The performance convinced the Welsh selectors that he was on form and they included him in the Welsh AAA team to compete against the English Universities and the Welsh Universities at Maindy Stadium, Cardiff, the following Saturday, 16 June.

The Festival of Britain was officially opened by King George VI and Queen Elizabeth on 4 May. Described as a chance for the British public to give themselves a 'pat on the back', the Festival would continue for five months, during which cities and towns were encouraged to enter into the spirit of the occasion by organising events that would get the public involved. Newport had decided to open two weeks of celebration with a triangular athletics meeting between Monmouthshire, Gloucestershire and Somerset, the afternoon to include an invitation 100yds sprint in which Ken had readily agreed to take part. This presented a problem as the meeting clashed with that due to be held at Maindy Stadium between the Welsh AAA and the universities. Some accommodating organisers and no little amount of common sense saw Ken able to compete in Cardiff, his race rescheduled to early in the programme allowing him time to get to Newport, where his appearance was set back to later in the afternoon.

Maindy Stadium was Wales' first purpose-built athletics venue. Recently opened, the running surface had not had chance to bed in and there was little likelihood of it producing any track records until it had settled into the firm surface required if athletes are to perform to their best. Ken and the track performed as expected; the sprinter following up his success in Penarth but in the slower time of 10.2. Outside the stadium a taxi was waiting to set off on the 15-mile journey to Kimberley Park in Newport, where things were well under way with a large attendance looking forward to seeing the international track and rugby star strut his stuff. With little time to prepare it was somewhat inevitable that the public would not see the Olympic athlete at his best and so it proved as he could only finish five yards off the pace in third place after being harshly treated by an overenthusiastic handicapper. The outcome of the race meant nothing in the great scheme of things, but his performance earlier in the day suggested Ken Jones was back in harness as Wales' fastest sprinter. All he had to do now was produce the same form where it really mattered.

A week later Ken Jones returned to Maindy Stadium for the 34th Welsh Championships. The athletes not only had to contend with the new track; on the day there was also a high wind to compete against. This made life particularly difficult for the sprinters but didn't prevent Ken Jones from firmly re-establishing himself as Wales' leading performer over 100yds and 220yds. Times of 10.3 and 23.2 were enough to see him crowned champion for the fourth time. Gareth Morgan from Bangor had won the 100yds in 1950 and in a thrilling final the pair matched stride for stride before the Olympic runner reclaimed the title by a matter of inches.

After three successful meetings in Wales it was time to think about the threat posed by some of the leading English sprinters, a threat that was never going to go away. The Welsh AAA entered a team in a triangular tournament held in Coventry at the end of the month. Teams from the North of England and the Midlands provided the opposition and for Ken this meant a meeting with Jack Gregory and a first clash with the new star of English sprinting, Doncaster's Brian Shenton. Gregory and Shenton took the level of competition beyond that which Ken had experienced in the short time since his return to the track, Shenton winning with Gregory second ahead of a disappointed Jones in third place. Brian Shenton's meteoric rise through the ranks of British sprinting had started in 1950 when he won the 200m at the European Championships after being selected originally as a reserve. Over both sprint distances, like so many before him, Shenton had to take the bridesmaid's role behind McDonald Bailey but these two looked certain to run in Helsinki in 12 months' time, leaving Ken to contemplate how good were his chances of selection.

He would learn nothing more in the course of the next two months. A recurring Achilles tendon injury prevented his appearance in the AAA Championships at the White City that saw McDonald Bailey at his imperious best, winning both sprints in 9.6 and 21.4, with Shenton in close attention.

When he was fit, Ken proved to be unbeatable on the Welsh circuit but his times had not improved since that first run at Penarth. In an inter-county match between Glamorgan and Monmouthshire at Neath he won both sprints in 10.2 and 22.9 but knew that to improve on these times he had to race against the best. His final chance in the season was at a meeting between the Welsh AAA and the AAA at Rodney Parade. Not only would McDonald Bailey take part, but there would be other leading sprinters in attendance, including Jack Gregory. This would give Ken the chance to see where he stood in the rankings at the end of the season and with his home crowd cheering him on the stage seemed set for a rousing finale. But it was not to be. Once again the tendon problem prevented him from appearing and he could only look on as McDonald Bailey ran 9.8 to equal the Welsh All-Comers record. Helsinki must have seemed a long way away.

CHAPTER EIGHT

NEW AMBITIONS

The injury that had kept Ken sidelined for the latter part of the athletics programme now impacted on the start of the rugby season. History has a habit of repeating itself and just as had happened 12 months earlier, but for entirely different reasons, his first outing was delayed until late October when, ironically, it was Leicester who provided the opposition. For 21 October 1950, read 20 October 1951. Fifty-two weeks after making his first appearance of the season following the Lions tour, Ken Jones now returned to the team fully recovered from the injury that had delayed the start of another. And for Rodney Parade read Welford Road; Newport supporters would have to wait a little longer to welcome the wing back to the fold on home turf. They didn't miss a lot, reports of the match confirming Ken played a fairly anonymous role in Newport's 16-3 victory. A week later normal service was resumed when the wing scored one of five tries as the Wasps were overwhelmed 31-3 at Rodney Parade. This was a resounding victory against a team that two weeks earlier had defeated Cardiff 11-9 and the winning margin was sufficient to waive any suggestions of local bias. Newport's great Welsh hooker and former

British Lion, Bunner Travers was the man in the middle when the appointed referee cried off due to illness; the telegram confirming his incapacity arriving at the club an hour before kick-off.

Bob Evans had succeeded Ken as club captain but what appeared to be a fairly innocuous knock on the knee that saw him limp off the field at Abertillery proved to be anything but. An operation was needed to repair a damaged cartilage, bringing an end not only to the captain's season but also his outstanding playing career. It was a sad day. Just as he had done in Ken's absence, Roy Burnett led the team and would continue in the role by right when elected captain for the next season.

By the end of November it was clear the club were not going to enjoy a repeat of the previous season's outstanding record, with two matches already lost and another drawn; the sum total of the debit side of the balance sheet in 1950–51. After losing at Cardiff in October, the second reverse came at the hands of Cambridge University, but three victories in which the team did not concede a point set the stage for the second meeting of the season with the Blue and Blacks, this time at Rodney Parade on 15 December. Newport had not lost at home since 4 March 1950. Cardiff were the victors on that distant day and it seems ironic that the same club would bring a record that extended to 37 matches to an end. That Newport were much the superior side was beyond dispute, a fact that even the most one-eyed Cardiff supporters would have readily acknowledged, but it meant nothing when referee Gwyn Walters brought proceedings to a close. Ken scored a first-half try, displaying great anticipation and even greater pace that saw him capitalise on some careless play in the Cardiff midfield, gather the loose ball and evade several despairing tacklers before touching down under the posts. In 1951 a five-point lead was often considered to be enough and as the game drew to an end there was nothing to suggest the home team would lose. The visitors had no

Of his 17 international tries, the second at Twickenham in 1952 is recognised as the best. From trailing 6-0 and with Lewis Jones struggling with a leg injury, the Welsh XV staged a grand recovery to take the spoils 8-6 in what proved to be the first leg of a Grand Slam. William Hook struggles to lay a hand on Ken.

19 December 1953 – Wales 13, New Zealand 8. The Welsh team standing left to right Dr PF Cooper (referee RFU), Clem Thomas, Sid Judd, Rees Stephens, Roy John, John Gwilliam, Courtney Meredith, Ivor Jones (touch-judge WRU), seated left to right Billy Williams, Gareth Griffiths, Bleddyn Williams (captain), Ken Jones, Dai Davies, front left to right Gwyn Rowlands, Rex Willis, Cliff Morgan, Gerwyn Williams. At the time of publication this was the last time Wales defeated the All Blacks.

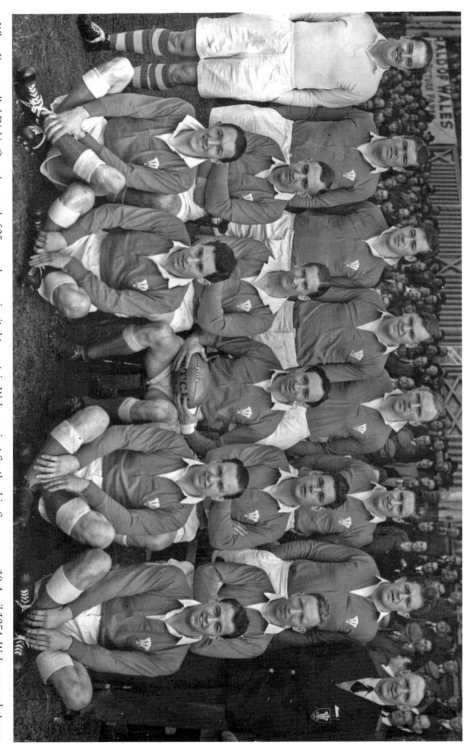

When Ken equalled Dickie Owen's record of 35 caps, he was invited to captain Wales against Scotland in Swansea on 10 April 1954. Wales won what was the last Championship match held at St Helen's but there would be no record breaking try to put the icing on the cake – Ken had scored what would prove to be his last try for his country against New Zealand.

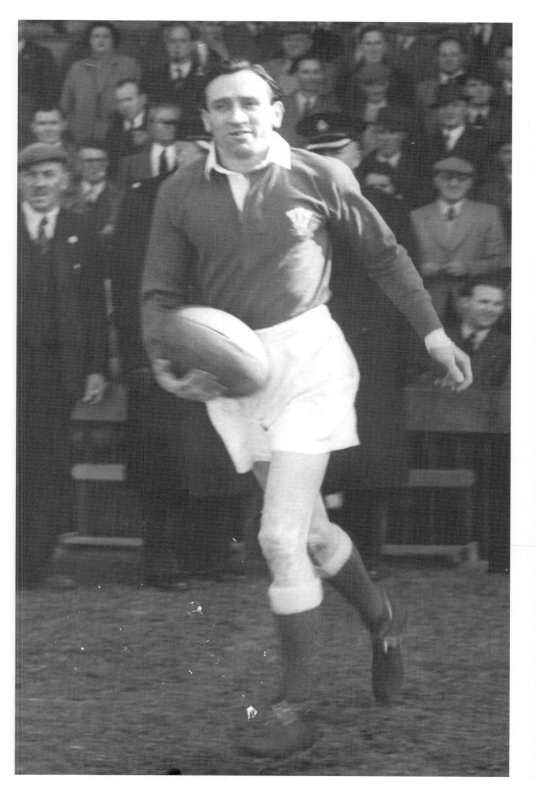

Leading out the Welsh team at Swansea.

Richard Thomas and Baldwin featured Ken in the company's inhouse magazine.

In 1953 Great Britain faced Sweden in Stockholm. Brian Shenton won the 100m with 10.7, Ken claiming second place in 10.8. The pair face the camera after a job well done.

Having elected not to compete in Auckland in 1950, Ken was keen to be selected for the British Empire and Commonwealth Games held in Vancouver four years later. The Welsh team shows Ken second from the left in the back row.

Ken on the podium as the New Zealand national anthem is played following Don Jowett's victory. England's Brian Shenton won silver.

On his return from Canada Ken could have been forgiven for thinking that his international days on the track were over. Far from it. Not only was he selected to represent Great Britain in the European Championships held in Berne a few weeks later but he was also chosen to captain the men's team. Here the full GB squad prepare to board the flight to Switzerland. (British European Airways)

The Newport seven-a-side team that defeated Ebbw Vale 6-0 in the final of the inaugural competition held at Rodney Parade at the end of the 1953–54 season.

In 1954 Ken Jones was the first to win the Empire News award which became the BBC Welsh Sports Personality of the Year. He is being presented with it by former Glamorgan and England cricketer JC Clay the chairman of the judges.

Ginger the cat was found in a hedge one night as Ken made his way home after a training session at Rodney Parade. He duly took over the Jones' household and remained a constant companion for the next 20 years. (Jones' Family Archive)

Wales met Ireland in Cardiff in 1955, the season the British Lions manager decided no player over 30 would be selected to tour South Africa. Here, the 33-year-old Ken Jones is about to be brought to ground as the 19-year-old Tony O'Reilly (left) watches on

His playing days may have ended but in 1958, Ken Jones' participation in the opening ceremony of the British Empire and Commonwealth Games held in Cardiff was the best kept secret in the Principality. He carried the baton bearing the Queen's message and hands it to the Duke of Edinburgh.

This Card is valid from JULY 4th to AUGUST 2nd, 1958, when certified by the Empire Games Village Authorities.

It entitles the holder to:—

Access to the Competitors Stand of OWN SPORT and to the Competitors Stand in CARDIFF ARMS PARK.

Access to the Dressing Rooms of OWN SPORT.

Access to and all amenities and facilities provided within the EMPIRE GAMES VILLAGE subject to the Village Rules and Regulations.

Right to FREE transportation as arranged and directed by the Organising Committee.

NOTE:—Photographing and filming of the British Empire Games for COMMERCIAL PURPOSES is forbidden unless officially authorised.

VIᵀᴴ BRITISH EMPIRE and COMMONWEALTH GAMES

CARDIFF 1958 WALES

BELCG

IDENTITY CARD

Nº 1656

NOT TRANSFERABLE

For Official Use Only

14-7-58
(Date)

(Signature of Holder)

ATHLETICS
(Sport) (Block Letters)

TEAM MANAGER
(Official Position) (Block Letters)

for Organising Committee.

JONES
(Surname) (Block Letters)

KENNETH JEFFREY
(Christian or Given Names) (Block Letters)

THE BRITISH EMPIRE AND COMMONWEALTH GAMES ASSOCIATION

of WALES
(Country)

certifies that the holder of this identity card is attending the Games in Cardiff in the stated capacity.

12-7-58
Date

Chairman or Sec

Ken Jones was Wales' team manager in 1958 and despite being one of the best-known individuals at Cardiff Arms Park he still needed to carry appropriate identification. Identity Card number 1656 appears to cover all eventualities.

On 8 November 1960 Ken Jones received the Order of the British Empire for services to sport from HRH Queen Elizabeth II at Buckingham Palace. Irene and Ken's mother join him for photographs outside the palace gates.

After hanging up his boots Ken Jones became the rugby and athletics correspondent for the Sunday Express, *a position he held for 28 years. Reporting aside, there was always a huge amount of correspondence to attend to.*

When the Australian tourists defeated Newport 8-4 in October 1947 the team included a strapping young man in the second row who would later become one of his country's finest ambassadors of the game. Nick Shehadie and Ken Jones reminisce over days gone by. (Jones' Family Archive)

Once retired Ken had time for holidays. Here he is with Irene

Ken in relaxed mood poses for the camera in the black and amber hoops of Newport RFC. At the time of his retirement he was the club's leading try scorer and featured at number eight in the list of appearances. (DR Stuart)

answer to a dominant Newport pack and resolute defence but Ben Edwards missed a couple of kickable penalties, and the visitors remained in contention. The gap was closed to two points by a Bill Tamplin penalty before an uncharacteristic error from Newport full-back Bob Hughes turned the game on its head. Cliff Morgan put a searching kick deep into the Newport 25 which Hughes failed to gather, leaving Cardiff loose forward John Nelson to collect the loose ball and score what was a match-winning try in the dying moments. Records are made to be broken but Newport's fine run of home victories really should have run a little longer; but such is life – *c'est la vie*.

C'est la vie indeed. Ken Jones was a sports master who also took English classes but how good his French was is very debatable. Six international appearances against France had seen him cross for four tries, very much enhancing his reputation across the English Channel where the rugby public love nothing more than to see the fast men in flight. And it was to France, specifically Cognac, that the Newport players and committee headed on 30 December. Not the best way to spend one's 30th birthday and wedding anniversary, but for Ken the train journey to Dover, the ferry crossing and the long haul south courtesy of the French railway network meant that the day would offer an acceptable alternative and be spent with those whose friendship he valued most. On another front it could be claimed that the timing of the tour was misplaced, with the Springboks due in Newport a week after the team returned from what would prove to be more than a rugby adventure.

The first official engagement on arrival in Cognac set the tone of things to come – a visit to the world-famous Hennessy brandy distillery. A civic reception held by the town mayor in honour of the visitors would be held later in the day, followed by an official banquet at La Brasserie du Coq d'Or during which the new year would be welcomed in. Consommé chevaux d'Ange; darne de colin à la Parisienne; contrefilet de boeuf roti; pâté de foie truffe du coq; plateau de fromage; fruits, etc., etc., etc. All washed down with vin blanc et rouge, champagne and café cognacs. Amongst all this *splendide hospitalité* some rugby was played, the first match against Union Sport Cognacais slotted in somewhere between the visit to the brandy distillery and that to the mayor's parlour.

Attention à Ken Jones! – Le rapide ailier du Pays de Galles, Ken Jones, est le plus fameux de cette equipe... Ken's reputation had certainly preceded him but atrocious weather conditions and a curtain raiser which did nothing to help an already churned-up pitch denied the 6,000 spectators a chance to see the 'flying wing' at his best, Newport happy to grind out a 6-5 victory.

The first day of 1952 saw the party head north to Nantes, where local club officials did their best to improve on the hospitality enjoyed in Cognac – le suprême de bar marechal and le contrefilet roti à la broche. Bass and sirloin steak stepping up to the mark in place of hake and roast beef with the usual *glaces* etc. to follow. Perhaps more wine conscious than their brandy quaffing neighbours, the Nantes committee included carafes of les vins blanc and a Medoc together with bottles of a 1948 Muscadet from the Loire region.

The second match was billed locally as a 'Rugby International' and saw Newport take on Nantes at le Parc Malakoff. The weather was much improved from the previous day and the pitch was in fine fettle for open rugby. Two tries by Bryn Meredith and Peter Davies and a Ben Edwards conversion saw Newport home 8-3, bringing a satisfactory finale to the brief sojourn into the south-west corner of France.

The following day, Wednesday 2 January, the party set off for Paris and the connection that would take them to Calais where they would board the homeward-bound ferry. A variety of memorabilia was collected en route but none of the items is as interesting as a cut-out black, handlebar moustache advertising 'The Pussy Chaser's Club'. Bearing in mind the old adage that 'what goes on tour, stays on tour' the player who collected this particular piece of nostalgia shall remain nameless, but Doug Ackerman's contribution to this work is recognised in the appropriate place. The crossing to Dover was particularly rough and few of the players were able to join Peter Davies for an organised sing-song – a regular feature of away trips. We know that Hedley Rowland, Roy Burnett and Billy Williams helped keep the tradition going but of Ken Jones there was no sign.

The Springboks had lost only one of the 22 matches played when they arrived at Newport. London Counties won a memorable victory at Twickenham by 11 points to 9 but the tourists had beaten the four home countries with a record-breaking 44-0 demolition of Scotland the highlight of the tour to date. Ken Jones and Malcolm Thomas were Newport's representatives in the Welsh team that played South Africa on 22 December but were unable to help Wales gain a first victory over the Springboks, who won 6-3. The tourists added a comfortable 17-5 victory in Dublin and on the Saturday preceding the Newport match, England were defeated 8-3 at Twickenham.

Newport had taken on the might of South Africa on three previous occasions. The matches in 1906 and 1931 were both lost but in 1912 the club registered a famous 9-3 victory. Being the first team to defeat the tourists, the club was presented with a Springbok head which still holds pride of place in the trophy room.

Looking at Rodney Parade in the early part of the twenty-first century it is difficult to imagine the crowds that once filled the famous old ground. It is not surprising that some of the biggest attendances were recorded in the late 1940s and early 1950s with the visit of Cardiff always attracting the greatest interest. To this day, the record attendance for a club match is the 27,000 that saw Newport in search of the elusive fourth win against the Blue and Blacks in March 1951 but the overall record at Rodney Parade was set in January 1952, when the fourth Springboks were the visitors. In the interests of safety it was decided the match would be an all-ticket affair and on this basis the official attendance of 31,000 has to be taken as accurate but it is possible that the figure could be adjusted upwards with the certainty that there were a few gatecrashers on the terraces.

It was purely by chance that Newport's 23rd match of the season came against the Springboks, who in turn were playing their 23rd match of the tour. Chance, however, had no part to play in the outcome of a game that saw the home side struggle to contain the visitors. A strong wind, a greasy ball and a sticky pitch should have worked in favour of the Black and Ambers but other than a period in the second half when Burnett made good use of the wind to keep the Springboks pinned down in their half, Newport showed little enterprise and were a well-beaten side come the final whistle. In winning 12-6, South Africa scored four tries to one and there could be no complaints from the record crowd other than the fact that Newport had not performed as well as expected.

There were those quick to point the finger at the French tour, suggesting the effect of the long journeys had not been helpful in the build-up to what was without doubt the biggest game in the club's recent history. Whether the damage was done in France, be it on or off the field, was irrelevant as the Springboks were an exceptionally good side and nothing less than 15 players performing at the very top of their game was ever going to be enough if a repeat of 1912 were to be seen. The Springbok management may have suggested that South Africa produced its best form of the tour against Newport but this was not required against a team that performed well below par. Even its star players were subdued, Ken Jones' major contribution to the game seen in defence, although he did show some deft footwork when dribbling on towards the Springbok line before the move broke down.

Dribbling aside, kicking was never recognised as one of Ken's strengths. Why kick the ball when you had the pace with which he was blessed? Recounting his teaching days at Newport High School, he recalled how at a training session with one of the junior teams the question of drop goals was raised. How did one do it? Never known to avoid any issue, Ken took up position on or about the 25-yard line, took aim and converted the perfect drop kick, mightily impressing the gathered schoolboys with his expertise. He admitted to being slightly fazed by the request for a demonstration having never before attempted to drop a goal. Following his success, he decided that his reputation would be best served if he never tried another one. A wise man should know his limitations and in the field of drop kicks and other boot-to-ball skills Ken Jones certainly knew his.

The Springboks returned to Wales to play the Barbarians at Cardiff on 26 January. Ken was selected on the unfamiliar left wing, which allowed England's John Woodward to play on the right. An abundance of talent that included Bleddyn Williams, Cliff Morgan and Rex Willis among the backs and Bob Stirling, John Kendall-Carpenter and Roy John in the forwards could do nothing to bring the South African juggernaut to a halt, the visitors winning their last match on British soil 17-3. Four more would be played in France before the Springboks could head home and but for the defeat against London Counties they would have returned to South Africa with an invincible record.

The Springboks may have conquered Wales and swept aside the challenges of Cardiff, Swansea, Llanelly, Newport, the combined forces of Neath and Aberavon and those of Pontypool and Newbridge but even that disappointing record failed to diminish the euphoria that followed the Welsh team's visit to Twickenham for the opening match of the championship. England's performance against the tourists when losing 8-3 had given much cause for optimism and having played both countries, the feedback from the touring side suggested Wales would find the going tough at Twickenham, However, such doom-mongers weren't to know that on 19 January 1952 Ken Jones would have one of his finest days in a Welsh jersey and the men in white would be able to do absolutely nothing whatsoever about it.

When England scored two unconverted tries in the opening quarter and Lewis Jones was forced to leave the field with a pulled thigh muscle, the huge Welsh contingent among the 73,000 spectators prepared themselves for the worst. Jones returned, but was a passenger throughout the second half and contributed very little to the cause, leaving his 14 colleagues with the seemingly impossible task of rescuing the game. Gone are the days when six points was a big deficit from which to recover but at Twickenham, the Welsh players found themselves with a mountain to climb.

This was the game in which Cliff Morgan came of age. In tandem with Rex Willis, his club scrum-half, Morgan put in the probing kicks that kept England on the back foot, released the outside backs with a series of precision passes and, on occasion, tested the English back row with an incisive break. One such effort saw the outside-half carve a gap through midfield before producing a delightful reverse pass to Ken Jones, who had ventured off his wing on a perfect running angle. With the England players suddenly finding themselves wrong-footed, all the wing had to do was gather the ball, shove it under his arm and take the shortest route to the line. He may have had 40 yards to cover but this was his territory and there wasn't a rugby player on the planet who could catch him when such opportunities came his way. With the conversion a formality for Malcolm Thomas the Welsh players suddenly found themselves back in a game they were desperate to win. Nothing ignites the Welsh spirit more than beating England and if victory is achieved at Twickenham, so much the better.

With all to play for in the second half the Welsh forwards set about their task with renewed endeavour while the backs were going through their paces with an added spring in the heel. Confidence was visibly rising and when the second Welsh try of the afternoon arrived, it was a direct result of control at a set piece together with some copybook passing by the three-quarters. The ball went through the hands in effortless fashion. The struggling Lewis Jones moved in off his wing to help create an overlap and 73,000 spectators rose as one, all eyes focused on the yawning space now exposed in the English defence. We are only talking about split seconds and half gaps but receiving the ball with both the time and the room in which to exploit his devastating turn of foot was all Ken Jones ever needed. A swerve off the right foot took him infield before he elected to move back outside the covering defence and make his way in a direct line towards the corner flag. Olympic sprinters don't get caught in such situations and the outflanked English defenders could only look on as the wing touched down for what proved to be the final and winning score of the match.

Ken Jones' two tries helped to gloss over what was a bruising encounter and when the dust settled the press went to town on what was variously described as – 'not rugby as we know it... this was sheer murder!...'; it had been a game of give and take but some of the give was 'too brutal to bear the name rugger...'; and there were suggestions that 'Jack Solomons ought to promote a return...'. As a result of all the shenanigans, eight minutes of injury time were added on at the end of the second half, an inordinately long period to defend a two-point lead.

Four years earlier the Great Britain 4x100m relay team were rightly denied a gold medal at the Olympic Games by evidence recorded on cine film. With the BBC intent on broadcasting sport, the cameras were in attendance at Twickenham and following the official dinner members of both teams converged on the Grosvenor House Hotel in central London where a screening of the match was shown during the London Welsh Rugger Ball. A head-on camera caught the second Welsh try in particularly fine detail with Ken's facial expressions clearly indicating his train of thought as the move unfolded or, as one reviewer wrote, '...you can almost see his brain at work...'. Still photographs of the try give even greater attention to detail, capturing perfectly the moment when the ball was grounded.

Advances in technology have taken photography to levels unimaginable in the early 1950s but even with such advanced equipment available it is doubtful if Ken's second effort at Twickenham could be improved on. The black and white print captures a sporting legend going about his business, as do so many of the photographs that recorded his glittering career. Importantly, they confirm how expertly he carried out the basics of the game. Whether it was carrying the ball in textbook fashion under his right arm; executing the perfect hand-off with his left; or completing a copybook tackle, seemingly all of Ken's skills came directly off the pages of every coaching manual. Throw electrifying pace into the equation and you are close to the definite article; the perfect wing three-quarter, a try-scoring machine. And just as he had left indelible memories on the spectators at Eden Park two years earlier, so did he run to glory at Twickenham. In the early 1950s there was no finer sight on a rugby field than the Blaenavon product in full flight.

When Ken joined Newport in 1946 he would have encountered a young, strapping second row forward from Pontypridd. John Gwilliam played 19 games for the club between 1946 and 1949, during which time he was a student at Cambridge University, from where he won the first of his 23 caps. On completing his studies, Gwilliam took a teaching post in Edinburgh, played for Edinburgh Wanderers and became Welsh captain at Twickenham in 1950 following the late withdrawal of Bleddyn Williams. He led Wales to a fourth Grand Slam but was also at the helm in 1951 when Wales came unstuck in spectacular fashion at Murrayfield. Dropped against France,

Gwilliam was recalled to lead the team against South Africa and asked to continue in the role at Twickenham. Such a brief resumé does scant service to Wales' most successful captain but include the next three matches in the 1952 championship and the picture becomes a little clearer.

Next up for a buoyant Wales was the visit of Scotland. A year on from the debacle at Murrayfield, Wales included only nine players who had been on duty in Edinburgh on that miserable day. In front of a record Cardiff Arms Park crowd of 56,000, the Welsh team was intent on registering a victory that would in some small way help to redress the previous season's disappointing result. In winning 11-0 they may have appeased some of those supporters who had travelled with high expectations 12 months earlier but in truth there was little about the performance to suggest Wales were likely to emulate the results achieved in 1950. Ken scored another try and Malcolm Thomas provided eight points with a conversion and two penalties – the Newport pair had scored all Wales' points against both England and Scotland. All Wales' points may have been scored by Newport players but the Big Five were not inclined to look further into the wealth of talent at the club until fate played a hand. Rex Willis broke his jaw against Scotland, which gave Newport scrum-half Billy Williams a chance to prove himself on the bigger stage when it was confirmed that he would win a first cap against Ireland in Dublin.

The match was also a first for Ken. Lansdowne Road was the only current international ground used in the Five Nations on which he had not represented Wales. Additionally he had scored tries at all the others; Murrayfield in 1947; Twickenham in 1948 and 1952; Stades Colombes in 1949 and 1951; and Belfast in 1950. Equally successful when Wales enjoyed home advantage, there were tries against Scotland at Cardiff Arms Park in 1948 and 1952 and against the French in 1950. St Helen's, Swansea also held fond memories, with Scotland in 1950 and England a year later both forced to watch on as the wing touched down. An unusual record was completed on 8 March as Wales secured the Triple Crown for the second time in three years when beating Ireland 14-3, Ken once again among the try scorers. Wales were certainly not as dominant as the team that had swept all before it two years earlier but were still good enough to beat the three home countries in a season when two of the matches were played away, which always makes a Triple Crown that much harder to come by. It appears to have arrived almost unnoticed, to have crept up on players and public alike, but two weeks later, a Welsh team that had rarely clicked into top gear throughout the championship would take to the field against France at St Helen's, Swansea, in search of a Grand Slam.

Despite doing everything conceivable to lose the match, Wales contained a spirited French team and ran out winners by 9 points to 5. The 1952 Five Nations Championship was a memorable one in as much as Wales registered a Grand Slam, but the fare on offer was often mediocre at best. This was particularly frustrating when one considers the wealth of talent on show, but as this was only the fifth time Wales had won all four championship matches it would be churlish to labour the point. To have performed so consistently in 1950 and again in 1952 was particularly gratifying for captain John Gwilliam, who together with Roy John, Dai Davies, Malcolm Thomas and Ken Jones played in all eight matches. Never seeing himself as more than one of the 15 players who make up a team, Ken would try to duck any individual praise. Admirable a quality as that certainly is, the statistics confirm that of the 16 tries scored by Wales in those two Grand Slam winning seasons, Ken Jones claimed eight of them. This brought his total to 15, leaving him just two short of the Welsh record held jointly by Reg Gibbs and John L Williams, the Cardiff wings who played during the three earlier Grand Slam winning campaigns of 1908, 1909 and 1911.

Ken Jones had long since decided that the French game would be his last of the season. This would mean missing Newport's last ten matches but the club were in pretty good fettle and would only lose one of the remaining fixtures. The reason for dispensing with the rugby boots as early as 22 March was quite straightforward; Ken knew that if he were to mount a serious claim for a place in the Great Britain team at that summer's Olympic Games there was some serious training to be done.

The early end to his rugby season meant that he appeared in only 18 of the club's 43 matches. This may have equalled the previous season's figure but fell short of what he would have liked. Extenuating circumstances there most certainly were, but Ken Jones wanted to play rugby and so few club matches over an eight-month period was not what he spent hours training for.

On a more positive note, his try count had increased from six to nine but these were not exactly earth-shattering numbers and were made to look even less significant when compared with what was happening on the left wing. Against Penarth at Rodney Parade in the final match of the season John Lane scored two tries. The first saw him equal the 60-year-old record held by the great Arthur Gould, who once scored 31 tries in a season, and the second took him into the club's record books.

With athletics now at the top of the agenda, Ken set himself a rigorous training schedule that would ensure he was fully prepared come the major meetings that would culminate with the AAA Championships at the White City on 21 June, following which the Great Britain team to travel to Helsinki would be announced. In a candid interview printed in the *South Wales Argus*, Ken readily admitted that while hopeful, he accepted that his prospects of gaining selection for the individual sprints were not good but remained optimistic that he would gain selection for the 4x100m relay.

The season got under way at Abertillery on 14 May when the annual Monmouthshire Police Sports included a series of challenge matches between the South Wales Athletics Association and Walton Athletic Club. Ken Jones' decision to sacrifice the end of the rugby season and concentrate on his sprinting paid off immediately when he won the 100yds in 9.8. This equalled the Welsh native record he already held with Swansea's Cyril Cupid, a Welsh champion from the early 1930s, and the Welsh All-comers record which the two Welshmen shared with England's Ernest Page and McDonald Bailey. Jones completed the sprint double, winning the 220yds in 22.7 to end a perfect afternoon at the track. At this early stage of the season he had posted positive markers and could look forward to the bigger events with a certain degree of optimism.

The first of these took place at Maindy Stadium ten days later when the Welsh AAA competed against the Midland Counties AAA. Ken was entered in the 100yds and 220yds and in the shorter sprint renewed his rivalry with Jack Gregory. The race produced a thrilling finish with Gregory gaining the verdict in even time, Ken running into second place a matter of inches behind the winner, the clock unable to separate them. A pulled muscle may have prevented him taking his place in the 220yds but he was generally happy with his season thus far. Early days for sure, but the two meetings confirmed that one of the senior figures on the circuit still had some mileage left in the tank.

Performances in the Monmouthshire AAA Championships would not normally alert the national selectors unless an extraordinary time was recorded. First and foremost the level of competition would be short of international standard but for an athlete looking to get some decent runs under his belt the event held at Rodney Parade would serve some purpose. As expected, Ken Jones won both sprints in addition to running the anchor leg in the sprint relay won by Newport Athletic Club. So far, so good.

That meeting was held on the Spring Bank Holiday Monday, leaving athletes five days to finish their preparations for the Welsh Championships to be held in Cardiff the following Saturday. The selectors had previously announced that only athletes nominated by the committee would be allowed to compete in the AAA Championships two weeks later, unlike previously when being crowned Welsh champion would mean automatic selection; now the winner would have to perform to an accepted standard.

Ken won both sprint finals for a sixth time with times of 10.3 and 23.1 and had done enough to ensure he would be at the White City. These times may have been good enough to secure Welsh titles but it was unlikely they would make an impression in London, where the competition was guaranteed to be of a much higher standard. And there was another cause for concern, one that had first reared its head four years earlier. There was no apparent reason why it worked its way back into the routine, but just as a champion golfer will suddenly find his swing has deserted him, Ken Jones was again having problems with his start. WO Williams had helped him on the training grounds in Bath but inexplicably, the problem had returned with a vengeance, with Ken slower than ever getting out of the blocks. This was serious; if things went awry in the first ten yards there was little hope of retrieving the situation in the remaining 90. There were meetings and tracks where he could get away with it but the AAA and the White City were not among them.

The 1952 AAA Championships got under way on the evening of Friday 20 June, concluding on the following day. Ken qualified for the semi-finals of the 100yds but was eliminated at the first stage of the 220yds. Now all his eggs were in one basket; he would have to qualify for the 100yds final if he was to have any realistic hope of Olympic selection. With the first two runners in each of three semi-finals progressing to the final there was no margin for error and when Ken was drawn against McDonald Bailey in his semi the odds shortened. McDonald Bailey was a much-improved performer from the one plagued by injury and illness in 1948 and now found himself firm favourite for both sprint titles. In some circles he was even being touted as a possible gold medallist in Helsinki. Jack Gregory was also in serious contention for Olympic selection along with Brian Shenton, as were some of the young pretenders, namely Nick Stacey, Alan Lillington and William Jack.

With three competitors expected to be confirmed in each of the sprints and six from which the relay team would be chosen it was clear that with seven men in pursuit of the six places, one would miss out. Ken's last chance to convince the selectors came in the 100yds semi-final but in McDonald Bailey and Jack Gregory he came up against two men who were simply better on the day. His starting problems compounded into a measurable distance that saw him two yards off the pace after the first ten and it was of little consolation that he was inches behind Bailey and Gregory in a close finish.

McDonald Bailey went on to win the final in 9.6 with Lillington and Shenton taking the minor places, and Jack in close contention in fourth. McDonald Bailey completed the double in fine style, followed home by Shenton and Jack; now it was the turn of the selectors to take centre stage and put together the team that would represent Great Britain in Finland.

McDonald Bailey, William Jack and Alan Lillington were chosen for the 100m with Bailey doubling up in the 200m alongside Brian Shenton and Nick Stacey. As expected, six athletes were included in the relay squad; Bailey, Jack, Lillington, Shenton and Stacey with Jack Gregory getting the nod ahead of his great rival. Bitterly disappointed as he most certainly was, Ken Jones was never one to dwell on such things, and neither was he slow in congratulating those chosen ahead of him. That wasn't what sport meant to the man and he would have backed his rivals all the way, both individually and as a team, in their pursuit of medals.

In Helsinki McDonald Bailey won a well-deserved bronze in the 100m, Lindy Remigino of the USA taking gold and Jamaica's Herb McKenley silver. How close the three athletes were at the tape is confirmed by the times – the three medal winners each clocked at 10.4. Bailey had to settle for fourth place in the 200m final and it was a similar story in the relay, where the Great Britain team of Bailey, Jack, Shenton and Gregory just missed out on a medal, the Americans making no mistakes with the baton to retain their title.

Closer to home it was the pairing of Col. Harry Llewellyn and Foxhunter that set the blood racing in the eastern valleys. Hailing from Llanover, a small village across the mountain from Blaenavon, Llewellyn and Foxhunter produced a clear round in the Grand Prix Jumping Team event to secure Great Britain's only gold medal at the Games. And it couldn't have come much later, Llewellyn completing his round in front of a packed arena minutes before the closing ceremony got under way.

That was on 3 August, by which time Ken had one eye firmly focused on the new rugby season, the club trials that would take place at the end of the month and the visit of Abertillery on 6 September. That was in the future and the Olympics were consigned to the record books but in between times he was timed at 22.3 over 220yds when running for the South Wales and Monmouthshire AAA against the Western Counties AAA at Maindy Stadium. The next Olympic Games would take place in Melbourne in November 1956, by which time Ken would be a matter of weeks from his 35th birthday, almost certainly ruling him out of contention. Two years earlier, the newly named British Empire and Commonwealth Games were scheduled to take place in Vancouver and the European Championships in Berne. These two major events in the athletics calendar provided a much more realistic target and as he brought a close to another season of mixed fortunes these now became the focus of Ken's ambitions on the track. Meanwhile, all that pent-up energy, frustration and explosive speed would be focused on the rugby field – in the black and amber jersey of Newport and the red of Wales.

All work and no play makes Jack a dull boy. So goes the saying, but what does all work and all play make Jack? For Jack read Ken; five years had passed since his return from India but there is no suggestion that Ken and Irene enjoyed anything resembling a holiday other than their honeymoon at the end of 1948. After failing to secure a teaching post on her return from Bath, Irene had settled into her job in the offices of William Adams but when the opportunity to return to teaching eventually presented itself she readily accepted. Not only was she now back in a job for which she was well qualified but it took her to Newport High School for Girls – Mr and Mrs Jones could walk to work together.

The extended summer vacation is normally viewed as a grand time for those in the teaching profession to recharge the batteries but when your husband is a top-class athlete whose appearance at meetings the length and breadth of the country was very much in demand, holidays had to be put on hold. There would be plenty of time for that when his body told him it was time for a rest.

Ken Jones was a good teacher. Popular with staff and pupils alike, he may have been prone to dishing out a painful punishment when appropriate, but his charges certainly held him in high esteem. Once settled into the academic world, Ken was particularly keen that the school rugby teams performed well and if the opponents were West Mon then even more so. Unfortunately, in his early years at Newport High, the First XV failed to live up to any expectations that having an international star to guide them may have produced. In 1950 and 1951 the senior team failed to win any matches before Christmas with a demoralising 57-0 defeat to West Mon in October 1951 the undisputed low point of many. Ken would have to wait until his fourth year at Newport High before he enjoyed a victory over his old school; in January 1953 West Mon finally accepted second best when losing 3-0.

Teaching, rugby football and athletics may have dominated every waking moment but there had been a new addition to the family who slowly but surely found his way into the routine and arguably elevated himself above all other interests. This was Ginger the cat, a stray that Ken had found as a kitten returning home to Summerhill Road one evening following a training session at Rodney Parade. Hearing the little mite's cries for help he explored further and retrieved the small bundle of fluff from the depths of a hedge. So small it fitted into his pocket; and he continued on his way wondering what Irene was going to say about his find. He need not have worried. Ginger would be a fixture in the Jones household for the best part of the next 20 years.

Ken had missed the first month of the previous two seasons and when the latest started it brought with it opportunities to enjoy some refreshing low-key rugby before getting down to the serious stuff. The season got under way with a seven-a-side tournament at Abercarn. Newport fielded a strong team and duly won the event, beating Abercarn and Cross Keys on the way to the final against Abertillery. Seven-a-side rugby was the perfect stage for men with great pace. The reduced numbers opened up the pitch and once Ken was in possession there was little to stop him and he scored four tries during the tournament. Chosen to play for Sir Wavell Wakefield's XV against the Harlequins at Twickenham on the opening Saturday of the season he ran in two more, the Harlequins winning 16-15 with a late try and conversion. There was also a guest appearance at Blaenavon in the club's match against Abergavenny, which brought another try in a 14-10 win for the home team, and two more followed when he turned out for a team put together by Bleddyn Williams in a fund-raising game against Exeter.

On 16 August 36 people lost their lives and thousands were left homeless when freak storms all but destroyed Lynmouth, a pretty little village situated on the north coast of Devon. The match was arranged to help the Lynmouth Relief Fund, with gate receipts of more than £300 donated to the appeal. This was rugby football at its best – a gathering of the game's finest for the benefit of others. Among those appearing alongside Bleddyn and Ken were the recently retired Jack Matthews, Cardiff half-backs Cliff Morgan and Lloyd Williams, with Bryn Meredith, Dai Davies and Ben Edwards alongside England star John Kendall-Carpenter in a strong pack. The result was of no significance but the 4,000 spectators were treated to some fine open play before the invitation team ran out winners by 26 points to 6.

Tries aplenty, but the pattern was not repeated where it really mattered – at Rodney Parade and wherever the road took the Black and Ambers. Comment appeared in the *South Wales Argus* that 'It was sad to see Ken Jones, one of the greatest wings of all time, virtually a passenger in his first game for Newport this season... the question arises whether Newport cannot devise some variety in their methods to make more use of this unique match winner. It is a fact that Roy Burnett travels more confidently in attack to the left... Newport should get the attack more regularly developing to the right.'

A later report on the match with Nantes–Cognac was headed 'Why did Newport starve Ken Jones?' Newport won a close match 12-11 but 'failed to use a match winning wing in Ken Jones. He had to wait until a minute before half-time before getting his chance. Given the ball with the room to move for the first time, 40 yards out, he used his amazing speed to outpace most of the defence...' etc., etc., etc. The old adage, 'If it's not broke don't mend it' should not be forgotten, particularly as Newport had been such a successful club in recent seasons. That Ken Jones scored ten tries in his first season at Rodney Parade and failed to reach double figures in the next five campaigns does suggest there was a certain imbalance in the middle of the field. But did it really matter? If there had been a drought on the left then maybe so, but while John Lane kept scoring and breaking records in the process there was little cause for concern.

Ken played in 32 of Newport's 44 matches in 1952–53, his highest number of appearances in one season since joining the club, and he finally began to register the tries expected of him with 18 scored during the campaign. His season remained relatively injury free with only a leg strain picked up in the volatile encounter with Nantes–Cognac in September ruling him out for three matches. His guest appearance for Wavell Wakefield's XV had clashed with the club's opening match and international calls prevented him appearing in another six. Therefore, of the 35 matches for which he was available, Ken Jones played in 32. This was a big improvement and nobody would have taken more satisfaction from it than the player himself, who was well aware that time was no longer on his side.

That 1952–53 season might not have seen the club perform as well as in recent years but the record still showed that 32 matches were won with seven lost and five drawn. Closer inspection reveals that in the three seasons between 1950–53, only South Africa, the Barbarians and Cardiff, three times, claimed the spoils at Rodney Parade. The place had become a fortress; times had rarely been so good for supporters of the town team. But there was a downside, there always is: Newport RFC would never reach such heady heights again.

Instrumental in much of Newport's success was the charismatic outside-half Roy Burnett. For far too long this great talent had been overlooked by the Welsh selectors but his turn finally came when he was chosen to partner Billy Williams against England at Cardiff Arms Park. Any chance of more Triple Crown and Grand Slam glory disappeared at the first hurdle. Beaten 8-3, the Welsh team failed on every front and few players would have been happy with their day's work. That the following three matches were all won shows how close to becoming the stuff of legend the Welsh team was, but the selectors had shown a clear intent when introducing six new caps against England, an indication that maybe it was time for some of the old guard to move on. Ken Jones scored his 16th international try against Scotland and ended the season with 30 caps but there could be no escaping the fact that for the first time in his international career, questions were being asked. How much longer could the great right wing, now in his 32nd year, be relied on to produce match-winning tries?

The routine was a familiar one. No sooner had the rugby season drawn to a close than the athletics meetings began to fill the calendar. Before he took to the track in earnest Ken received the news that he was to lead Newport for a second season. His first as club captain, while entering the record books as one of Newport's finest, had been far from satisfactory for a player restricted to 18 appearances. With the New Zealand All Blacks arriving in October for a tour that would include matches against Newport and Wales there was much to look forward to but for now it was time to dust off the spikes and find out if there were any young aspirants waiting to hijack Ken Jones' position as the undisputed fastest man in the Principality. Just as the doubters had expressed negative opinions within rugby circles so too were there those followers of Welsh athletics who thought that a sprinter nearer 32 years of age than 31 was living on borrowed time. And it was only time that would provide the answers.

Much as he would have liked to shy away from the limelight, by 1953 Ken Jones was a celebrity and the demands on his time were proving difficult to accommodate. The curtain was finally brought down on the rugby season with a charity match held at Pontypool Park that saw Ken assemble a glittering array of talent to play a side selected from local clubs in aid of the Welsh Church Laymen's Appeal. The summer of athletics got under way in similar low-key fashion with the Weston Biscuits' Sports Day. Held at Llantarnam, halfway between Newport and Pontypool, the organisers had not been so bold as to invite the Olympic star to compete; rather, they wanted him as guest of honour with the principal duty of officially open the meeting. This was an indication of what lay ahead and such events would come to play a big part in Ken's calendar in the coming years, when the invitations would greatly outnumber the slots in the diary available to accommodate them.

The Welsh Championships, after being held at various venues throughout South Wales since its inception in 1907, was now a regular fixture at Maindy Stadium. Over the years many athletes had made their mark on the meeting but none with such regularity as Ken Jones, who had won six titles at both 100yds and 220yds, but in 1953 there were plenty who fancied their chances of dethroning the star. Nineteen competitors joined him in the heats of the 100yds, with 21 entered in the 220yds, and you can bet your bottom dollar that not one among them was older. This may well have been a meeting that saw youth come to the fore with nine of the 16 men's events won by competitors aged 22 or younger, but in the sprint finals, all any of the young bucks saw of the reigning champion was his back and a clean pair of heels. Age proved to be no barrier with Ken retaining his titles in 10.2 and 22.7 and with considerable ease.

Seven days later there was a renewal of the Monmouthshire Police Sports at Abertillery, which again incorporated a match between the Welsh AAA and its English counterpart. Wales were well beaten, losing the match by 75 points to 41, but Ken clipped a tenth of a second off both his times at Maindy Stadium in winning another notable double. He also ran a magnificent final leg in the sprint relay to overcome a large deficit and break the tape two yards ahead of the AAA's anchorman. Winning is rarely less than a rewarding experience but nobody had to tell Ken that the big guns had not found their way to Abertillery. There had been no McDonald Bailey or Brian Shenton in attendance or any of the other leading sprinters from across the border. As ever, these men were waiting for the bigger stage and that would come at the White City Stadium two weeks later.

Ken had always met his match in the AAA Championships. This was usually in the shape of McDonald Bailey, who recorded a seventh sprint double in 1953. Unlike the situation Ken found in Wales, where there was nobody who could provide a sustained challenge to his reign as champion, McDonald Bailey had several outstanding sprinters waiting in the wings, ready to capitalise on any perceived shortcomings. But there weren't any shortcomings. Only Brian Shenton had beaten Bailey during the season but at the White City over 10–11 July the Trinidad-born sprinter was imperious. Ken Jones produced his season's best performances in the heats of both sprints with 10.0 and 22.4 and in the 100yds final he clocked even time again, but that was only good enough to see him home in fourth. He made up the numbers in the 220yds final and his prospects of being selected to race against France in August were not good. There were also the away matches against Germany and Sweden which would bring the season to a close but again, his chances of being selected were slim.

'Gone north' was an expression all too familiar to rugby players and followers of the game. Quite simply, the expression referred to rugby union players who had been enticed to accept lucrative offers to play rugby league and with the majority of the league clubs found in the north of England, so came the term. There was only one reason for this change of direction – money. For the not inconsiderable sums paid as a signing-on fee and a weekly wage, players could make their living doing much as they had when playing rugby union, something which held great appeal for those finding it difficult to make ends meet. Since the formation of the Rugby League in 1897 many players had signed on the dotted line and nowhere had the exodus been more apparent than in South Wales. Ken Jones had looked on as players he knew left for pastures new; Newport prop Reg Blakemore had won his first cap with Ken against England in 1947 and soon after signed for St Helens RLFC; Ray Cale was another star of the Welsh team in the post-war years and he also moved to the Lancashire club in 1950. More recently rugby league had captured a major signing when Wales and British Lions star Lewis Jones joined Leeds RLFC.

Rugby union to rugby league was an obvious move, even allowing for the variations in the Laws of the two codes, but athletics to rugby league doesn't hold the same connotations. Jack Gregory had upset union officials when he turned out for Huddersfield RLFC when stationed in the town during the war. He was banned from returning to union by the RFU and only the intervention of the Army RU helped his cause. The unusual circumstances which had brought about his appearances in a rugby league team were finally accepted by the RFU and Gregory was allowed to return to the union game after serving a year's ban. Gregory aside, the threat of the professional game had not impacted on athletics but that changed in July 1953 when McDonald Bailey signed papers to join Leigh RLFC for an undisclosed sum, thereby bringing to an immediate end his days as a sprinter.

The immediate beneficiary of this move was Ken Jones. Called up to replace McDonald Bailey in the 100yds against France at the White City, the substitute produced his best time of the season when claiming third in 9.9 behind René Bonino of France and Brian Shenton, who were also clocked at 9.9 in a blanket finish. A chance meeting in the athletes' canteen between the new rugby league signing and his replacement saw McDonald Bailey pumping his friend for any advice on the oval ball game: 'Keep out of the way of the big men' was all that was forthcoming.

By an unusual set of circumstances Ken had regained his place in the Great Britain team in what was a new age for British athletics. By 1953, only a few of those athletes who had competed for Great Britain in the 1948 Olympic Games were still in contention and with McDonald Bailey now gone, links were becoming hard to find. In the men's team selected to tour Europe at the end of August only hurdler Harry Whittle, middle-distance runner Bill Nankeville, high jumper Ron Pavitt and hammer thrower Ewan Douglas had competed at Wembley but with the recent defection of McDonald Bailey the name Ken Jones could now be added to the short list. Joining these 'veterans' were a new generation of athletes led by the middle- and long-distance runners, Gordon Pirie, Chris Brasher, John Disley and Chris Chataway with Roger Bannister, perhaps the most famous of the new names, unable to travel due to medical examinations.

The final meetings of the season saw a return to metric distances. Ken surpassed all expectations by running into second place in the 100m in Berlin, beating Brian Shenton in the process, before following home the same athlete in both sprints in Stockholm a few days later. Five years on from the London Olympics, the Welshman was clocking times over the 100m barely one tenth of a second slower than his best in 1948 while managing to maintain his performances over 200m. These were remarkable achievements that suggested there might be more big days at the track to come. The British Empire and Commonwealth Games and the European Championships were now less than 12 months away and Ken Jones was even more determined to appear at both.

CHAPTER NINE

A FAMOUS TRY AND MUCH, MUCH MORE

Ken Jones was determined to be involved from the outset in his second season as captain of Newport RFC. After competing in Stockholm he arrived home late on Friday night but on Saturday 5 September led the club out at Rodney Parade for the opening match against Penarth. Looking further ahead, the next 12 months held much to savour; hardly anything new, but there would not be many more such years and Ken was going to make the most of this one.

The captaincy of Newport was a responsibility he held dear and on the international front there was a chance to equal Dicky Owen's record of 35 caps, Wales playing five matches during the season with a mouth-watering encounter with New Zealand in December. Newport would also play the tourists, the highlight of the club's 42 scheduled matches, and Rodney Parade had been chosen as the venue for the first Welsh seven-a-side competition that would bring the season to a close in April.

The athletics season also promised to be a memorable one. The Welsh Championships and the AAA equivalent would again play a significant part in helping to identify those who would represent Wales at the British Empire and Commonwealth Games in Vancouver, which would start on 30 July, and Great Britain at the European Championships in Berne a month later. In amongst this hectic schedule Ken Jones would celebrate his 32nd birthday but, as ever, the only numbers that interested him were those on the scoreboard at the final whistle and the ones on the face of the timekeeper's watch at the end of a sprint. You are only as old as you feel and in 1953, Ken felt about 25 years of age, maybe even 20. Mind over matter; it was as simple as that.

The game against Penarth was the one hundredth meeting between the two clubs and apart from two periods, the late nineteenth century and the early 1930s when Penarth were led by the great Welsh full-back Jack Bassett, Newport had usually come out on top, winning 81 of the matches to date including all those played since the Second World War. Much the same was expected when the teams took the field but an early eight-point lead was squandered by the home side and Newport were lucky not to come unstuck in an exciting finale that saw the visitors having to settle for an 11-11 draw when a surprise victory looked the more likely outcome. Seven days later it was Bristol who were leading as the game entered its final stages but a late penalty goal saw Newport claim a share of the spoils in another drawn match. Comfortable victories against Swansea, twice, and Neath settled the ship but Cardiff and Gloucester both defeated the Black and Ambers in October and Ken's second stint as club captain had fallen short of his first by the end of the month.

On 31 October the All Blacks began their much-anticipated fourth tour, defeating Southern Counties 24-0 at Hove. With the exception of Oxford and Cambridge Universities and the Combined Services, English opposition was provided by such regional sides, while in Ireland, the provinces of Ulster and Munster would stand alone in their bid for glory. North of the border, Glasgow and Edinburgh would join forces and there were fixtures included against South of Scotland and North of Scotland combinations.

Clubs in England, Ireland and Scotland must have been envious of how the rugby map in Wales was carved up with matches against the major tourists regularly awarded to their counterparts in the Principality. Llanelly, Cardiff, Swansea and Newport had been granted the plum fixture and combined teams from Abertillery and Ebbw Vale, Pontypool and Cross Keys, and Neath and Aberavon would also get their chance to claim a famous victory.

With Wales due to play New Zealand in December trial matches were arranged earlier in the season with the first held at Swansea on 14 November. This was unfortunate timing as it clashed with Cardiff's first visit of the season to Rodney Parade. Club fixtures were never postponed because of such inconveniences and Cardiff in particular were under strength with six players on duty at Swansea, Newport less so with three. Ken Jones was forced to sit out both matches, a twisted knee picked up in training the cause for concern. There would be another trial match in December before the selectors announced the team to face New Zealand and with Newport favourites to avenge October's defeat, the captain could sit back in the committee box and enjoy a rare Saturday off.

Club matches were once 70-minute affairs with only internationals and other major games played over 80 minutes. All the tour matches were to be played over the extended period and with this in mind, Newport and Cardiff agreed to stay on the field ten minutes longer in preparation for the All Blacks. The public may have been promised more playing time for their money but the absence of so many star players ensured the turnout fell well short of the record-breaking numbers seen a few years earlier. Despite the numerous changes in personnel, it was the visitors who took the day in a disappointing match notable for an uninspired first-half performance by the entire Newport team. Things may have improved in the second period but Cardiff held on to win by 5 points to 3 and could now focus on the match against New Zealand in seven days' time.

Long gone are the days when Wales could welcome the All Blacks with a certain degree of confidence that the national side would claim victory and one of the clubs produce an upset. By 1953 the two countries had met three times, with Wales 2-1 up in what would become an extended, albeit one-sided, series of matches. Llanelly became the sixth team to find the latest All Blacks too good, going down 17-3, but things were very different in Cardiff where the home team, under the captaincy of an inspired Bleddyn Williams, recorded a famous 8-3 victory. As the Blue and Blacks celebrated, in the rugby outpost of East Anglia, the Black and Ambers were left licking their wounds as the students of Cambridge inflicted a fourth defeat of the season on the Welsh club with an unexpected 15-11 victory. Ken returned to lead the team after sitting out three matches nursing his knee but failed to lift Newport, and another poor first half ended with the visitors trailing 12-3, leaving too much to do in the second period.

The All Blacks left Wales and headed for Scotland to play three matches before returning via Leicester and Camborne. Swansea would entertain the tourists on 12 December and a week later it would be the turn of Wales in the first international of the tour.

The final Welsh trial took place on 5 December with Ken Jones and Lyn Davies Newport's only representatives. On the same day, Newport welcomed Bristol to Rodney Parade and despite fielding a near full-strength side were beaten 9-3. It was unfortunate that five years after running in the 4x100m final at Wembley, Ken Jones was in Cardiff looking to secure his place in the Welsh team to play New Zealand while Jack Gregory was scoring a hat-trick of tries for Bristol against his old friend's club. The Welsh selectors were not likely to drop the 30-times capped Newport wing but there was no room in the team for Davies, who lost out to his namesake, Dai Davies, the former British Lion who had experience of New Zealand rugby having featured in two Tests in 1950.

The Welsh team showed six changes, one positional, from that which had beaten France in March. Gerwyn Williams replaced the injured Terry Davies at full-back; Gareth Griffiths moved into the centre to replace Alun Thomas, Gwyn Rowlands was introduced for a first cap on the left wing; Rex Willis returned at scrum-half; Courtney Meredith joined the front row; and a first cap was awarded to Glyn Davies of London Welsh at wing-forward. Davies was forced to withdraw from the team, his place taken by Sid Judd, who had played against the French and scored a try for Cardiff when the club defeated the tourists four weeks earlier. Judd's inclusion brought Cardiff's representation to six with Bleddyn Williams asked to continue as captain.

Five of the team had played Test rugby in New Zealand three years earlier – Ken Jones, Bleddyn Williams, Rex Willis, Dai Davies and Roy John. The New Zealand selectors included four men who had appeared in the series in Bob Scott, Tiny White, Kevin Skinner and Laurence Haig. Some familiar faces, but the All Blacks bore little resemblance to the side that had won the fourth Test three years earlier.

This was the third meeting between the two countries to take place at Cardiff Arms Park, both previous encounters resulting in Welsh victories. Only Teddy Morgan's try separated the teams in 1905, a match that had long since entered rugby folklore as the result of a 'try' by Bob Deans not allowed by the referee. Much had been written about the events that unfolded at the famous stadium almost 50 years earlier, most of it by people who were not there, but the result stands and it helped create the great rivalry forged between the two countries.

In 1935, a classic encounter was decided by the bounce of a ball in the game's dying moments that saw Wales home by a point – 13-12. Things were very different in 1924. The invincible All Blacks won all 32 matches played and Wales could offer little to contain one of the best New Zealand teams, losing by 19 points to nil. That match was played at St Helen's, Swansea, so it was a question of whether or not it would be third time lucky for New Zealand or could Cardiff Arms Park prove to be Wales' trump card once again?

The first Welsh home match to be transmitted live on television did not deter 56,000 spectators from descending on the famous ground and they were not disappointed. It was to become one of those 'I was there' occasions. New Zealand were still smarting after losing to Cardiff and when Sid Judd pounced for a try following an uncharacteristic error by full-back Bob Scott it was as if the clock had been wound back four weeks. Judd had scored Cardiff's first try following a cross kick that caused some confusion in the New Zealand defence; now the same player was on hand to score in almost the exact same spot. Some untidy play saw the ball booted upfield by Judd with Ken Jones setting off in rapid pursuit. The wing was first to the ball and showed some deft football skills to hack it on into the All Blacks' 25 before catching the retreating full-back in possession. Scott desperately tried to find Kevin Skinner but the ball fell short and into the welcoming arms of the Cardiff wing-forward who crashed over the line. The added points saw Wales five points up but the score did not give a true reflection of proceedings as it was the New Zealand forwards who were the dominant force. It was only a matter of time before the balance of play was reflected on the scoreboard, firstly Ron Jarden reducing the deficit with a penalty then the same player adding the conversion of a try by Bill Clarke to put the All Blacks 8-5 up at the interval.

When Gareth Griffiths was forced to leave the field after ten minutes of the second half with a dislocated shoulder, few would have given the Welsh team any hope of retrieving the situation. But Wales held on, thanks mainly to a sterling effort from the forwards, reduced in number with Clem Thomas used as cover for Gwyn Rowlands on the left wing who now found himself in the centre in place of the injured

Griffiths. How uplifting it must have been to see Griffiths return to the field, his shoulder restored to its proper place after a painful ten minutes in the dressing room. This show of bravery was the inspiration Wales needed and for the remaining 20 minutes it was the men in red who looked the more likely to take the spoils. With Thomas restored to the pack, the forwards took the game into the New Zealand 25 and forced a penalty which Gwyn Rowlands had no trouble in converting to level the scores. Ten minutes remained. Ten short minutes for Wales to turn what at one stage looked a certain defeat into an improbable victory. Ten long minutes for New Zealand to take stock, regroup and try to salvage what they could from the game.

Clem Thomas had won his first cap against France in 1949. There was a three-year wait for the second, which came against Ireland in 1952, since when he had only missed one game, the defeat by England earlier in the year. On the eve of the New Zealand match there was some concern that the outstanding Swansea wing-forward would miss out again. Thomas was involved in a fatal road accident earlier in the day. An innocent party caught up in a tragic incident and understandably, this was an experience that would have caused him much mental anguish. There were suggestions that he should stand down from the team but support came from a quite unexpected source when Bill Ramsey, treasurer of the RFU, persuaded the Welsh selectors to stick with Thomas as he clearly wanted to play.

In Wales' hour of need it was Clem Thomas who had been drafted onto the left wing following Gareth Griffiths' brief departure. Who knows if he garnered any understanding of what the men out wide actually do during that brief spell, but when he found himself on the left touchline, deep in New Zealand territory, the forward certainly looked at ease with his lot.

Comfortable he might have been, but a decision had to be made and there was no time to dwell on it. Only Bleddyn

Williams was on hand but obviously struggling with a torn thigh muscle. Then there was the not insignificant matter of several All Blacks who had him firmly in their sights and were getting much too close for comfort.

'Why did I cross kick at that moment? Well, I had to do something... so I just booted and hoped I had done the right thing.' Clem Thomas executed as fine a left-footed cross kick as one could wish to see. The ball bounced in no man's land and hung about at chest height waiting to be collected. Ken Jones covered the distance between his onside position and the ball in record time; onlookers doubted he had ever run 30 yards quicker, certainly on a rugby field. Ball safely gathered, the wing swerved to his right before moving inside to leave any defenders clutching at air with only Ron Jarden able to get a hand on him as he crossed for what proved to be the winning score. This was Ken's 17th try for Wales. Often claimed to be the best, it is certainly the most famous but whether it compares with his second effort at Twickenham in 1952 is open to debate. Ken Jones won his 31st cap against New Zealand and while there would be 13 more appearances for his country, what could not be realised at the time was that there would be no more tries.

Ken may have scored the winning try against New Zealand but his overall performance during the 80 minutes attracted some criticism. One of the broadcasters providing live commentary of the match suggested that in scoring the try Ken had made his first contribution to the game and there were others who felt much the same.

Taking up the cudgel on the wing's behalf, Jack Davis, writing in the *South Wales Argus*, castigated such criticism, drawing attention to the fact that Ken had created the first try, made two tackles on Ron Jarden when the New Zealand left wing seemed certain to score and executed a precision perfect cross kick, collected by Courtney Meredith who lacked the speed to capitalise on the effort and was brought down short of the line. And he had scored the all-important try. Ken Jones was no stranger to criticism and it is unlikely that any adverse reporting would have impacted on him beyond the level of a minor irritation.

If proof of the popularity and high esteem in which the general public held Ken Jones were needed it arrived in the form of a readers' poll conducted by the *Daily Express* at the end of the year. Asked to vote for the outstanding sporting achievements of 1953, among those selected were Stanley Matthews, who finally won an FA Cup winner's medal when Blackpool beat Bolton Wanderers 4-3; Gordon Richards, who won his first Derby aboard Pinza at what was his 28th attempt; Alec Bedser, who bagged 39 wickets when helping England regain the Ashes; and rugby's Ken Jones, who was held responsible as 'ten million televiewers [sic] stood on the sofas, knocked aside lampshades as he sprinted in for the winning try for Wales against the All Blacks on 19 December. The greatest wing three-quarter of our time...'. If there were a couple of hacks who felt differently, so be it. Ken Jones had nothing left to prove.

After a decidedly unimpressive first half of the season, the record at the end of the year confirmed that of 20 matches played, Newport had lost six and drawn two. With the arrival of the All Blacks less than a month away the club had three matches in which to address the problems that had been apparent since the opening fixture against Penarth. The year got under way with a win at Cross Keys but a cold prevented the captain taking his place against Llanelly at Rodney Parade.

The Newport forwards may have looked lively around the field but were once again comprehensively beaten in the tight, the area where much improvement would be needed against a New Zealand eight who had outmuscled everything they came up against, Cardiff and Wales included. Newport did beat Coventry on the Saturday before the big game but there was little on show to suggest there would be an upset five days later.

Neither was there, but in going down 11-6 the Newport XV rose to the occasion to give the All Blacks a thorough examination in every department. The tight five warmed to their task and rightly earned plaudits in the press and things could have turned out very differently if the place kickers had stepped up to the mark. Malcolm Thomas and Peter Davies squandered several chances and one wonders why the young centre Brian Jones was not handed the responsibly after landing a long-distance penalty to bring the home team within two points; only the captain could answer that. But kicks were missed, they often are, and New Zealand were the better side on the day and fully deserving of another hard-fought victory at Rodney Parade.

As Newport were preparing for the All Blacks, the Five Nations Championship got under way at Twickenham. Wales travelled to HQ with only Gareth Griffiths, still recovering from his shoulder injury, and Bleddyn Williams, a late withdrawal, absent from the side that had defeated New Zealand. Rees Stephens was chosen to lead a team that, but for Ken's winning try, may well have shown more changes. Twickenham's first all-ticket match restricted the Welsh presence to 10,000 and those lucky enough to get in saw England deny Wales a draw by scoring a try in the game's final moments. England deserved the 9-6 victory if only by virtue of scoring three tries to Wales' one, but a spate of injuries that saw Gerwyn Williams, Rex Willis and Billy Williams spend time off the field did not help the Welsh cause. Hero of the hour he may have been a month earlier but Ken endured 'an idle afternoon' at Twickenham, reports suggesting the player did not receive a pass during the match.

All rugby players in Wales were idle for a three-week period when a blanket of snow covered the country. The accompanying ice caused the postponement of most fixtures, including the visit of Scotland to St Helen's, the match rescheduled for 10 April. When normal service was resumed, Newport welcomed Leicester to Rodney Parade.

Selected to play for the Barbarians against New Zealand the following week, there was some concern when Ken left the field at half-time carrying a pulled leg muscle. Initial prognosis suggested he would not play for three or four weeks but with the help of the magic hands of Ray Lewis, he made a rapid recovery and was able to take his place for a third appearance against the tourists. Interviewed about the injury, Lewis said: 'He is the fittest man playing rugby union football and that helps when he gets an injury. His recuperative powers are terrific. He loves training – that's his secret. He does a PT master's job all day, yet he is out training on Newport Athletic Ground in the evenings and he will train by himself if there is no one else around!'

Ken was a guest on a BBC radio programme in the week leading up to the Barbarians match. Asked about his career plans he suggested that there was no reason why he could not play rugby for 'another three or four seasons at least. But the number of caps will depend on the WRU...' Inevitably, the forum led to questions regarding his finest moments as both an athlete and a rugby player. Beating McDonald Bailey and Alastair McCorquodale at Uxbridge in 1948 when he ran a personal best of 9.8 contradicted earlier suggestions that competing in the Olympics headed the list but there was no hesitation when nominating his try against New Zealand in Cardiff as his defining moment on a rugby field.

The All Blacks wound up the British part of their tour with an emphatic 19-5 defeat of a star-studded Barbarians XV. Often criticised for their dour, win-at-all-costs approach, the tourists now threw caution to the wind and scored four splendid tries with the Barbarians response coming from a Gareth Griffiths' try converted by Ian King. Only two of the 28 matches played to date had ended in defeat with two others drawn; Cardiff and Wales gained notable victories with Ulster and Swansea doing the next best thing. A brief trip across the English Channel produced two unexpected defeats, South-West France and France both causing major upsets. A rearranged fixture against South-Eastern Counties was played at Ipswich before the party headed home via Canada and the United States, where five matches were comfortably won.

It would be ten years before the arrival of the fifth New Zealand All Blacks but any thoughts of another Welsh victory would have to be put on hold. For how long? Who knows. At the time of writing, 58 years have passed during which the two countries have met on no fewer than 24 occasions, New Zealand winning every one. Not a record to be proud of but one which tends to focus the mind on a December day in 1953 when 15 Welshmen dug deep and Ken Jones scored his last international try.

With the Scotland match postponed until later in the season, all roads led to Dublin and this time the Welsh selectors did set about their task with vigour, change very much on the agenda. Roy John, Dai Davies and John Gwilliam won their last caps at Twickenham, as had the unfortunate Gerwyn Williams, whose shoulder injury brought his career to an end. For the trip to Ireland, first caps were awarded to Neath full-back Viv Evans, who at 34 years of age belittled any arguments as to when a player should hang up his boots, something that would have not escaped the notice of the youngster on the right wing; the Llanelly centre Denzil Thomas and second row Rhys Williams were introduced; as were Newport's loose forward Leighton Jenkins and hooker Bryn Meredith. Neath's Brian Sparks was another new face in the back row, bringing the number of new caps to six, and with Bleddyn Williams still unavailable, Rees Stephens continued in the role of captain. Was Ken Jones' place on the wing under threat? We will never know, but there were Welsh appearance records that were definitely under threat and the Newport player had his sights firmly set on breaking them.

Wales won a close match in Dublin, a late drop goal by new cap Thomas the deciding score, and continued in winning form when beating the French 19-13 in Cardiff. Rees Stephens' late withdrawal from that match saw the captaincy pass to Rex Willis, the third player to lead the team during the season. Come the end of the Five Nations, a fourth name would be added to the list. Having played against Ireland and France, Ken Jones now had 34 caps to his name. The Welsh record of 35 was held by Swansea half-back Dickie Owen, who was first capped against Ireland in 1901, the day Swansea full-back WJ Bancroft won the last of his 33 caps, the record Owen would eventually improve on. Unlike Owen, Bancroft's caps had been won consecutively and Ken made this particular record his own when making a 34th consecutive appearance against France. Selected to play in the postponed match with Scotland, Ken Jones would equal Dickie Owen's record and if he could score a try he would also become Wales' top scorer in that department.

Appropriate then that the Welsh selectors should honour Ken with the captaincy against Scotland. It was to be the last championship match played at St Helen's, where both Owen and Bancroft had performed with such great distinction for the All Whites of Swansea (Wales would return to the ground to play Tonga in 1997) and there was a poignant moment before proceedings got under way when the 83-year-old Bancroft came down from the stand to congratulate the Welsh captain on his achievements. The match, played in April, saw an improvement on the indifferent weather so often served up on international days. With the sun on their backs the Welsh team produced a match-winning performance, running in four tries in a 15 points to 3 victory. A fitting end to the season which saw a three-way tie for the Championship; England, France and Wales each winning three of the four matches played. All that was missing was a Ken Jones try. Newspaper photographs show how close he came to claiming the record when two promising runs saw him forced into touch at the corner flag by a desperate defence.

Any thoughts of Newport enjoying a season to rank among the best had long since been dismissed. Come April, there were still ten fixtures to fulfil, a chance to redress the balance perhaps, but the month went on record as one of the worst in the club's history when five of the ten matches were lost with another drawn. Miserable reading for those ardent followers of the club's fortunes but the end of the campaign did offer a chance to bring the disappointing season to a close on a high. For some time there had been talk of launching a National Seven-a-Side competition. Newport secretary Bill Everson and chairman RS Snelling had gathered support from the senior clubs and the WRU agreed to extend the season by a day to accommodate the event. The decision to allow the tournament to take place at Rodney Parade on 1 May proved to be prudent, 7,000 spectators turning out for a feast of rugby which saw the host club win the first staging of a tournament that would run for 42 years.

Sixteen clubs took part in the inaugural event, which was a knock-out competition. Seven-a-side rugby is a fast game played over two seven-minute halves with the final extended to 20 minutes' play. And if a team included men with pace, as they all did, then the idea was to get the ball to the speedsters as often as possible. Newport included the fastest man in rugby and Ken Jones lived up to his billing, scoring two tries in the first round to send Swansea packing. Next it was Newbridge, a 9-0 victory steering Newport into a semi-final with Penarth. Ken was back on the scoreboard with a try late in the second half that saw the hosts home 6-3 and a place in the final where they would meet Ebbw Vale, conquerors of Llanelly in the other semi-final.

Sevens is pretty much non-stop rugby with players getting few opportunities to take a breather. Brian Jones, who would later gain a reputation as a fine exponent of the shorter game, recalls some advice received from his captain after he had given fruitless chase in the first-round match against Swansea with the game already won. Ken knew that the short, sharp bursts of speed that seven-a-side rugby demanded would soon take their toll and to set out on a needless chase would dig deep into the energy bank. This, coming from someone who regularly trained in short, sharp bursts, was advice not to be ignored. In later years Jones would pass it on to others as Newport became recognised as the leading practitioners of seven-a-side rugby in Wales.

Lining up for Newport against Ebbw Vale in the final were Ken, Graham Ross, Roy Burnett, Brian Jones, Malcolm Thomas, Doug Ackerman and Dick Shepherd. Ross opened the scoring in what was the last rugby match of the season and, fittingly, it was Ken Jones who, receiving the ball near his own goal line in the second half, set off on a run that saw him swerve and outpace the Ebbw Vale players, who could do little but watch on as he ran the length of the field for the final try of the season. Members of the winning team received a silver tankard as a memento for their afternoon's toil and the club would hold the cup in its trophy room for 12 months until the tournament's first renewal.

Newport may have enjoyed an indifferent season but on the international front, 1953–54 provided Ken Jones with some memorable moments in a distinguished career; records were broken and equalled; the All Blacks were beaten; and Ken Jones had been awarded that highest of accolades when he was invited to captain Wales. He was on a high and there was more to come as spring headed into summer, a time when many rugby players would turn their attention towards enjoying a hard-earned rest or playing some club cricket. For Ken there would be no respite as he approached an athletics season that would see him satisfy personal goals to rival those recently achieved as a team player.

The athletics season started with a bang. On 6 May at Iffley Road, Oxford, three university graduates worked together in a concerted effort to run the first sub-four-minute mile. It had been talked about for many years but despite a plethora of great middle-distance runners setting off with high hopes, the 4min 01.3 record set by Sweden's Gunder Hägg in 1945 still stood. On the basis that three minds are better than one, the sums were done, the split times worked out and when Chris Brasher and Chris Chataway set the perfect pace an attempt on both the world record and, more importantly, the four-minute barrier, was on.

Roger Bannister took up the pace as he entered the final lap with less than a minute at his disposal, but it was enough. Bannister completed those final 440yds in 58.9 seconds to record a time of 3min 59.4 and earn himself a permanent place in the history books. Having taken so long in coming there was a certain inevitability that on 21 June at a meeting in Finland the Australian John Landy would not only become the second man to run a sub-four-minute mile but in doing so he also broke Bannister's record when recording a time of 3min 57.9.

The summer of 1954 already promised to be an exciting year for British athletics, with both the British Empire and Commonwealth Games and the European Championships taking place, and the recent publicity surrounding the mile suggested there would be increased public interest when the major championships took place in England and Wales.

Ken Jones was one of five athletes chosen to represent Britain at an international meeting held in Cologne on 30 May. Competing in the 100m and 200m the Welshman found an American serviceman stationed in Berlin too good on the day. Jim Golliday won both events, Ken having to be content with second place in the longer sprint. The rugby season had been particularly long and hard so it is not surprising that being asked to almost immediately turn one's attention to international athletics would not come easily.

Somewhere between the meeting in Cologne and the Welsh Championships at Maindy Stadium on 19 June Ken suffered a calf muscle strain that put his appearance in Cardiff in doubt. The 1954 meeting was to be an unofficial trial for the

British Empire and Commonwealth Games; success would certainly strengthen an athlete's claim for selection while failure would leave the individual with much to prove in the five weeks before the team departed for Canada. There is little doubt Ken Jones should not have competed in the Welsh Championships. His training was seriously disrupted after returning from Germany and he appears not to have done any in the week leading up to the meeting. Ray Lewis knew Ken was in a lot of pain and strongly recommended he withdraw from the competition.

'If I don't take part I might never race again...' was Ken's simplistic approach to the issue, with his desire to compete in Vancouver appearing to override all other considerations. He had elected not to represent Wales in Auckland four years earlier and would not be competing in 1958, leaving Vancouver as his only chance to represent Wales at a major games. So with his confidence at an all-time low and in desperate need of a fillip, Ken set off to Cardiff on the morning of 19 June fearing the worst.

His name was John Gilpin. Originally from Newport, 24-year-old Gilpin ran in the colours of Exeter Harriers having moved to the city in 1941. Employed in the building trade, he was the reigning Western Counties 100yds champion and at Maindy Stadium on 19 June 1954 he brought to an end the record of Kenneth Jeffrey Jones, who had won seven of eight Welsh 100yds titles contested since the war, only his departure for New Zealand in 1950 breaking the sequence. Gilpin won the final in 10.2 with Ken second in 10.4, the veteran gaining with every stride following a bad start. This was familiar territory but whereas in the past he had been able to make up any lost ground before reaching the tape he was found wanting in 1954. Ken would never look for excuses but his continued optimism as reported in the press during the week building up to the championships belied the fact that he was struggling to overcome a recurring injury problem and to those closest to the sprinter, defeat would not have come as a surprise. To those very same people, the surprise would come later in the afternoon with the running of the 220yds.

The disappointing run fresh in his memory, Ken took his place in 220yds. Such was his desire to win, he may well have viewed the final of the longer sprint as one of the most important races of his career. There is little doubt that the pain barrier had to be broken and to do this the risk of any long-term damage had to be ignored. There was a lot at stake when the starter fired the gun to set the six finalists on their way but there was only going to be one winner; one man who wanted the title more than any of the other finalists – and that man would not be beaten, crossing the line fully two yards ahead of his nearest rival. The winning time of 22.5 equalled his best in the event recorded five years earlier and lays testament to the fact that Ken threw caution to the wind, went for broke and triumphed. In the space of a few short hours his season had turned full circle and there would be no looking back.

There is little doubt that in the early weeks of May he was saddled with an injury that, in the words of one of the most respected men in the field of physiotherapy, was 'career threatening'. This in turn certainly impacted on his mental preparation for the big races and his confidence going into the Welsh Championships was not at a level associated with success.

But Ken Jones prevailed, and a week later he was back at the same venue representing Wales in both sprints in a triangular meeting against the Northern Counties and the Western Counties. He turned the tables on John Gilpin in the 100yds, winning in a wind-assisted time of 9.9 with the Exeter Harrier two yards behind in second place. The only available photograph of the athletes as they cross the line shows Ken looking lean and mean as he strides to victory with the rest of the field in his wake; the oldest competitor in the field putting the younger pretenders to the sword. His winning time of

22.7 in the 220yds was slower than clocked a week earlier but Ken looked to be enjoying a welcome return to form, one that the selectors would find hard to ignore.

A regular competitor at the AAA Championships he might have been, but Ken only had one notable performance to reflect on, his third place finish behind McDonald Bailey in the 220yds in 1949. Five years later he produced his best overall performances at the White City but these counted for nothing as they were not enough to take him into the first three in either event. Ken finished fourth in both sprints, his even time in the 100yds one tenth of a second behind the first three home, who were all clocked at 9.9. In the 220yds he was a distance behind Brian Shenton and George Ellis, who both recorded 21.5, Shenton getting the verdict.

Notwithstanding that athletes were preparing for Vancouver, the Great Britain selectors decided it prudent to announce the team to compete in the European Championships in Berne immediately with the proviso that they would leave the door open for any athlete who produced an outstanding performance in the interim.

It was probably no surprise when Ken's name was not among those announced to the press on Monday, but there was better news elsewhere. The Welsh selectors had also been busy and when the results of their deliberations were made public, he was invited to take his place in both the 100yds and 220yds in Vancouver.

Wales' participation in Vancouver may not have been seriously under threat but to ensure the team of competitors and officials represented the best talent available, financial support was much needed. A grant of £1,000 had been received from the Canadian Games Council to cover travel expenses but the fund showed a significant shortfall. With the Games less than a month away the target figure was still to be reached and public appeals were announced through the local press in a final attempt to reach the required £5,000. Any late problems would have been extremely embarrassing, as Wales was hoping to host the Games in 1958. With the withdrawal of Nigeria and Singapore the field was left open for a Welsh victory and it was important that the national team should be in Vancouver when the announcement confirming where the Games would be held in four years' time was made.

On Wednesday 13 July the 24-strong party made up of 21 athletes and three officials were invited to a send-off lunch hosted by the Lord Mayor of Cardiff, Alderman George Ferrier, at Cardiff City Hall. The function was the last held in the team's honour before they departed for Vancouver by air, the days of long-haul travel being undertaken by sea thankfully a thing of the past. With sufficient money in the pot, the Welsh squad arrived at its destination fully looking the part in scarlet blazers, cream shirts, green ties and cream trousers or skirts. There were red dragons on the breast pockets of the blazers and ties, the ensemble topped off by a white hat with a green band sporting the Prince of Wales' feathers. Wales were dressed to kill!

Early reports suggested the running track at Vancouver's Empire Stadium had bedded in well and those local athletes who were allowed to test the surface confirmed it was very fast. Built at a cost of £534,000 with a 35,000 capacity, the new stadium was designed in the shape of a horseshoe with the open end facing a spectacular backdrop overlooking the Coast Mountains. The much talked about running track was a mix of 55 per cent cinder and 45 per cent clay but the contestants on the first day of competition were not so impressed with evidence that the surface was already breaking up and would need constant attention if it were to hold firm.

Trinidad's Mike Agostini would undoubtedly have disagreed with this premature prognosis after creating a new Games record when winning the 100yds final in 9.6. The next four athletes were all credited with 9.7 and in sixth place was Wales' Ken Jones, who in running 9.8 equalled his all-time best performance for the event. Ken had run a respectable 10.0 in his heat and ran into third place in the semi-final with another 9.8 lifetime best. Local newspaper reports advised that the Welshman was 35 years old, whereas he would not be 33 until the end of the year, but for a man who was somewhere in the lower thirties these were impressive performances.

Ken would later go on record as saying that his expectations when he left for Canada were not high. He hoped to perform well but beyond that saw little reason for optimism. His times in the 100yds may have given him cause to revise his earlier pessimism and although coming sixth in the final he was the only British representative, which would not have gone unnoticed elsewhere. Ken could now focus his attention on the 220yds, where he hoped to progress to a second final which would send him home in high spirits.

Ken found himself drawn in the last of six heats. With only the first two finishers in each progressing to the semi-finals there would be no time to ease up and look over the shoulder for any late threat; second would be good enough but first place much better. That his winning time of 22.4 was the slowest of the six heats was of no concern; all that mattered was a place in the next round and it was good enough for that. The second semi-final saw Ken alongside Agostini and England's George Ellis. This time it would be the first three across the finish line who would earn a place in the final. It was the Englishman who broke the tape but Ken was a close second in 22.1, an unbelievable 0.4 better than any of his eight Welsh Championship winning times.

On 5 August Ellis and Jones joined the Australian Hec Hogan, local hero Harry Nelson, New Zealand's Don Jowett and England's Brian Shenton in what was expected to be a highly competitive race, with Jowett and Shenton favourites to strike gold. Drawn inside Shenton, Ken's only objective was to stay in touch, believing his old adversary would certainly be in contention for a medal. By adopting this tactic, Ken ran a much faster first 100 yards than he would normally have considered and as the runners hit the straight he was in unknown territory but well in contention. Lungs burning and with every muscle and sinew telling him to stop, Ken Jones produced the finest individual performance of his long and distinguished athletics career. Jowett claimed gold with Shenton getting the silver, both runners given the same time of 21.5. In third place and winner of the bronze medal was Ken Jones in 21.9 – he had run faster only once before when clocking 21.7 for 200m in Oslo in 1949.

A big gathering was expected at Newport station on 13 August to welcome home Ken and John Brockway, who had won gold in the pool, but the celebrations were going to have to wait. Things had started badly when it was discovered that the safe holding the team's return air tickets and other documentation had been broken into. There followed much form-filling and red tape before replacements were issued but once airborne, much worse was to follow. The Super Constellation airliner bringing the Welsh team and other British competitors home experienced trouble with the undercarriage as it prepared for its early morning arrival at London Airport. Heavy ground mist compounded the problem and after circling London for an hour it was decided that the plane should be rerouted to Manston aerodrome in Kent, where it finally touched down at 9.15am.

Safely on the ground after their nerve-wracking experience, the passengers were then subjected to a further delay as Manston was not in the habit of receiving transatlantic flights and did not have the ground staff to cope with such numbers. They would also have to wait in line behind passengers from another plane that had been rerouted and landed ahead of them. Hours passed before disembarkation could begin and after clearing customs the Welsh party made its way to London by train for the onward journey to South Wales. When Jones and Brockway arrived at Newport several hours behind schedule it was to find hundreds of patient supporters still filling the platform, among them family, friends and representatives of Newport Athletic Club, Newport Harriers and Maindee and Newport Swimming Clubs, all wanting to pass on their congratulations to two local men who had done Wales proud.

Back from Vancouver, Ken could now devote some time to organising the house he and Irene had bought before he left for Canada. The move from Summerhill Avenue to Fairoak Lane in Croesyceiliog was a short one but, regardless of distance, it still involved the normal packing and unpacking, painting and decorating, and there was a garden to tend, lawns to cut, hedges to trim. With the rugby season and the new school term still three weeks away the Joneses could certainly put the time to good use. Three weeks during the summer without the demands of training or competing was a novel experience and looked forward to with some relish but elsewhere in the country, as Ken and Irene set about unpacking the tea chests and opening the pots of paint, plans were being hatched.

After his success in Vancouver, the question Ken was asked above all others concerned his future in the sport. While he had every intention of continuing with rugby there had to be a question mark over his career on the track. Perhaps now was the time to leave the sport? Bow out gracefully on a high after his recent exploits rather than risk one more season in which the John Gilpins of this world would be after his scalp.

As we know, the probable Great Britain team to compete in the European Championships in Berne between 25–29 August had been announced immediately following the AAA Championships in July.

Team manager Jack Crump and his fellow selectors were limited to two competitors in each event and although they left some selections open the majority of athletes were confirmed, including those who would contest the sprints. Brian Shenton, George Ellis, Ken Box and Alan Lillington were the men selected five weeks earlier and the quartet would also make up the 4x100m relay team. Only Shenton had been successful in Canada, leaving the selectors with one of several difficult decisions that had to be made before the final squad was confirmed.

Marathon runner Jim Peters experienced a tragic end to what proved to be his last competitive race when collapsing inside the Empire Stadium only 200 yards from the finish. His place in Berne was taken by Geoff Iden and in the women's team Shirley Hampton (later to become Mrs Gordon Pirie) was called up in place of Heather Armitage in the 200m. And there was a new name included among the men's sprint specialists. Ken Jones replaced the Durham University student Alan Lillington in the 100m and was also included in the sprint relay team alongside Ellis, Box and Shenton – the unpacking would have to wait.

On the team's arrival in Switzerland, Jack Crump confirmed that for the first time the Great Britain team would have two captains. Long jumper Jean Desforges (later to marry BBC commentator and coach Ron Pickering) was chosen to lead the women's team, and the men would be captained by Kenneth Jeffrey Jones. This was a fitting honour to give a man who had been at the forefront of British athletics since the war and a timely thank you to one of the true gentlemen of sport.

Ken enjoyed his role as team captain. He was a vociferous supporter of his colleagues' efforts in the track and field events and did all he could by way of encouragement in quieter moments away from the arena. When it came to the 100m heats he pulled another rabbit out of the hat to qualify for the semi-finals but found the best of Europe too good – although his time of 10.7 was only a tenth outside his personal best – leaving him to bow out gracefully after what would be his last individual appearance on the track. From a seat in the stands Ken applauded George Ellis as he produced his best form to take the bronze medal in the 100m final and again when the same athlete completed a fine double with another bronze in the 200m.

Great Britain's only gold medal on the track came on a fabulous final day. Roger Bannister headed the Dane, Gunnar

Nielsen in the 1500m and in the 5000m Chris Chataway won silver, not behind the hot favourite Emil Zátopek, but the Soviet sailor Vladimir Kuts.

Individual events over, the track was cleared for the relay finals in which Great Britain was well represented. The women's team ran well in the 4x100m to finish fourth and the men's' 4x400m team crossed the line in first place, fully two yards clear of the French. Following the race the Hungarians lodged an appeal after one of the team was tripped by Britain's Peter Fryer, an appeal which was upheld and led to the disqualification of the Great Britain quartet. Memories of London 1948 but with a very different outcome.

This left the 4x100 men's relay, in which Great Britain would line up alongside Hungary, the USSR, Czechoslovakia, Italy and Sweden. Ken Box was on the first leg and would hand the baton to George Ellis; Ken Jones would take over and run his favoured bend before passing on to Brian Shenton. All the quartet had to do was complete the baton changes within the prescribed boxes and run like the wind. No four Brits had run the 4x100m relay in a faster time. They were electric. Box, Ellis, Jones and Shenton ran the perfect race; great sprinting and excellent changeovers saw them break the Championship record with a time of 40.8. The only problem was that the Hungarians also broke the existing record but in a time of 40.6; Great Britain had to settle for the silver medal.

The decision would not be made until the following year but time would confirm that Ken Jones ran his last competitive race on 29 August 1954 when he won that European Championships silver medal in the 4x100m relay to go with that won in the same event at the Olympic Games in 1948 and the individual bronze in the 220yds in Vancouver earlier in the year. It would prove to be a fitting end to an outstanding career. Ken would make one more appearance at a major athletics meeting but that was four years away. In the meantime there was much more rugby to be played.

CHAPTER TEN

A RECORD, AND THE BAND PLAYED ON

On 1 December 1954 a function held in honour of Ken Jones took place in the gymnasium at Newport Athletic Club. This was one of several events staged during the last few months of the year, all arranged with the sole purpose of recognising the extraordinary sporting accomplishments achieved by this modest man.

Ken was never comfortable when he was the focus of attention and would sit, head bowed forward, as distinguished speakers eulogised on his performances on the rugby field and the running track. More than 400 people managed to get into the gym to hear tributes from the Mayor of Newport, Councillor Maurice Selby; WR Thomas, president of the WRU; and WE Fisher, president of the Welsh AAA. Newport Athletic Club president FH Dauncey presented Ken with a framed studio portrait to be hung in the club and RS Snelling, the club's chairman, confirmed that the committee had unanimously decided that Kenneth Jeffrey Jones be made an honorary life member of the club. This was ratified at the AGM held on 29 July 1955.

The principal guest was Lord Aberdare, a member of the IOC and president of the British Empire and Commonwealth Games Council for Wales. He spoke at length about Ken's life, leaving no stone unturned in giving a detailed account of the Blaenavon schoolboy's journey to international stardom. Illness prevented Harold Abrahams attending but he sent a message in which he wrote: 'There are few men in athletics for whom I have greater admiration, and may I add affection, than Ken Jones.' And writing on behalf of the RFU, president WC Ramsay confirmed 'the very high regard which everybody in England held for his outstanding performance in rugby football'. Then it was the turn of the guest of honour.

Modest he may have been but it wasn't only on the rugby field or athletics track that Ken Jones was good on his feet. It may have come with the territory of being a schoolmaster but he was comfortable speaking in public and on this particular occasion was at his best. He went to great lengths to emphasise what Newport Athletic Club meant to him, how he quickly became 'steeped in the traditions of the club'; how one's 'personal enjoyment or satisfaction is not gained merely by scoring tries but by playing the game and by being among friends and sportsmen...since I have been here that is exactly what I have found'.

Referring to those who had already spoken, Ken asked: 'What can I say? My past has been revealed, my present has been laid bare – only my future can I keep to myself....' And he did. There was no formal announcement that he had retired from athletics, nor did he give any indication regarding how much longer he planned to play rugby other than to say that his greatest wish was to be part of a Newport team that beat Cardiff four times in a season.

Talk of improving on his record number of caps came later when questioned by journalist Mervyn Thomas. Irishman George Stephenson held the world record of 42, causing Ken to remark: 'If I play in all four internationals this season and next it would give me one more...if I get so near the record it would be silly of me not to try and crack it.' The question of age never entered Ken's thought process. In 29 days' time he would be 33 but that counted for nothing. He wanted to play against England in January; wanted to help Newport lay to rest the Cardiff jinx – it wouldn't happen in the current campaign, the two matches played to date ending in a draw and a Cardiff victory; and there was also a British Lions tour to South Africa in the summer of 1955.

At the end of the year, an award was introduced that would recognise Welsh sporting achievements from across the spectrum before arriving at an overall winner – Wales' leading sports personality. *The Empire News* was a Sunday newspaper with a large circulation in Wales. When readers were invited to submit a list of ten Welsh sports stars for consideration by a panel of judges in their search for a Welsh Sportsperson of the Year, it was inundated with replies. Maybe it was the chance to vote for a particular favourite or simply the attraction of the cash prize on offer, but either way the Welsh public responded in great numbers before the cut-off date arrived.

The ten names suggested by Miss Beryl Thomas from Swansea won the £100 prize and now it was left in the capable hands of a panel of five judges to determine the first winner of the award. There had been many outstanding performances during 1954, leaving the judges a most difficult task. By selecting five individuals who would have contested such an award if one had existed during their own illustrious careers, the responsibility was in safe hands. Glamorgan and England test cricketer JC Clay; Cardiff City and Wales footballer George Edwards; former Wales outside-half Cliff Jones; Olympic gold medallist Lt Col. Harry Llewellyn; and boxing legend Jimmy Wilde each reached the top of their chosen field. All of them had been there and done it.

Miss Thomas' selection included footballers Ivor Allchurch and the mighty John Charles; Glamorgan cricketers Alan Watkins and Wilfred Wooller, who at the age of 42 had achieved recognition as a leading county cricketer to complement his success as an international rugby player in the 1930s; steeplecasher John Disley, the Welsh team captain in Vancouver; golfer Dai Rees, who lost out to Peter Thompson in the Open Championship; young tennis prospect Michael Davies, from whom much was expected; John Brockway, winner of Wales' only gold medal in Vancouver when claiming the 110yds backstroke title; boxing's young flyweight star and new Empire Champion, Dai Dower; and, representing both rugby and athletics, Ken Jones. A veritable who's who of Welsh sport in the early 1950s.

John Disley, Dai Rees and Ivor Allchurch would be future winners of the annual award now known as the BBC Welsh Sports Personality of the Year, but the first name inscribed on the trophy was that of Ken Jones. The Capital Cinema on Cardiff's Queen Street was the venue for the presentation held on 25 February, and it attracted huge interest throughout Wales. Not only were 3,000 members of the public in attendance, the BBC covered the event live on radio with recorded footage to be shown on television at a later date. Unlike in later years when the recipient's name is not revealed until the last moment, in 1955 Ken was told he had been chosen to receive the award before the presentation, with Dai Dower confirmed as runner-up and Wilf Wooller named in third place.

Writing to Ken on 9 February, David Cole, editor of the *Empire News*, confirmed the award and the arrangements for the evening ceremony. Ken and Irene were invited to a cocktail party before proceedings got under way at the cinema, where he would be expected to say a few words after being handed the trophy by JC Clay. This was the beginning of what has become a most prestigious award in Welsh sport, notably because it brings performers from all fields of activity together in its search for the most outstanding amongst them. No easy task, but all the more rewarding for the recipient. As

Ken considered the great names he had been bracketed with, immense pride and humility would have been uppermost in his mind.

The postman delivering mail to the Cardiff offices of the *Empire News* may have had reason to curse his luck as he struggled with the large quantities generated in response to the search for Wales' leading sports personality. Elsewhere, similar groans would have been heard from his counterpart delivering mail to 13 Fairoak Lane. Letters congratulating Ken arrived from all quarters, bringing invitations to make a guest appearance at a local sports day or rugby match. Sports forums were a popular social event in the 1950s. These were evenings organised by local clubs and institutes at which an invited panel of celebrities discussed current topics before taking questions from the floor. Ken was a frequent guest on such occasions.

Altogether, there were far too many to accommodate, but in among all these requests for part of his time there were some that were rarely refused. Ken was ever mindful of his past. Consequently, organisers of functions held in Blaenavon or by Jones' West Mon School Old Boys Association, the Old Chelts (St Paul's Cheltenham), the RAF and Newport Athletic Club were rarely disappointed.

Then there were the autograph hunters, those hardy individuals prepared to stand in line outside changing rooms and parked cars hoping to get a signature in a book or programme that would one day be looked on with fond memories or end up under an auctioneer's hammer, such items now much sought after. For those who couldn't wait patiently after matches, there was always the post and many a speculative letter was forwarded c/o Newport RFC or simply addressed to Ken Jones, Croesyceiliog. These would all receive a reply.

His generosity knew no bounds and there are numerous instances on record when a charitable cause or hospital received an international jersey to be used for fund-raising. So much so that, regardless of his 44 appearances for Wales, the whereabouts of only two jerseys is known – the immediate family have one and the other is to be found 12,000 miles away. The jersey worn when Wales beat New Zealand in 1953 is now on display at the Rugby Museum of New Zealand in Palmerston North.

Then there is the story of a young lad from Tredegar. Ten-year-old Bernard Morgan was born with a debilitating illness and confined to a wheelchair. A lover of the cinema and Welsh rugby, Bernard had two heroes – the American movie star Roy Rogers and the Welsh rugby star Ken Jones. In due course both received letters from Bernard asking for nothing more than an autograph, but his requests touched a nerve and both superstars decided there was more that could be done than simply add their name to a letter.

On a visit to London, Roy Rogers sought out the help of the *Sunday Graphic* newspaper where arrangements were put in place to have a temporary telephone line set up at the Morgan house allowing the famous cowboy to make a call to Bernard. Later, a model of Roy Rogers' horse Trigger arrived from America, only to be withheld until the duty was paid. Eventually someone, somewhere showed a little common sense and compassion, allowing Bernard to receive his gift.

Having already replied by letter and enclosed a signed photograph, Ken then took it upon himself to obtain the signatures of international rugby players. The collection was impressive and what better way to get it to Bernard than in person. Unannounced, he arrived on the doorstep of 58 Rhoslan, Sirhowy, to present the autograph collection to an excited young lad and there was more, the Welsh international also handing over his jersey from the England match played at Twickenham earlier in the year. Of all Ken's sporting memorabilia that was so unselfishly passed on to worthy causes, none can have been more gratefully received or given greater pleasure than the jersey that found its way up the Sirhowy Valley.

Unassuming individual he may have been but Ken was never fazed by appearing in public, something identified by personnel at the BBC. He featured on radio and television sports programmes talking not only about his own career, but contributing insightful comment on much else that was current in the world of sport. Be it with Alan Weeks over the radio network or alongside Peter Dimmock on *Sportsview*, a weekly programme that attracted one of the Corporation's biggest audiences, Ken's contribution was always worth listening to. *World Sports* and *Boys' Own* were among many magazines and newspapers to feature lead articles on Ken and he even appeared on the cover of the *Radio Times* in July 1955, the photograph showing the blanket finish of the 100yds final at the previous year's AAA Championships.

Then there were the more quirky claims to fame, those that went outside the box and viewed life from a different perspective. The fortunes of Pontyscrum RFC were faithfully chronicled in the 'Dai and Ianto' cartoon strip that featured in Saturday's *South Wales Echo*. Following the fortunes of a club and its players, a group of individuals unlike any seen around the rugby grounds of Wales but with traits all too readily recognised, the main protagonists welcomed the players of the day into their world with the name Ken Jones often found in the speech bubble.

On occasion, creator and artist Jon included a caricature of Ken to help with the punchline but if that failed to raise a smile the weighing machines found in most Woolworth's stores may have helped. Owned by the British Automatic Company Ltd of London, the machines generated a card which recorded the details in stones and pounds on one side and a themed picture on the other. The cards became highly collectable and in 1954 the manufacturers produced a series showing leading sportsmen and women – Ken Jones weighing in at number 6.

On his return from Berne, Ken was very guarded when asked about his future in athletics. 'I have not made up my mind yet... Remember, I can still do better than even time.' This was certainly true and there is nothing to suggest that in eight months' time he would not be able to compete against the best British sprinters; but there were other factors to take into consideration. He had experienced eight consecutive years during which the opportunities for some free time, time to spend with Irene, were rare. Realistically, there simply weren't any. While he was not under any pressure to ease up on the hectic schedule – Irene was his number one supporter and never complained about the demands on her husband's time – common sense told him the situation could not continue indefinitely.

The next major athletics event would be the Olympic Games in Melbourne in 1956 and it would be another two years before the Commonwealth Games and European Championships reappeared on the calendar. Ken knew the likelihood of being selected for any of these major meetings was pretty remote, which would leave him the pursuit of more Welsh titles as his principal goal. There had already been signs that his reign as Welsh sprint champion was coming under threat, so why not get out at the top? Leave the sport with the knowledge that he was the best Welsh sprinter in 1946 and still the best when he bowed out from the sport eight years later. And with the British Lions heading for South Africa at the end of the season, surely that should be his next target, which would rule out the prospect of any athletics if he was selected to tour.

Then there was his career in teaching. No other job could have fitted in better with Ken's personal agenda than PE master at the local grammar school. Rarely did his timetable interfere with the training sessions and matchday arrangements imposed on a leading rugby player while in the summer the extended school holiday enabled him to travel the country and compete in the major athletics meetings.

Few occupations may have fitted in with these demands but Ken knew that there was more money to be made outside teaching, the only downside being that he would have much less time at his disposal if he were to go in search of it. Among the avenues explored over the next two years was the post of assistant chief welfare officer with the Steel Company of Wales and a position with the Dunlop Sports Company, neither of which came to fruition.

In 1955, Eric Evans, secretary of the WRU, passed away. Evans was only the fourth man to hold the position since the formation of the union in 1881, but during his term of office (1948 to 1955) he proved to be an outstanding administrator with exacting standards and his successor would need to be a man of the highest calibre. Understandably, there was much interest in the post from those within the Welsh rugby fraternity. The announcement of the vacant position attracted applications from 83 candidates, eventually reduced to a shortlist of eight. The fourth estate 'unofficially' identified those under consideration and were spot on when naming the candidates. Eurof Davies, Jim Dark and Raynor Jones already held senior positions within Welsh rugby and Sidney Harris was a well-known first-class referee, but it was the other four names that attracted most interest. Ken Jones, Rees Stephens and Bleddyn Williams had represented Wales during the 1954–55 season and if one of these were to be offered the post it would bring an immediate end to their playing days because of the strict parameters in place covering the thorny issue of amateurism. Making up the list was WH 'Bill' Clement, who had played for Wales in the 1930s and toured South Africa with the Lions in 1938. Jim Dark, Rees Stephens and Bill Clement were invited for final interviews before the committee members cast their votes, Glyn Stephens withdrawing from the ballot due to his relationship with one of the candidates. The voting ended with Stephens and Clement receiving 12 votes each and Dark a distant third with two. A second ballot, this time with Dark's name withdrawn, confirmed Bill Clement as the fifth Secretary of the WRU, an office he held for 25 years.

Ken knew that any thoughts he might have harboured concerning his retirement from athletics could be put on hold as he began to focus on yet another rugby season. Watching players old and new vying for recognition at Newport's final trial, his uppermost thoughts were to get out there among them, pull on the black and amber jersey once more and set about doing what he did best. But it would have to wait.

For the first time since returning from India in 1946, Ken decided to listen to the messages being sent to his brain from various parts of his body, messages telling him that a long-overdue rest was needed. There was no injury to nurse, no illness to get over, simply a need to recharge the batteries after a particularly hard summer of athletics competition which had also involved extensive travel. It would have gone against all he represented, but Ken Jones was an absentee from the club's early-season training sessions and sat out the opening matches against Swansea, Bristol and Neath.

Secure in the knowledge that he was in the peak of physical fitness, Ken was taking time to get himself mentally prepared for the new season and anything that lay beyond. He may not have known how much sand was left in the hourglass but he did know that none of that which remained was going to be wasted.

It wasn't just Ken who enjoyed the support of his wife at Rodney Parade. Irene had joined the Ladies' Committee soon after its formation in 1946 and by 1954 was one of its most active members. Somebody had to feed the players following training sessions, cater for the teams after matches and organise the food arrangements for any official functions. All this and more came under the auspices of the committee and the capable hands of, among others, Mrs Ken Jones, Mrs Vernon Parfitt, Mrs Jim Hawkins, Mrs Alf Panting and Mrs Bill Everson. And whether or not he was wanted, on those nights when he opted out of training, Ken would help with the sandwiches and pour numerous cups of tea before making his excuses and doing a runner when the time came to wash the piles of dishes mounted high in the kitchen. Nothing short of a nuisance really, not knowing what to do with the time he found at his disposal during the self-imposed break.

Malcolm Thomas had been chosen to succeed Ken as captain for the 1954–55 season and would be re-elected the following year and again in 1956. The club enjoyed great success during his tenure, particularly in 1954–55 and 1955–56 when only 11 of the 81 matches played were lost.

The Welsh Club Championship was always open to criticism but it did serve a purpose in producing a leading club each season. The problem lay in the fact that there were great disparities to be found among the fixture lists of the clubs involved. While many fixtures may have been replicated there were also a great number that weren't; neither did the clubs play the same number of matches in a season. This made the awarding of points for a win or draw totally impracticable and heralded the introduction of a system based on a club's individual performance. It was measured as a percentage – played 20, won 10, lost 10 – 50 per cent; the club with the highest percentage rate of success declared that season's champions.

With an ongoing table regularly updated and published in the *Western Mail*, supporters were able to keep up to date with events, becoming reconciled to the fact that one's club was at the top, the bottom or somewhere in between, allowing the Welsh Club Championship to take its place as the recognised measurement of a club's standing in the great scheme of things. Newport regularly figured among the top three but had only won the title once since the war. Ken Jones had led the champion club in 1950–51; now it was the turn of Malcolm Thomas to try and lead the Black and Ambers back to the top.

He would have to be patient. The season got off to the

worst possible start when the new captain broke his leg in a trial match and he did not lead the side out until 18 December, by which time the season was almost half over. The injury effectively ruled out any chance of Thomas playing international rugby come the new year, which in turn meant any hopes of touring with the British Lions in the summer were also likely to be dashed.

Fortunately for Newport, Brian Jones was now fully committed to the club after serving with the Royal Navy, while John Roblin, for whom many predicted a bright future, had just joined. When Cambridge Blue Harry Morgan, yet another centre of some distinction, also made his way to Rodney Parade, the club appeared to have an embarrassment of riches in midfield to cover for the captain during his absence.

There are no shortage of theories that try to explain why Ken Jones had so many lean seasons at club level when measured by the number of tries scored. Not forgetting the massive contribution he made in other areas of play, people expected much more, and it is difficult to comprehend why they were so often disappointed. The player himself never felt deprived if those around him were running in the tries – provided somebody did he was happy – but there were many who paid the entrance money just to see him perform.

Like it or not, Ken Jones was one of the stars who put bums on seats, but unfortunately he couldn't be expected to run in tries from great distances on a regular basis; certainly not if he wasn't seeing much of the ball. The most popular theory aired suggested that players find it more natural to pass to the left than the right, unless they are left-handed when the reverse is seen. When questioned, Ken was inclined to go along with this but in truth it doesn't bear close inspection as there is a long list of right wings whose try-scoring feats are well documented. Another obvious reason would be that for most of his career Ken Jones was a heavily marked man, opposing sides ever alert to the threat he posed.

But the explanation is likely to be much more straight-forward. It all comes down to the fact that the men out wide, the fastest on the field, are only as good as the players inside them, and in earlier seasons Newport's midfield players were often found wanting. Not so in 1954–55. The speed with which scrum-half Onllwyn Brace was able to get the ball away from set pieces and Roy Burnett's good hands ensured that whichever pairing was selected from Jones, Morgan and Roblin, the men out wide benefited. Between them that season, Ken and John Lane broke the club record for the number of tries scored by a pair of wings, Lane claiming 23 and Ken 21, the most he would score for the club in any season. Lane had claimed the individual record three years earlier, possibly contesting the theory that there were times when all was not well in midfield, but with Ken Jones now benefiting from the men inside him there was much to enjoy.

When Malcolm Thomas returned to the team he immediately slotted in, a most versatile player who was equally at home in the centre, at outside-half or on the wing. With the captain back in harness, the wings continued to run in the tries and with only two of the remaining 23 matches lost, Newport were runners-up in the championship.

It seems that the bigger the occasion the more memorable the try. Ken Jones had scored several extraordinary tries on the international stage, some that would be talked about as long as the game is played, but in club rugby one try in particular stands head and shoulders above all others. On 16 October Gloucester arrived at a rain-soaked Rodney Parade, a heavy morning downpour having left its mark on the pitch to make conditions underfoot treacherous and leave ball-handling skills in the lap of the gods. Garfield Owen kicked an early penalty for the home side midway through the first half but there was little else to report until smooth passing moved the ball to Ken Jones, who received it on halfway with his opposite number and the Gloucester outside centre in close attention. The Newport wing somehow contrived a path between them and set off on a side-stepping run that wrong-footed every player who tried to stop him. One, two, three times he stepped off his right foot before changing direction and setting off on a swerving run that took him clear, leaving a 20-yard sprint to the line.

It is not difficult for pundits and spectators alike to get carried away in the heat of the moment and without the help of television footage later generations are left to form their own opinions, but the wide coverage the match received from local press and those journalists who had travelled from the West Country confirms the try was something special. 'One of the best tries ever scored at Rodney Parade...'; '...deserves to rank among the finest the flying Welsh wing has ever scored...'. These set the tone, but perhaps the comments found in the *South Wales Argus* are the most reliable. In his role of rugby reporter for the local newspaper Jack Davis would have seen most of Ken's games for the club and when he wrote 'I say that it was the finest try Ken Jones ever scored...', then maybe it should be taken as read.

The tries may have been totting up for Newport but for a second successive championship Ken failed to add to his 17 in a Welsh jersey. Wales beat England, Ireland and France but a disappointing performance at Murrayfield was enough to deny the team a Triple Crown and Grand Slam. The 14-8 margin may not have been as comprehensive as the 19-0 drubbing handed out four years earlier but it was every bit as unexpected. Scotland came into the match on the back of 17 consecutive defeats and with Wales leading 3-0 at half-time and apparently well in control, the bad run looked like being extended. A fine try by Arthur Smith, a student at Cambridge University making his debut on the right wing, tied the scores, from which point the Scots began to take control. Smith's fine performance would not have escaped Ken's notice, and neither did that of another young man included at centre for Ireland a month later.

Wales bounced back from the Murrayfield defeat with a 21-3 victory at Cardiff Arms Park over an Irish team that was completely outplayed in a final quarter that saw the home side score 18 points, including four tries. At 3-3 the outcome hung in the balance and the final score may have flattered Wales but, even in defeat, it was the young Irish centre who was immediately identified as a star in the making.

Tony O'Reilly was two months short of his 19th birthday when he won his fourth cap in Cardiff, Arthur Smith a few years older at 22 when he was introduced to the Scottish side. Ken was now 33 years of age, playing some of the best club rugby of his career and more than holding his own when it came to the international stage. But 1955 was the year when age mattered if you were a leading rugby player. The year in which Ulsterman Jack Siggins, the man chosen to manage the British Lions on the forthcoming tour to South Africa, determined that no player over the age of 30 would be considered for selection. This immediately ruled out Ken and fellow Welshmen Bleddyn Williams, Rex Willis and Rees Stephens; four players who had toured with the Lions in 1950 and who were still comfortable on the international stage. Higgins may well have got it right, the Lions sharing a thrilling Test series 2-2 while playing some of the most entertaining and enterprising rugby that followers of the game in South Africa had ever witnessed, but for Ken and those similarly denied the chance to tour it was a bitter blow.

If there are better players available, current form is suspect or injury plays a hand, then failing to gain selection would not be a problem. However, not to be considered because of one's perceived 'advancing' years is a judgement difficult to accept. There is little doubt that Ken Jones would have thrived on the hard playing surfaces found in South Africa. Neither the Lions nor the Springboks had a player among their ranks who could match the Welshman for pace alone and that the followers of the game in a country where he would have been most at home on a rugby field never saw him in action was particularly sad.

It was not quite the same as spending three months in South Africa, but Newport's three-match end-of-season tour to Devon did see Ken back on the road and enjoying the camaraderie of those he was involved with week in week out during the course of the season. The three matches were won but on the final Saturday of the season, Cardiff surprised the hosts and reigning champions by winning the second Welsh Sevens tournament at Rodney Parade. Newport accounted for Abertillery and Llanelly in the earlier rounds before beating Cross Keys in the semi-final while Cardiff beat Pontypridd, Aberavon and Newbridge on the way to the final and, importantly, had not conceded any points. The large crowd enjoyed six hours of entertainment before the climax of the afternoon produced a thrilling 20 minutes of seven-a-side rugby. With minutes remaining the teams were tied at 3-3 but there was little doubt that Cardiff were the better side, which was confirmed when Gordon Wells crossed for his fifth try of the afternoon.

Ken Jones' decision to retire from athletics was finally announced in April. It came as no surprise, regardless of the fact that he had been very non-committal about his future during the winter months. In a press interview he stated categorically that he had run his last race but would continue to play rugby for at least one more season. It was his intention to spend time coaching any promising sprinters, but in a forthright attack he questioned both the youth of the day and the town councils. Speaking as one who was in regular contact with teenage boys, he bemoaned the fact that too many became disillusioned with sport if their ambitions were not quickly realised. Far too often there were instances of boys with great potential falling by the wayside. With the British Empire and Commonwealth Games coming to Cardiff in three years, now was the time to begin serious training but suitable facilities were few in number and it was in this area that the councillors were seen to be failing their communities.

There were very few purpose-built running tracks in Wales and while the Ken Joneses of this world were prepared to put up with the inconvenience of having to travel some distance to train, many other promising youngsters were not. Newport Town Corporation had confirmed that a purpose-built facility would be ready in 1956 but the news was not so good elsewhere. As one leading journalist so eloquently put it, 'training facilities for Welsh youth would be a better investment than many of the costly architectural monstrosities which seem used chiefly for bebop sessions, whist drives and political hot airing...'; meaning Ken would have his work cut out in the search for the next generation of track stars.

For the first time in his life Ken Jones had a lengthy period of time on his hands, seven or eight weeks, unheard of in recent years. He and Irene had settled into Fairoak Lane and he could now catch up on all those jobs around the house that previously had to 'wait until tomorrow' and there was a garden to tend, a pastime that would become a passion later in life. But you could only spend so much time odd jobbing – what to do?

The move to Croesyceiliog meant Ken and Irene now had to rely on public transport to take them to Newport. Ken had travelled from Bristol to Bath each day when he was teaching at Bathwick Junior School and though his time living in Newport had allowed him a little longer in bed each morning, the change in circumstances caused minimal disruption. But there had to be a better way of getting around, something that would allow him those precious extra few minutes in bed in the morning. Ken Jones decided to take to the road – he learnt to drive. What is now taken very much for granted was quite the opposite in 1955. The days of a man walking in front of a car waving a red flag had long since disappeared but the motor car was still regarded as a luxury which not many families were able to afford. And if Ken was to continue his search for a new area of employment, then the ability to drive would certainly widen the horizons.

When the Newport players assembled for pre-season training a glance across the dressing room would have confirmed that Ken Jones had enjoyed his summer break, which had included a holiday in Bournemouth. Used to having their colleague return in the peak of fitness after the athletics season, the sight of a few extra pounds spread about his angular frame would not have passed without comment. Once back into the strict regime Ken quickly got rid of any excess baggage but he did carry more weight in those final seasons, all in the right places, and was certainly a stronger player for it.

This was the season he hoped to break George Stephenson's record but he would need to play in all four championship matches to do so. The main threats to his long reign on the right wing looked likely to come from the Cardiff pair CL 'Cowboy' Davies and Gwyn Rowlands. Both were capable enough to handle the game at the higher level and the returning British Lions, Gareth Griffiths and Haydn Morris, provided other options. Elsewhere, Neath's Keith Maddocks and the Aberavon flyer John Collins were not about to take a back seat and let the city slickers move in. Little doubt then that Ken would have to be at his best if he were to retain his place in the Welsh team. Anything less would not be good enough.

Ken went into the 1955–56 season fully expecting it to be his last. He made no secret of the fact and, fresh from his long summer break, was happy to consider any invitation to play outside the club and international windows. As Newport kicked off the season beating Penarth at Rodney Parade, Ken was playing for an Invitation XV selected by Dr Glyn Hughes against Blackheath in an exhibition match at Twickenham. A spectacular hat-trick of tries helped the select team to a 38-14 victory, suggesting the player was in fine form and more than ready for what might lie ahead in the coming months.

An opportunity to play for Blaenavon presented itself two weeks later. A midweek fixture against Abertillery saw his home town club struggling to raise a side due to an early season crop of injuries that was compounded by work commitments. Abertillery had started the season with three convincing victories but at Blaenavon's Recreation Ground the run came to a halt. Word of Ken's participation drew a large crowd and they were treated to an outstanding individual display that highlighted his defensive qualities rather than his potency as an attacking force. Ken put in tackle after tackle, twice giving chase to deny the visiting side what should have been certain tries. Following this fine example the Blaenavon players raised their game to record a well-earned 6-6 draw against a team expected to wreak havoc.

Disappointed to have missed out on the British Lions tour, Ken was invited to play for a Lions XV against a Wales XV, the match played at Cardiff Arms Park on 22 October as part of the WRU's 75th anniversary celebrations. Twelve players who had toured South Africa were joined by Ken, Malcolm Thomas and Rees Stephens from the 1950 Lions while the Wales XV boasted an impressive line-up that included many current and future international players.

The large crowd was entertained to a feast of rugby that saw the Lions XV run out winners by 20 points to 17. After being forced to accept that his last appearance in the Lions jersey was in Australia, not only did he find himself back in the famous colours but there was one more try to add to those scored in New Zealand five years earlier.

Following defeats at Bristol and Gloucester in the early weeks of the season, Newport put together an impressive run of victories that would eventually extend to 17 and continue through to the end of January, by which time of the 24 matches played only the two West Country clubs had spoiled the record. Included among the matches won were two against

Cardiff. If Ken did retire at the end of the season there could be no better way of bringing down the curtain than having realised his dream of playing for the first Newport team to defeat Cardiff four times.

There was an unexpected appearance at centre when the club travelled to Herne Hill to play London Welsh. Harry Morgan's late withdrawal saw Malcolm Thomas move to stand-off. Ken replaced him with Graham Ross taking over on the wing. As seen against Plymouth Albion some years earlier, once again Ken proved to be the catalyst. He set up a try for Geoff Whitson, another for Graham Ross, scored two himself and made several important tackles to nullify dangerous attacking movements. With three members of the Big Five present it was a timely reminder that there was still plenty of gas in the tank and Vince Griffiths, Dai Jones and Ivor Jones may well have pencilled in Wales' right wing for the opening match of the championship at Twickenham. How could a man one month short of his 34th birthday still be such an invaluable member of a team? Ken Jones was proving to be something of an enigma and when he scored five tries against the Watsonians on Boxing Day it appeared that all he had to do was avoid injury and his place in rugby's hall of fame would be assured.

Ken's involvement in competitive athletics had ended when he announced his retirement from the sport earlier in the year. With Cardiff due to host the British Empire and Commonwealth Games in 1958, the organisation of such a high-profile event needed to be up and running well in advance. The British Empire and Commonwealth Games Council for Wales had delegated responsibility to an Organising Committee that would 'proceed in all aspects in conjunction with the Council for Wales'.

Under the chairmanship of Col. Sir Godfrey Llewellyn, the first meeting of the committee took place in the Council Chambers at Cardiff City Hall on Friday 18 November. In attendance were almost 70 distinguished individuals who, together with those unable to attend, would make up a body of 100 men and women responsible for the organisation of the biggest sporting event yet to be held in Wales. Ken was both honoured and flattered that Sir Godfrey had invited him to become a member of this august group of individuals. The chairman knew that input from someone who had experienced major athletics meetings as a competitor would be invaluable. Ken readily offered his services and remained involved until the Games got under way in July 1958, when he would be invited to carry out one last act before finally laying his boots and spikes to rest.

Ken Jones rarely said no. His personal timetable would have to be particularly stretched for him to decline any invitation to a worthwhile cause. Sporting stars finding themselves in similar circumstances today would open any conversation with the question 'How much?' but life was viewed very differently in the 1950s. It would be foolish to suggest that Ken's willingness to oblige left him out of pocket, as all reasonable expenses could be claimed without impacting on his amateur status, but nothing could ever compensate for the innumerable hours spent fulfilling engagements. By agreeing to be part of the Organising Committee, many more hours would have to be spent at the beck and call of others, but this was Ken's life and he wouldn't have had it any other way.

New Year's Eve found him not at a family gathering or a party with friends but in Dublin for yet another of the invitation matches that in previous seasons he may well have declined. The Irish RFU arranged a match between an England–Wales XV and an Ireland–Scotland XV to celebrate the opening of a new West Stand at Lansdowne Road and had invited the leading players of the day to take part. The very nature of the occasion suggested a none too physical, fast and open exhibition of rugby football would be the order of the day, but this did not put off representatives of the four home unions' selection committees attending. The England–

Wales combination won by 18 points to 15 and again it was the Newport wing who caught the eye, scoring two classic wing three-quarter tries courtesy of some fine centre play by Malcolm Thomas. If the current season were to be his last, then the first half certainly ended on a high with nine tries coming his way in four matches spread over eight days; seven for Newport in the games played over Christmas and two in Dublin.

When the Welsh team to play England at Twickenham was announced, Ken Jones was included on the right wing for his 40th consecutive cap. Unlike in recent seasons, Newport's recent rich vein of form was at last recognised. Garfield Owen, Malcolm Thomas and new caps Harry Morgan and Onllwyn Brace joined Ken in the backs with Bryn Meredith and Leighton Jenkins included in the pack. The seven players provided the club's biggest contribution to a Welsh team since the 1890s. England were beaten 8-3 and two weeks later Scotland lost 9-3 in Cardiff to set up a Triple Crown match at Lansdowne Road in March. The seven Newport players retained their places for the Scottish match with little effect on Newport, which continued in its winning ways despite the handicap of having so many first-team stars on international duty. At both club and international level, the season was promising to be memorable. Then the students from Cape Town and Stellenbosch Universities arrived at Rodney Parade.

They may have toured as a South African Universities team but the squad of players came from the two leading universities in the Western Province – and for students, read mature men. Of the team fielded at Newport, Dawie Ackermann and Butch Lochner played in the Test series against the 1955 Lions and Pat Montini, Jan du Preez, Brian Pfaff, Piet du Toit and captain James Starke were all destined to play for the Springboks. Students in name, but here was a team made up of outstanding rugby players, which goes some way towards putting Newport's unexpected 6-3 defeat into perspective.

Australia in 1947; South Africa in 1952; New Zealand in 1954; and now a team representative of the world of academia in South Africa. Ken played in all four matches without enjoying that special glow that comes when part of a winning club side against overseas opposition.

Victory against Leicester immediately restored the equilibrium, then it was a trip to the Arms Park for the much-anticipated third encounter of the season with the Blue and Blacks. Severe frost claimed most of the day's fixtures but a covering of straw ensured the match would go ahead. Played in front of a big crowd, it was nail-biting stuff, much of the game dominated by the two packs of forwards with the Newport eight marginally coming out on top, and at the final whistle only a Malcolm Thomas drop goal separated the sides.

Ken suffered a painful knee injury in the first half but chose to remain on the field. This was a match he probably prioritised above all others at that point in time and he was not going to see Newport reduced to 14 men with so much at stake. He always argued that nobody knew his body better than he did himself but that dogmatic philosophy had been known to fail him in the past.

As the next few weeks could see him rewrite the history books, Ken's decision to carry on playing in Cardiff may be considered somewhat foolish, but perhaps it confirms what mattered most to him at this late stage of his career. The victory meant that Newport had now beaten Cardiff in four consecutive matches, but as the first took place in the previous season it counted for nothing. Three down, one to go.

Rarely did clubs meet in consecutive fixtures, but as luck would have it Newport's next scheduled match would see Cardiff at Rodney Parade in two weeks, after which Wales would travel to Ireland for the match in which Ken could equal George Stephenson's record. The choice was fairly straightforward: should he play against Cardiff in the knowledge that any injury would prevent his appearing in Dublin; or should he stand down from the Newport team and watch from the stands as his club endeavoured to break the Cardiff jinx? If all went well in Dublin the same scenario would occur later in the month, with Newport travelling to Aberavon the week before Wales were to play France in Cardiff when it was hoped Ken would make the record his own – decisions, decisions.

Ken's dilemma was the subject of much speculation. The two-week break was timely, the injured knee had responded well to treatment and if Ray Lewis had every confidence Ken would play in Dublin, he made it clear he didn't want him turning out against Cardiff. A rigorous 90-minute workout thoroughly tested the damaged knee and Ken had no hesitation in declaring himself fit to play and in doing so resurrected memories of an identical situation five years earlier, one that may well have clouded his judgement.

In his first season as club captain Ken had found himself in a race against time to prove his fitness to play in the final match against Cardiff, Newport having won the first three. On that occasion his efforts failed, leaving him with little option but to look on as his team were held to a 3-3 draw. Now, with the added knowledge that such a moment may never come his way again, he was reluctant to let the team take the field without him. The Newport selection committee would have no part in the decision, happy to leave it to the player; but not so Ray Lewis, who remained adamant Ken should not play.

The build-up of fluid around the knee may have been removed but the slightest knock could see the problem re-appear and Lewis was concerned there would not be enough time between matches to work his magic again. It became a drawn-out battle of words, the outcome of which saw a greatly disappointed Ken Jones concede defeat.

With John Lane also on the injured list, Graham Ross and Ken Sergeant were selected; but this particular story had more mileage in it. When Ross reported unfit on the Saturday morning, the only remaining option was to introduce an inexperienced player either into the centre or on the wing, a huge gamble in a match of such importance. Cometh the hour, cometh the man. Far from happy after being omitted from the team, Ross's withdrawal gave Ken the necessary ammunition to win the argument he had lost two days earlier and the captain led his team onto Rodney Parade in front of over 20,000 spectators for the club game of the season.

Yet again, it would be good to be able to report that Newport beat Cardiff for the fourth time in that 1955–56 season but they didn't. It would have been the stuff of fairy tales; something to tell the grandchildren; another of those 'I was there' moments. But it wasn't to be. Leading 6-0 at half-time courtesy of a John Anderson drop goal and a penalty by Norman Morgan, Newport had looked much the better team but the match was turned on its head in a five-minute spell that saw the visitors claim two converted tries.

Contained by the Newport back row for much of the first half, the mercurial Cliff Morgan was at his tactical best in the second. Probing kicks were executed with great precision and when he decided to run with the ball, so the alarm bells rang out for the home team. Two tries were the immediate result of the outside-half's enterprise and if the second conversion needed the help of an upright to secure the points, the end result was that Newport were four points down.

The home pack set about its task with renewed vigour and was rewarded when prop forward Des Greenslade pounced on a loose ball wide out with only minutes remaining, taking the score to 10-9. Norman Morgan's conversion attempt could win the match and rarely can 20,000 people have been so quiet at a ground famous for the vociferous support received from the terraces. But it wasn't to be; the players of both teams compelled to look on as Morgan's kick sailed wide of the uprights. Newport 3, Cardiff 1 – game over.

There was little time to dwell on what must have been a

massive disappointment with the Welsh team set to leave for Dublin on Wednesday. For the third consecutive match, Newport had seven representatives in a side that would travel in search of a Triple Crown. Having played throughout Wales' recent Triple Crown winning seasons in 1950 and 1952 and against England and Scotland in the current championship, Ken and Malcolm Thomas could join an elite group of five players who had played in every match of three Triple Crown winning campaigns if Wales were successful at Lansdowne Road. John Williams, Billy Trew, Dickie Owen, George Travers and Jim Webb played in all nine matches in 1908, 1909 and 1911, but before anyone could join that elite group of individuals there was a mountain to climb.

The Irish media and public were full of praise for the Welsh wing who was about to equal a record established by an Irishman in 1930. George Stephenson sent a telegram to Ken on the morning of the match offering his heartiest congratulations, and there was a special welcome from supporters when he ran out at Lansdowne Road, but for 80 minutes, 15 men in green set about spoiling the day. British Lions manager Jack Siggins was well aware of Cliff Morgan's bag of tricks and the Irish players had got to know him particularly well when the stand-off played for Bective Rangers. 'Cripple the root and the tree falls' were Siggins' instructions to wing forwards Marney Cunningham and Ron Kavanagh, and so it proved, Morgan unable to shake off the immediate attentions of the Irishmen. That the Welsh pack was so comprehensively outplayed did not help the outside-half but it was Ireland's day, the final 11-3 score failing to confirm the home team's dominance.

So Ken Jones was now officially the most capped rugby player in the world. For 14 days the honour was shared with Stephenson, but on 24 March he led the Welsh team out at Cardiff Arms Park and the record was his. The players who followed him onto the field were much changed from those who appeared in Dublin: Gwyn Rowlands replaced Lynn

Davies on the left wing; Rex Richards and Ray Prosser took over from Billy Williams and Courtney Meredith in the front row; Leighton Jenkins moved into the second row at the expense of Rhys Williams; and there was a new back row with CD Williams, Russell Robins and Geoff Whitson called up to take over from Jenkins, Brian Sparks and Clem Thomas. With Whitson called up for his first cap, Newport's complement became eight.

The occasion was certainly a memorable one for those associated with Newport RFC, but the match itself failed to live up to expectations, proving to be something of an anticlimax. Wales won 5-3 but the winning try was the subject of much debate with most critics reporting that the home team were extremely fortunate to record the victory that confirmed them as Five Nations champions. And what of Ken Jones on this historic day? Well, he certainly had his work cut out in defence, where he was as reliable as ever, but one correspondent claimed that the only pass he received was from Onllwyn Brace in the dressing room after the match when he handed him the match ball!

A record-breaking 18th try would have been the icing on the cake but Ken's try-scoring days for Wales were a thing of the past. It was 12 matches since he had scored against New Zealand, which led to suggestions that he was only included in the team as part of an underhand scheme concocted by the WRU in an attempt to wrest the record of the world's most capped player from the Irish. What tosh! Ken Jones was the best right wing in Wales for ten years and his superior fitness levels and the little bit of luck that all sportsmen occasionally rely on saw him through a decade of uninterrupted international rugby. That such disparaging comments could be heard, not only outside Wales but also throughout the valleys, was nothing short of shameful.

Malcolm Thomas' second season as Newport captain improved on his first, with the club topping the Club Championship and reclaiming the Welsh Seven-a-Side trophy. Five matches were lost: the South African Universities and Cardiff won at Rodney Parade and in April, victory at the Gnoll saw Neath join Bristol and Gloucester as the only clubs to defeat Newport on the road. On the international stage, the club would never again be able to boast eight players in the same Welsh team, neither could a Newport player lay claim to the record for the number of appearances in a Welsh jersey.

If the old adage suggesting that a sportsman should quit while still at the top was to be heeded, then now was the time for Ken Jones to call it a day. His club was riding high, Wales were champions and he had played more international rugby than anyone else. On a personal note, he had made the decision to take his career in a different direction and would leave Newport High School for Boys in the summer to take up a position in sales with a leading tyre manufacturer. Everything that would allow him satisfactory closure on his days as a distinguished sportsman appeared to have fallen into place. All that was now required was some official announcement through the press confirming what had been expected since the start of the season when he went public in suggesting it would be his last.

But why retire? Was Ken Jones really ready to lead a sedentary life? Definitely not. Anyway, Newport still hadn't beaten Cardiff four times in a season – what greater incentive did a man need?! Ken decided to follow the lead of a group of men aboard the *Titanic* on that tragic day in April 1912 when the ill-fated liner collided with an iceberg. As did the members of the *Titanic's* dance band, Ken Jones decided to play on.

CHAPTER ELEVEN

FROM PLAYING TO WATCHING

W hen Ken Jones packed his bags on his final day at Newport High School he believed life was never going to be the same again. He was about to enter the world of nine to five, a five-day working week with a holiday entitlement of 20 days plus the statutory Bank Holidays; Christmas, Easter, May Day, etc. In 1949, Ken had entered the teaching profession on an annual salary of £390, a figure just beneath the threshold at which income tax kicked in. Seven years later, his salary might have increased to £685.10.0 per annum but with the taxman now taking his share, Ken was taking home less than £50 a month. The long summer breaks and extended holidays elsewhere in the year were no longer important to him. Now it was time to address how much money arrived in the bank at the end of each month, time to find out if the grass was greener beyond the world of teaching.

His new job as a sales representative for an Oxfordshire-based tyre company would see him cover a territory extending from Monmouthshire through the Forest of Dean to Gloucester and Cheltenham and including the areas around Bristol and Bath in the West Country. Much of this territory was already well known to him, as indeed was the name Ken Jones known to many of the customers he would be visiting. And when it came to seeking out new accounts, it is unlikely that his knowledge of the components that went into making tyres for motor cars or the suitability of one product over another would impress potential customers; it was his name that was guaranteed to open the necessary doors.

From putting schoolboys through their paces in the gymnasium or on the playing fields and using any free time to do some personal training, Ken now found himself behind the wheel of a car for extended periods as he drove the network of roads across the length and breadth of south-east Wales, Gloucestershire and Somerset. This was a time when the only way across the Bristol Channel was by ferry, the M4 motorway and Severn Bridge still a few years from completion. Life on the road required a certain stamina and much patience, but sitting down for hours at a time was totally alien to a finely tuned athlete and compensatory measures would have to be taken to maintain the status quo. Fortunately Ken Jones was prepared to put in the extra hours of training now required and it was a fit and healthy-looking 34-year-old who turned up for the Newport trials at the end of August.

He approached the new season with exactly the same mindset that had driven the previous campaign. This time, however, there would be no added pressures on the international front, no records waiting to broken. And if the Big Five decided that having a 35-year-old playing on the wing was not the way forward, then so be it. Club rugby was likely to dominate, and after seasons in which he was restricted in the number of appearances, then 1956–57 would go some way to redressing the balance. At the final reckoning, Ken played in 33 of Newport's 43 matches, equalling the number of appearances of 1952–53, and but for his continued involvement with the national team and a few invitation matches there would have been more.

The first invitation to lure him away from Newport duty came on the opening day of the season. Twelve months earlier, Glyn Hughes had assembled a star-studded team to play the Wasps at Twickenham, and now it was the turn of Arthur Rees to do the same. Rees won 13 Welsh caps in the 1930s before rising to the rank of Squadron Leader in the RAF during the Second World War. Then followed a glittering career in the police service and much involvement with various sports in an administrative capacity.

The players he invited to Twickenham included England's Peter Jackson and Louis Cannell; Jack Kyle of Ireland; Scottish forward Jim Greenwood; the French pair Michel Vannier and Henri Domec; and, from Wales, Rhys Williams and Bryn Meredith. Ken enjoyed these matches, which were played with a certain abandon. They also gave him the chance to meet up with friends from beyond the Welsh borders and when he was given the honour of leading these famous names out at Twickenham his day was complete. He played a big part in helping the invitation XV overcome a spirited Wasps team, his major contribution to the afternoon coming by way of a trade mark try that began with a series of side-steps and ended under the posts for the biggest cheer on an afternoon that drew many big cheers from the large crowd. AM Rees' XV won the match 13-8 while, back at Rodney Parade, Newport got the season under way with an 11-3 victory over Penarth.

No matter how fit an individual is, maybe he shouldn't be executing electric side-steps on the opening day of the season. Either way, Ken's return to club rugby was put on hold due to a pulled leg muscle that kept him out of action for the next three weeks. Bristol and Neath were beaten before Newport travelled to Swansea with Ken Jones named on the right wing. Torrential rain fell all morning and continued throughout the match, which at one point looked like being called off. With the pitch quickly turned into a quagmire it was left to the two packs of forwards to play among themselves and the match ended in a scoreless draw.

Two weeks later, any dreams of gaining the four precious victories over Cardiff were laid to rest when the clubs shared 12 points at Rodney Parade. Ken scored his first try of the season in Newport colours within three minutes of the start but as the match unfolded it became clear there was little to choose between the sides. If Newport squandered a couple of chances that might have won the game, then the Cardiff defence deserved to take something home with them and a draw was deemed to be the right result on the day.

Ken's place on the right wing for Newport seemed assured for as long as he wanted it, an assumption based on the fact that he was never going to outstay his welcome, continue playing beyond his sell-by date. Things were very different with Wales. Even if the great Ken Jones had played 43 consecutive international matches, when the Big Five sat down to select the team to play England in January it would be chosen on form not fame.

The three trial matches produced the usual conundrums, but what did become clear was that Llanelly's Geoff Howells offered a serious alternative on the right wing. He played particularly well when the Whites defeated the Reds in the first trial at Rodney Parade, but it was a wonderful hat-trick of tries that helped the Possibles overcome the Probables in the final trial at Cardiff Arms Park that sealed Ken's fate. Newport had travelled to Stradey Park a week earlier, going down to a strong Llanelly team in which Howells was prominent. Ken Jones missed the chance to impress those selectors in attendance, having travelled to Birkenhead to represent the UAU Past and Present against another touring team from the South African Universities.

There would have been some satisfaction taken from the 6-3 victory after Newport's defeat a year earlier, but the knowledge that his Welsh place was under threat would not have rested easily.

On reflection, the invitation to play for the UAU might have been declined, a trip to Stradey Park a more considered option. Maybe choosing to travel north instead of west gives some indication of how Ken viewed what remained of his career. Things might have turned out differently if he had seen some of the ball in that final trial, but perhaps it was time to move on. When the team to play England was announced, Howells was included on the right wing for his first cap and there was also a first appearance for Neath's Keith Maddocks on the left with KJ Jones listed among the non-travelling reserves. It seemed that Welsh rugby was witnessing the end of an era but, as is so often the case, there was one final act still to be played out.

England defeated Wales in Cardiff. A Fenwick Allison penalty goal, awarded when Maddocks was caught in an offside position, was the only score of a disappointing match that left the selectors still searching for the right formula. In two weeks' time, Wales were due to travel to Murrayfield to play a Scottish team that had started the championship with victory in Paris. When the Welsh side was announced it was confirmed that four players who had appeared against England were dropped and there was one positional change. Lloyd Williams was called up for a first cap at scrum-half, where he would link with club partner Cliff Morgan; Robin Davies and Brian Sparks replaced Clem Thomas and Rory O'Connor in the back row; Geoff Howells moved across to the left wing at the expense of Keith Maddocks; and Ken Jones earned a recall on the right wing for his 44th cap.

For those who like their packages neatly wrapped, without any doubt, the point when Ken Jones should have bowed out of international rugby was after playing in a winning side against France at Cardiff Arms Park in a match that saw him become rugby's most capped player. That would have been the perfect end to an international career that had spanned ten seasons; 43 caps won through ten championships with the additional matches against Australia, New Zealand and South Africa thrown in. Ken's omission from the team that lost to England was probably made more with the future in mind than due to any lack of form. Similarly, his immediate recall does seem to be a knee-jerk reaction. Either way, the next five seasons would highlight the selectors' problems in searching for a replacement on the right wing. Eight players would be called upon, of whom only Aberavon's John Collins reached double figures in the number of caps won. Unfortunately there was no fairy-tale ending at Murrayfield. No final dash up the right flank for a match-winning try that would set a new record. Wales were beaten 9-6.

The 1957 Five Nations Championship brought to a close an era that featured one of the greatest international players of all time and the resurgence of Newport as one of Wales' finest clubs. This was confirmed on 24 March 1956 when no fewer than eight players were included in the Welsh team that played France. When the two countries met on 23 March 1957 it was a very different story, with no players from the club on view. There would be other great clubmen who would stamp their mark on Welsh rugby but Ken's ever presence on the international stage was finally over – it had been a great journey.

Malcolm Thomas' third season as Newport captain may not have reached the heights of the previous two but a good sequence of results in the latter part of the campaign was enough to take the club to third position in the championship table. The season ended on a high at the now well-established Welsh Seven-a-Side competition, which took place at Swansea on 27 April. After defeating Pontypridd and Newbridge in the early rounds Newport scraped home in the semi-final, beating Neath 12-10 to set up an all-Monmouthshire final with Abertillery. It took a mighty effort from the Newport team before they retained the title.

Abertillery were the surprise package of the tournament with future international stars Haydn Morgan and Alun Pask in outstanding form. The reigning champions found themselves 8-0 down but, able to call on all the experience gained from the three previous finals, the Black and Ambers rallied to run out eventual winners by 11 points to 8. This brought the season to a fitting close and Ken could look back on another successful campaign with no regrets. But there was one oversight that must have rankled with the player.

The British Empire and Commonwealth Games were now little more than a year away. The WRU, together with the other home nations and with the cooperation of the Cardiff club, arranged a match, the proceeds of which would go towards the games' fund. Closely involved in the various organising committees, it seems not unreasonable to assume that one of the first names on the team sheet would have been that of Ken Jones, but he was not invited to take part in this one-off occasion that saw a Welsh XV beat an International XV 17-16. Played two weeks after Wales won 19-13 in Paris, only two of the players on duty at Stade Colombes were missing from the Welsh XV, three-quarters Geoff Howells and Graham Powell. Maybe the selectors wanted the team to have another outing as part of the rebuilding process, or possibly Ken declined an invitation to play, which seems highly unlikely. Whatever the reason, on 6 April, Wales' most famous rugby and athletics star was playing for Newport at Plymouth while a Welsh XV turned out at Cardiff Arms Park for a cause most dear to his heart – how strange is that?

If Ken needed any confirmation that his time as an international rugby player was over then this incident, regardless of why he was not involved, provided it. Looking ahead, if he were to turn up for training in August then Newport would have him completely at their disposal for the first time since he joined the club in 1946. The odds against Ken Jones playing beyond the 1957–58 season were extremely long, at the very least double carpet or 33–1 in bookies' parlance. When it was confirmed there would be one more season, his final appearance at many of the club grounds he had graced over the years brought out the crowds, eager to see him in action one last time.

The season may have got off to a bad start with home defeats at the hands of Penarth and Ranji Walker's Invitation XV but when Cardiff won by 3 points to nil at Rodney Parade on 5 October Ken knew that his one remaining ambition as a player would not be realised. By the turn of the year Newport had lost seven matches with a further three drawn and there was every likelihood that 1957–58 would be its worst post-war season to date. Among the doom and gloom of the first half of the campaign, one match stood out above all others; that against the fourth Australian tourists, who visited Rodney Parade on 23 November.

Ken was the sole survivor of the Newport team beaten by the third Wallabies in 1947, and he now had a final chance to enjoy success in a Newport jersey against one of the southern hemisphere's major rugby-playing nations. When Jack Hurrell and Leighton Jenkins scored tries together with a conversion and drop goal by Norman Morgan for an 11-0 victory, Ken was able to tick one of the two remaining empty boxes in his personal portfolio. The tourists may have lost 14 of the 30 matches played on the British Isles sector of the tour but the defeat at Rodney Parade was the biggest and Newport were the only side against which the Wallabies failed to register any points. As for that other box; Cardiff would always nettle him but, at the end of the day, nobody's perfect.

With no outside distractions, Ken played a full part in Newport's season, appearing in 32 of the 42 matches. One fewer than in 1956–57, but once again confirming his ongoing commitment to the cause in those final years. The hat-trick of tries scored against Newbridge in the previous April took his total for the club to 133 and put him in second place in the list of Newport's leading try scorers. Only the great Arthur Gould with 136 had scored more, and it was only a matter of time before that long-standing record would be broken. Ken's record-breaking try came against the Watsonians with the number increased to 146 by the end of the season. His 292 games for the club put him in seventh position on the all-time list, but he could only watch as his world record number of international appearances was improved on when Jack Kyle won a 45th cap at Twickenham before improving the figure to 46 against Scotland at Lansdowne Road. The goalposts had been moved and would continue to be; 50 years later the record held by Australian scrum-half George Gregan stood at 139.

It would be 20 years before Ken's record number of Welsh caps and tries would come under threat; statistics that would hold sway until the great teams of the 1970s set the rugby world alight.

So, how did it all end? If one were perfectly honest it would have to be said that Ken Jones' final appearances for Newport were also something of an anticlimax. Those responsible for compiling the fixture list may have been a bit more helpful. When the last home match of the season took place against the Barbarians on 8 April, five away matches were still to be played followed by the Welsh Sevens, which in 1958 were held in Cardiff. When the Barbarians arrived at Rodney Parade for that last home match of the 1957–58 season they faced a team unbeaten in its last 13 outings. Led by current England captain Eric Evans, the visitors fielded a particularly strong back division made up entirely of Scottish and Irish internationals. Arthur Smith and Cecil Pedlow were familiar names from Ken's international days but Gordon Waddell, Ken Scotland, Mickey English, Andy Mulligan and Dion Glass represented the next generation.

Both teams stood aside, allowing Ken the opportunity to soak up the welcome as he ran onto the Rodney Parade turf for the last time. Spectators filling the large grandstand joined those on the terraces, standing as one in recognition of a truly great clubman who had played the game with distinction while maintaining a level of modesty that deserved every moment of the extended applause.

The match rose to the occasion with Newport running out 13-8 winners but there was no try from the right wing, although Ken did make the initial break that led to the Bryn Meredith try that secured victory in the final minutes of what was a thrilling encounter. Ken Jones was carried shoulder high from the field to further applause, knowing that in a few short weeks it would all be over. Before the final curtain could be brought down there was a little more rugby to be played and four days later Newport set off on their end-of-season tour of the West Country and matches against Plymouth, Devonport Services and Exeter – a well-trodden path.

With comfortable victories against Plymouth and Devonport, Newport arrived in Exeter in good shape with the unbeaten run now extended to 16 matches. Record crowds had welcomed the players at Plymouth and the Services' ground and it was the same when Newport ran out at Exeter. In the visitors' dressing room minutes before the teams were due to take the field Ken approached Norman Morgan, Newport's full-back and recognised goal kicker, with a most unexpected request. He had kept it to himself throughout his long career but with time running out Ken had little option than to make known his ambition to attempt a kick at goal. What could Morgan say? The outcome of the match could depend on the success or otherwise of a place kick which led to a compromise; if Ken scored a try under the posts then Morgan would hand over the kicking duties.

Two first-half tries by Geoff Whitson and one by Jones, who touched down nearer the corner flag than the posts, gave Newport a 15-6 interval lead and there had been no further scoring as the match entered its final minute. With one last attacking move the Newport backs freed the right wing, who had the pace and wherewithal to beat the defence before making his way to the posts for that all-important touchdown. A smiling Norman Morgan looked on as Ken placed the ball before executing the perfect conversion to great acclaim from players of both teams and the enthusiastic crowd, who would have been fully aware that they were watching a unique moment. When the boots were hung up for the last time Ken's scoring record for Newport RFC would now read – 146 tries, 1 conversion.

If the final curtain could not be lowered after the Barbarians match, then Exeter on a pleasant April evening would have provided a reasonable alternative, but there still remained away trips to Neath and Llanelly. It was at these rugby strongholds in west Wales that Ken Jones would make his final appearances in the 15-man game before finally bowing out at Cardiff Arms Park in the Sevens. As was to be expected, Newport found both the Welsh All Blacks and the Scarlets less than compromising opponents and after going down by the narrowest of margins at the Gnoll, Newport beaten 6-5, Llanelly piled on the misery, winning convincingly by 11 points to 6.

The Barbarians or Exeter might have provided satisfactory closure but two end-of-season defeats away from home certainly didn't. Some compensation could be taken if Newport were to retain the Welsh Sevens title and in so doing make it three wins in a row in the tournament. With victories over Maesteg, Cardiff and Neath in the early rounds only Ebbw Vale stood between the Black and Ambers and the trophy. On paper there looked to be only one winner; Jones was joined in his last appearance on a rugby field by Clive Lewis, Harry Morgan, Norman Morgan, Brian Cresswell, Bryn Meredith and Glyn Davidge. Ebbw Vale were the tournament's surprise package and in beating Newport 10-5 in the final proved to be anything but the icing on the cake.

Despite the sting in the tail of Newport's long and hard season it is not difficult to argue that for Wales' most capped player there could only be one ground, other than Rodney Parade, on which to end his playing days. Cardiff Arms Park had been witness to many of Ken Jones' finest moments on a rugby field but it had also been the scene of some of the most disappointing, notably the defeats at the hands of the resident club when all else tended to pale into insignificance. The beauty of sport is its unpredictability, the fact that on occasion even the biggest underdog can steal the thunder of the greatest of champions. Ken experienced both the highs and the lows during his distinguished careers in athletics and rugby football but at the final reckoning the overall statistics weighed comfortably in his favour in both arenas.

When asked which of the many feats of derring-do figured uppermost in his personal list of recollections Ken was never less than diplomatic: it could have been the try that brought about the downfall of the New Zealand All Blacks; the drama surrounding the relay at the 1948 Olympic Games; his tour with the British Lions; leading the Great Britain athletics team in Berne at the European Games; his record number of appearances for Wales; the 1954 British Empire and Commonwealth Games; or his life-long love affair with Newport Athletic Club and Rodney Parade. Undecided he may have been about these and many other notable achievements, but assured a place on any shortlist was a day in July 1958 that would take him back to Cardiff Arms Park where for one last time Wales' finest sportsman would be the focus of attention.

With the rugby season over, the contractors could move into the Arms Park and begin the task of making it ready to host a major athletics meeting. As at Wembley Stadium in 1948, surrounding the famous pitch was a greyhound track used by Cardiff Greyhound Racing Club for much of the year. This provided a popular diversion from the rugby football for which the ground was famous but if Cardiff was to host a successful Games then the dogs would have to find a temporary home at which to chase the hare. The issue became the subject of much debate before all the involved parties finally agreed that the greyhound racing would be relocated, the track dug up and a six-lane, purpose-built cinder running track constructed in its place. It was a bit of a squeeze, only inches separating the outside lane from the public enclosures, but all the international standards were met and any doubts that may have been raised regarding the suitability of the venue were finally laid to rest.

Athletics being only one of several sports to cater for, suitable venues had to be found to accommodate other activities sure to attract much public interest. A purpose-built swimming pool was positioned adjacent to the stadium while the boxing competition would be held at nearby Sophia Gardens. With the exception of the rowing events, which were held in north Wales, the Games took place in and around the city of Cardiff. The athletes' village was built on the RAF base at St Athan, from where the competitors would be bussed the short distances to the various venues. More shades of Wembley in 1948, when Ken Jones was among the many competitors housed at RAF Uxbridge from where they too were bussed to the stadium and the other designated locations.

The £300,000 cost of staging the VIth British and Empire Commonwealth Games in Cardiff seems small change when compared with the money spent on hosting major sporting events in the twenty-first century; amounts counted in billions rather than thousands. The Organising Committee carried out many fund-raising events and before the games got under way more than £100,000 of the projected outlay had been raised. When the dust finally settled, the number crunchers would report that the Games made a profit in excess of £35,000, a remarkable achievement when one considers the lack of any sponsorship or corporate involvement. In 1958, Cardiff showed what a group of committed individuals could get done and how the Welsh public fully supported the whole process – build it and they will come!

When it was announced that a message from Her Majesty Queen Elizabeth II was to be sent by relay from Buckingham Palace to Cardiff, there was much speculation as to who the last runner would be; the person given the honour of carrying the baton containing the missive into the stadium and handing it to the Duke of Edinburgh. The first leg from the palace was run by a trio of athletes: Roger Bannister, Chris Chataway and Peter Driver were chosen to start the journey which saw the baton carried from London, through the Midlands and into Wales with hundreds of chosen representatives from local clubs and schools running legs of one or two miles. Each would have a story to tell, each would remember the small part they played in getting the message to Cardiff, but for the person chosen to run the shortest leg, the honour would be the greatest. From the dressing rooms in the bowels of the stadium, onto the track, where one circuit would be completed before arriving at the dais, was little more than 500 yards but the final runner would be carrying the expectations of a proud nation with him every step of the way. Beyond the inner sanctums of committee rooms and council chambers, the identity of the mystery runner remained a well-kept secret.

One person who was privy to the name of the last runner was to be found in a private ward at Panteg Hospital, Pontypool. On her doctor's recommendation, Irene Jones was admitted to hospital in June, 20 weeks before she was due to give birth. Earlier complications had resulted in heartbreak for the couple so desperate to start a family and this latest pregnancy could well be the last opportunity they would have. Three babies had each been born prematurely, none of the two boys and girl surviving beyond 24 hours.

In hospital there would be doctors and nurses constantly on hand and all the necessary tests and monitoring could be done on a regular basis leaving nothing to chance; all Irene had to do was be a good girl, do as she was told, relax and let nature take its course. Not easy when your husband is about to meet a member of the royal family in front of 30,000 spectators plus untold numbers who would watch the celebrations unfold live on television. And it was on television that Irene watched Ken enter the stadium and begin his lap of the track before coming to a halt in front of the Duke of Edinburgh. Ken had set up the small television in the ward earlier in the week and on the day Irene invited the duty staff to join her and watch the BBC coverage of the opening ceremony. The surprise shown by the doctors and nurses when the cameras focused on Ken making his way around the track confirmed the secret was well kept, certainly within the confines of Panteg Hospital.

In the weeks building up to the Games there was much speculation that the track was not up to scratch. Ken Jones was one of those invited to try it out and confirmed it as 'first class. In fact it is as good as any I have ever seen or raced on'. Readers of the *Sunday Express* would also have learned that after training on it, the New Zealand team also spoke favourably of the new surface, 880yds runner Don Smith considering it 'as good as the White City'.

The article from which these quotes are taken was one of the first filed by Ken Jones in his new vocation as a sports journalist. Not a full-time job – the tyre industry continued to pay the bills – but it saw Ken follow in the footsteps of such Welsh rugby luminaries as Vivian Jenkins, Wilf Wooller and Bleddyn Williams, who had all turned their hand to reporting at the end of their playing days. Ken found himself in good company on the sports pages of the leading Sunday paper; Danny Blanchflower wrote on football; Denis Compton covered cricket; and before becoming a best-selling novelist, Dick Francis reported on horse racing. Writing for the *Sunday Express* would become a year-round occupation for Ken as he covered both athletics and rugby football and he would continue to contribute to the newspaper for the next 29 years.

Ken's was a gentle introduction to the world of journalism, lead writer Alan Hoby contributing the major pieces. That would change come September when he would report on rugby at both club and international level, but it was in the press box at Cardiff's Games that he started to learn his trade. The first piece of actual reportage appeared on 20 July. Under the heading 'Gardner Felt at Home!' Ken Jones wrote 'At 5.8 [*sic*] pm yesterday starter JW Aspland set off the greatest sprint final in the history of the Empire Games and 9.4sec later Jamaican Keith Gardner was crowned the fastest man in the Empire...' So began an unexpected change of direction and a week later Ken was eulogising how 'Never have I felt prouder to be a Welshman than when the sixth Empire and Commonwealth Games [*sic*] ended in a blaze of glory at the famous Cardiff Arms Park yesterday. And Welshmen everywhere can be proud of the way in which these Games have been presented...' Ken quickly got into his stride behind the keys of a typewriter and in the following years readers would come to expect nothing less than informative and insightful words from someone who had been there and done it – the byline 'Ken Jones' guaranteed essential reading.

On Sunday 17 August 1958 Philip Jeffrey Jones was born at Panteg Hospital. For the fourth time Irene had given birth to a child several weeks prematurely, and with young Philip weighing in at only 4lb there was once more cause for concern. The baby survived those crucial first 24 hours, he survived the next day and the one after that and as the measurement of time began to be counted in weeks, so did his chances of survival improve. Irene had entered hospital in June and in October she was finally allowed to leave, taking with her a son who now weighed more than six pounds; it was the happiest day of Mr and Mrs Kenneth Jones' lives.

Fairoak Lane became the scene of much coming and going in those first weeks but the family soon settled into a routine familiar to many. While father went off to work Monday to Friday, mother would stay at home and look after the new arrival with Ginger the cat trying to decide what to make of it all. Weekends would see Ken tending the garden, washing the car and driving his family to Blaenavon on Sunday afternoons – a typical picture of domesticity in Britain at the end of the 1950s.

The joy of Philip's arrival was tempered by the death of Ken's father, Jack Jones passing away two weeks after the birth of his grandson. Working in the mines was not a healthy occupation and after a long fight with pneumoconiosis, Jack joined the large number of men who died as a result of working long hours in the dust-filled atmosphere found underground.

Saturdays were much as they had always been, with Ken going off to an athletics meeting or rugby match, but now he was involved from the outside, from the confines of the press box. Often he would be found sitting at the back of the grandstand at Rodney Parade in the designated press seats from where he could file his reports by telephone, but his role as roving reporter took him to all the major clubs. In those early months he reported from Cardiff Arms Park, Stradey Park Llanelli, St Helen's Swansea, Abertillery Park and Penarth. He also covered the Welsh trial matches and identified the Pontypool centre Malcolm Price together with London Welsh loose forward John Leleu as men ready to win their first caps. He was also among the first to champion the cause of a young student from Carmarthen Training College who played a few games for Swansea during the first half of the season.

When the Welsh team to play England in Cardiff was confirmed, Price and Leleu were included, as was 20-year-old Dewi Bebb, who would play on the left wing after only five first-class matches for Swansea. Reporting on the match, Jones was able to highlight the performance of Bebb in particular, who scored the game's only try to give Wales a 5-0 victory, and there were also favourable comments on Price and Leleu.

Readers would quickly recognise that there was more to Ken Jones' columns than they might have expected from one who spent his playing days out on the wing. He showed a complete understanding of all aspects of play and, as seen when he recognised the three aforementioned players, was a respected observer of new talent. More importantly, he was always ready to discuss a player's shortcomings and nothing could have been more difficult than when this involved someone he had recently shared a dressing room with. Wales' disappointing performance in Paris in 1959 attracted some adverse comment and how hard it must have been to report that 'Malcolm Thomas had a poor game at outside-half'. The 11-3 defeat marked the end of Thomas' international career.

In 1960, Ken decided to leave Bicester Tyres and set up in business on his own. He would remain in the industry but put the knowledge and experience gained over the past four years to his own advantage. Ken Jones Tyres opened depots in Newport and nearby Caerphilly and would continue to trade for the next 13 years. This was also the year in which he received recognition for his services to sport from on high. Ken would have lost count of the number of functions organised in his honour by the people of Blaenavon and Newport but this latest invitation was very different. When the letter bearing the impressive insignia landed on the doormat it bore news of a most unexpected nature – Ken Jones was included in the Queen's Birthday Honours List and was invited to become an Officer of the Order of the British Empire.

A memorable day in London saw the Jones family arrive at Buckingham Palace in force, Ken's mother and sister Phyllis accompanying him and Irene on the journey to the capital. With only two additional invitations extended to each recipient it was Irene and Ken's mother who proudly watched as he stood in front of Queen Elizabeth to receive his medal. Then it was outside for the photographs that would record the event for posterity, Ken smartly kitted out in top hat and tails as his nearest and dearest proudly looked on.

The decision to set up in business on his own was not only significant based on the financial ramifications involved but was one that would impact on life in general. It may have been many years coming, but by the 1960s Ken Jones was at last enjoying something resembling a private life, one in which the demands on his time from the traditional sources had all but dried up. This was no bad thing after the years in which he was considered 'public property', years during which there was rarely time to get away from the attentions of the media and the man on the street.

Ken had never been one to seek out the limelight and within a few years of playing his last match he could relax in the knowledge that, while it was nice to know that somebody might point him out as he walked down the street, rarely would he be approached for an autograph or be expected to talk about Saturday's match on demand.

By establishing his own business and calling it Ken Jones Tyres, he was effectively forfeiting all such privacy by putting himself back in the public domain, where he would undoubtedly be expected to enter into long conversations with customers and tradespeople about the current state of Welsh rugby and athletics.

Having sacrificed the holidays and free weekends associated with the teaching profession for a regular nine-to-five job, Ken now had to accept that while being self-employed had obvious advantages, it also meant working much longer hours, never being able to totally switch off from the daily routine. If this in itself were not sufficiently demanding, having to drive from Croesyceiliog to Caerphilly and Newport on a daily basis also became an additional burden, but one which could be easily remedied.

In 1964, the Jones family upped roots and headed west, beyond Newport to Cardiff and a new home in the city's affluent Roath Park area. Overlooking the large lake at which the city folk spent much of their leisure time, the new home was only a short distance from Caerphilly and the tyre depot on Nantgarw Road while at the same time being within easy driving distance of Newport. Living in Cardiff also offered the added bonus of making the journeys to Neath, Llanelli and Swansea much shorter when the *Sunday Express* wanted to cover the big matches taking place in west Wales.

Ken Jones enjoyed 12 seasons playing first-class rugby football, seasons in which the game underwent few significant changes in the Laws. Fine tuning would best describe the majority of Law amendments introduced between 1946 and 1958, with the reduction in value of a drop goal from four points to three and the awarding of a try after a player's momentum had carried him over the goal line the notable exceptions. During his 29 years in the press box the game underwent many further changes, changes that were introduced in an attempt to make the game more appealing to players and spectators alike – to put the accent on the scoring of tries.

How Ken would have enjoyed the wide open spaces made available by the new offside Laws introduced at scrum and line-out; the outlawing of a direct kick to touch out of hand unless a player was inside his own 25-yard line; and the increase in the value of a try to four points. These improvements were well received by a man who knew only too well what it was like to stand on the touchline waiting for the ball, but interviewed in 1971 he took the opportunity to air his discontent with much that was happening to the game within Wales.

The great Welsh teams of the 1970s would do much to promote rugby union and perhaps Ken Jones was a little premature when suggesting that there were not as many good players around as in his day, that the general standard was not as high, but other observations were pertinent in relation to the game, not only in the early 1970s but into the twenty-first century. He bemoaned the fact that the number of schools at which the game was played had reduced and that there were many alternative pastimes in which pupils could indulge themselves, and he accurately pinpointed the demise of so many valley towns as a major concern.

Many of the great players had learned the game at the smaller clubs found nestled in the network of valleys before gravitating to the major clubs dotted along the coast. How important then that the Newports and Cardiffs should be developing local talent at a time when the traditional sources of talent were so under threat. Looking further ahead, he feared the almost certain arrival of leagues would have a detrimental effect on clubs in Wales, and then there was the added threat of professionalism. Talk of players being paid to play rugby union football was like a red rag to a bull. Kenneth Jones deplored such a suggestion, would never condone it and when the inevitable happened in 1995, it saw him dissociate himself from the game for good.

Those comments made in 1971 regarding the quality of the players plying their trade at the time were drastically reviewed as the decade unfolded. Ken's enthusiasm for the game and the players who took Wales to new heights in the 1970s leapt off the pages.

Ken Jones had played a significant role in what became known as the second Golden Era of Welsh rugby, and nothing would have given him greater pleasure than to be able to report on the uplifting performances that produced three Grand Slams and five Triple Crowns in the third. Ken was never sparing in his praise for Gareth Edwards, Barry John, JPR Williams, Phil Bennett, Gerald Davies, Mervyn Davies, the Pontypool front row and the many other stars of the day.

He also wrote with great enthusiasm when Edwards broke the Welsh try-scoring record, which Ken had shared for over 20 years. The scrum-half notched up his 18th against Ireland in 1976 and two weeks later Ken watched as his individual record of 44 caps was bettered by the same player – defining moments in the career of Welsh rugby's finest. As Edwards prepared to make his record-breaking 45th appearance, Ken Jones discussed the prospect with fellow *Sunday Express* reporter Michael Boon.

> *How will I feel? Perhaps a little sad… but also some pride of my own that the man who takes the record from me has made an impact on rugby that almost defies description. Out of this world… I dislike trying to make comparisons but the case of Gareth Edwards is an exception. He is simply a super great. The finest player of my lifetime of watching, playing and reporting rugby football. Haydn Tanner and Rex Willis for example were superb scrum-halves but Gareth stands above them both and above all others too.'*

Although playing different positions in different eras, comparisons between Jones and Edwards are inevitable. Jones' record as an international athlete elevates him beyond rugby alone while Edwards' competence as a gymnast, tennis player and potential international hurdler also take his all-round athleticism further than the rugby field. As Ken recognised, '…he (Edwards) illustrates the advice I have given so often to rugby players; never go to sleep in the summer. In fact my dedication to athletics was greater than my dedication to rugby. In the summer I trained six days a week and competed on the seventh.'

Reporting from the Welsh Championships held at Maindy Stadium on 25 July 1964, Ken saw Lynn Davies win the 100yds in 9.6 before setting a new United Kingdom all-comers and AAA National record in the long jump with a leap of 26ft 4 inches (8.02 metres). Few outside the sport would remember Lynn Davies as a sprint champion, his gold medal in the long jump at the 1964 Olympic Games in Tokyo the lasting impression of his distinguished athletics career. However, he was one of the first to improve on a record created by Ken Jones who would in due course advise his readers that all he once laid claim to had been passed on to others.

At the end of 2010, Gareth Thomas was Wales' most capped player with 100 appearances to his name and Shane Williams had scored 51 international tries. With the advent of a fully integrated metric system and automatic timing, Ken Jones' Welsh records on the track cannot be compared with the performances of athletes running 50 years later. Hand-recorded times on a stopwatch are a thing of the past but those once held by Ken were all broken before timing systems were improved. His 9.8 record for the 100yds was improved by Ron Jones and Lynn Davies to 9.5 and the 100m record of 10.6 recorded at the 1948 Olympic Games was lowered to 10.3 by Berwyn Jones and Ron Jones. Ken also created a new hand-timed record of 21.7 for the 200m in Oslo in 1949, which was broken by Ron Jones before resting with Howard Davies of Newport Harriers, who clocked a time of 20.8 before the use of stopwatches was finally dispensed with.

There can be little doubt that Ken Jones enjoyed his years in the press box. This second 'career' continued into his 66th year, a period of 29 years that saw him keep company not only with Vivian Jenkins, Bleddyn Williams and Wilf Wooller, but also men for whom rugby journalism was a full time occupation: JBG Thomas and John Billot of the *Western Mail*; John Reason of the *Daily Telegraph*; the *Guardian*'s David Frost and Pat Marshall of the *Daily Express* among them. In his final years as rugby correspondent for the *Sunday Express*, some of the names more familiar to the reading public in the twenty-first century had joined the press corps, including Stephen Jones of the *Sunday Times*, Peter Jackson, who moved from the *South Wales Echo* to become rugby correspondent with the *Daily Mail*, and David Hands of *The Times*. All fair men whose astute observations came to be reckoned with, men with whom Ken shared a love and understanding of the game.

The passion the game of rugby football generates in Wales is highlighted when the national team plays in Cardiff. All roads lead to the city, and people from all walks of life find themselves united in a common cause. In the 1970s in particular, the great deeds performed by the great players and great teams of the day reached a worldwide audience and if you were a Welshman living away from home, when Wales were playing at Cardiff Arms Park was the time to head back.

The Royal Hotel on Cardiff's St Mary Street was a favoured watering hole of the Welsh Rugby Writers' Association of which Ken was a member, and it also attracted the many celebrities who would arrive in the city on match day. Ken Jones kept company with the likes of Richard Burton and Elizabeth Taylor, Stanley Baker, Peter O'Toole and Richard Harris when Ireland were in town, and other famous figures from the world of entertainment, all keen to listen to one of Wales' finest discourse on the game which they all loved.

Interviewed in 1971, Ken Jones enthused over the proposed introduction of a Welsh Cup, a knock-out tournament that would give the small clubs a chance to compete against the big guns and produce the occasional upset.

In the following years he would visit many of the smaller clubs in the Principality in search of an upset to report, a David and Goliath contest that saw the underdog triumph. Blaina, Hendy, Crynant, Taff's Well, Senghenydd and Ysrtadgynlais all welcomed the rugby legend into their clubhouses on days when they played host to the likes of Cardiff, Llanelli or Bridgend. Such matches saw grass roots rugby at its best, but any suggestions regarding the introduction of leagues were treated with something tantamount to disdain. He realised that the additional competitive edge that a league structure that included promotion and relegation would bring to the game could only lead to one thing – professionalism.

When the WRU first tried to introduce leagues as far back as 1908, the proposal met with resistance from the major clubs and came to nought. In 1975, a similar scheme was put before the member clubs, of which 72 per cent were in favour, but again it was the wishes of the big clubs that, although they were very much a minority, once again carried the day. Ken's days as a reporter were in the past when the WRU finally introduced a four-league structure in the 1990–91 season. The invitation to participate was extended to 38 clubs: a Premiership Division in which ten clubs would take part; eight clubs would contest the First Division; and Divisions Two and Three would each include another ten clubs.

Sponsored by Heineken, the Premier Division winners would receive a cheque for £23,000 and in the lower leagues, the Division One champions would be presented with £14,750, the top club in Division Two £10,450 and the winners of Division Three a very welcome £5,750. The writing was on the wall. If players weren't already receiving a financial backhander for their services they soon would be and Ken Jones' greatest fear looked to be a racing certainty – you wouldn't get double carpet on this. It was just a matter of time before rugby union would become a professional sport.

CHAPTER TWELVE

THE CLOCK STOPS

If Ken Jones had belonged to a later generation and had elected to play professional rugby, what would his earning potential have been? Hypothetical this may be but it is safe to say there would have been a lot of money on the table. Other than by following up the interest shown by rugby league clubs, which he rejected out of hand, Ken's long involvement in sport could never pay the bills, never put food on the table. It was money earned during the seven years spent teaching at Newport High School and the subsequent career move into selling, together with Irene's income, that set up the couple, allowing them to buy a house and lay the foundations for a solid financial future.

With a semblance of security in place, it was a brave move to set himself up in business, put his name over the doors and hope the customers came flocking through them. That they did, and in sufficient numbers to reward the proprietor with a comfortable lifestyle, cannot be solely as a result of any goodwill the name Ken Jones carried in the local community. Undoubtedly there would have been an initial influx of business generated by the prospect of meeting one of Wales' finest sportsmen as the new tyres were being fitted, but this was a short-term fix and not the basis on which a sound business could be built. That would be based on hard work, competitive pricing and the three most important factors – location, location, location.

For a decade or more Ken Jones Tyres was a successful business, but by the 1970s outside influences began to come into play, factors over which a hard-working, self-employed retailer had no control. Factors up against which the name above the door counted for nothing: industrial unrest that led to strike action being taken; the closure of the docks; a wages and prices freeze; the three-day working week; and national power cuts. All these and more conspired to make life extremely difficult.

More significant to Ken's situation was the opening of the first Kwik-Fit tyre depot in Edinburgh in 1971, which was soon followed by many more outlets throughout the UK. Here was a national company offering a complete service at very competitive rates which made life difficult for small, independent retailers and it was with a mixture of disappointment and relief that Ken Jones Tyres ceased trading in 1973.

When he turned his back on the teaching profession in 1956, it is highly unlikely Ken would have envisaged ever returning to it but following the closure of his business, that is exactly what he did.

By 1973, the family had moved back to Newport, buying a property in Bassaleg, a village to the west of the town which was home to a grammar school with a fine reputation for academic and sporting achievement and where Philip would complete his school days. The son of a famous rugby player carries a certain level of expectancy if he decides to play the game at school, and laying claim to a famous father is not always something to be shouted from the rooftops. So found Philip Jones as he made his way through the school teams, playing in the unlikely position of prop forward before later moving back to the second row.

His father was instructed that under no circumstances was he to walk down to the school playing fields on a Saturday morning to watch his offspring perform. No different to any other proud father interested in following his son's progress, Ken disregarded such pleas and was often to be seen standing on the touchline as Philip kept his head down trying to pretend he wasn't there. This led to much banter between father and son, but Philip perhaps held the advantage with the knowledge that what Ken knew about the intricacies of the front and second rows of a scrum wouldn't fill the back of a postage stamp and an impasse of sorts was arrived at.

Fortunately for Philip, his father's return to teaching was not at Bassaleg High School but at Croesyceiliog Grammar School, a stone's throw from Fairoak Lane where the family were living when Philip was born. Ken spent one summer term at the school before transferring to nearby Llantarnam High School, where he would spend 11 years until retiring in 1986.

At 53 years of age there was no return to the gymnasium and playing fields but a working day spent in the classroom that saw Ken teaching the most fundamental of subjects – English. In many ways things had travelled full circle from those early days in teaching, the obvious exception being that come Saturday, rather than making his way to the team's changing room, Ken now headed for the press box.

Never for a moment thinking he would return to his chosen profession, Ken soon found himself embracing the education system with renewed enthusiasm and his second spell would last six years longer than the first. It all came to an end in June 1986 and a year later Ken Jones submitted his final report to the *Sunday Express*. Retirement beckoned.

The family continued to live in Bassaleg until Philip completed his formal education. For three years Ken travelled the comparatively short distance to Llantarnam but in 1976 the opportunity to buy an attractive property on the outskirts of Newport and only a stone's throw from the school proved far too attractive a proposition to pass on. Once more the boxes were packed and the short haul across the town saw the Jones family decamp to Pillmawr Road, Malpas.

A large property, Tregarth sits in half an acre of landscaped gardens which do not look after themselves. Fortunately, Ken had acquired a love of gardening and was blessed with green fingers which were put to good use at every opportunity. The school day over, he would return home and immediately set about tending the garden: cutting the large lawns and hedges; maintaining the flower beds and vegetable patch; and undertaking the basic groundwork during the winter months that would ensure all was ready come spring.

The routine continued for ten years until Ken received his last pay cheque. A quarter of a century later people would hold mixed views on the thorny issue of retirement and pensions. For some, the attraction of being paid off at 50 or 55 years of age proves irresistible while for others, having both the opportunity and ability to continue doing the day job well into their sixties and beyond is equally desirable. But for Ken, calling it a day at 65 seemed about right – goodness knows he had done his bit. There may have been a few unwanted pounds in the most obvious places and his waist measurement might have increased a tad but overall, here was a fit and able-bodied man ready to make the most of his retirement.

With Philip settled at Bassaleg Grammar, the chance to return to teaching saw Irene join her husband in the profession she had also elected to pursue many moons before. This time there would be no walking to work together before parting company at the top of the school drive. All farewells would be on the drive at home before Ken headed to Llantarnam and Irene set off for Maindee School in Newport, a short distance from Summerhill Avenue, bringing back memories of those early days when the couple originally settled in the town. Irene remained at Maindee until her retirement in 1984.

To maintain a high level of fitness for an extended period of time requires dedication. It not only means an intensive training regime but making sacrifices that are not always easily accommodated. For many years rugby and beer were synonymous with each other – play hard and play hard would be a fair description of a typical match day. As a generalisation and on a scale of one to ten, a prop forward would be in the first division when it came to the after-match celebrations and a wing or full-back down in the fourth. There have been some notable exceptions, but Ken Jones wasn't one. No surprise there, but elsewhere things were very different indeed. Ken smoked, enjoying a cigarette or two or three. Now that is surprising!

Herbert Lewis, a former colleague at Newport High School, likened the atmosphere in the masters' common room to a London fog, from which we can only assume that abstinence was of little significance. Ken was a contributing factor rather than a passive smoker but there are great differences of opinion on this. Irene Jones is adamant that Ken didn't take up smoking until later in life, after his playing days had ended. Others beg to differ.

One close associate in the changing room offered the theory that 'Jonesy would smoke ten cigarettes a day during the rugby season but reduce it to five when he was in training during the summer months...'. You pay your money and you take your choice. If Ken did enjoy the occasional puff or two during his playing days then good luck to him, and any such habit certainly didn't appear to impact on his performances. Today's fitness and health experts would argue otherwise, suggesting he might have produced better performances without the influence of the wicked weed. But what the heck! The days of being frowned upon when lighting up were a long way off. In the post-war era the very opposite prevailed, so why shouldn't a leading sportsman, one who didn't get a sou for his labours, partake if he chose to do so?

Ken Jones

In 1987, rugby union took another important step on the road that would lead to its becoming a professional sport. The first Rugby World Cup took place in New Zealand where, against all the odds, Wales played admirably to reach the semi-finals where they met a New Zealand team that would go on to win the tournament. By defeating Australia in a play-off, the Welsh team secured third place, leading to talk of another golden era. A Triple Crown in 1988 provided more cause for optimism but it proved to be a false dawn. The national team quickly fell from grace with all talk of a golden era soon put on the back burner, replaced by condemnation and ridicule. Wales won only eight championship matches between 1988 and 1995 and lost all nine played against the southern hemisphere powers, some in most disturbing fashion when 30, 40, 50 and, on one particularly bad day at the office, 60 points were conceded.

The WRU saw the introduction of leagues as a way of improving all-round standards. Ken Jones had always been outspoken in his opposition to such a move but when the 1990–91 season got under way he had to sit back in the hope that time would prove him wrong. After determining how many clubs would constitute each league, Newport RFC was disappointed to find itself in the second tier. At the end of the season the club would be crowned champions of the First Division and promoted to the Premier Division. This was timely as Newport Athletic Club was due to announce its new president, a successor to RT 'Bob' Evans who had decided to stand down from the position. At the first suitable opportunity nominations were invited from committee members. Proposed by Evans and seconded by chairman Brian Jones, the next on the list of distinguished men elected president of the famous club would be Kenneth Jeffrey Jones.

This honorary position was the highest accolade the club could bestow. By recognising the enormous contribution made by Ken Jones during his long association with Newport Athletic Club the committee made a popular choice, one which met with no opposition when the raised hands were counted. Ken's involvement with the actual running of the club was minimal, but by having such a high-profile individual as its president, whenever the need to roll out the red carpet arose, then the right man was in place to conduct any formalities.

With no written mandate regarding the tenure of a president, his election was viewed as long term and well it might have been if not for a set of circumstances beyond the control of any committee at Newport Athletic Club, circumstances that saw Ken resign and totally sever any connection with the game that he had played with such distinction.

Before such dramatic events unfolded there was an opportunity to revisit the country where he had played some of the best rugby of his career. In 1993, the British Lions under the captaincy of Scotland's Gavin Hastings toured New Zealand and it was that highlight of the rugby calendar which prompted the return. Joining Ken on board the plane for the long flight to the Land of the Long White Cloud was Bleddyn Williams. The pair were feted, wined and dined, treated to the finest hospitality on match days, and lauded wherever they went; followers of the game in New Zealand ever mindful of the great players of yesteryear.

It was a three-week trip that resurrected the wonderful memories of 1950, while also presenting the opportunity to meet up with many of the All Blacks who had proved such formidable opponents. But how times had changed. In 1950, a total of eight players from the Cardiff and Newport clubs toured with the Lions; now there wasn't a representative from either. Not since the early missionary tours of the 1880s and 1890s had both clubs been ignored by the selectors. In a squad dominated by 17 players from England, the Welsh contingent was a disappointing five, which only confirmed the current plight of the game in Wales.

The visit 'down under' not only allowed Ken to take a trip down Memory Lane but it also went some way toward confirming what the future held in store. The rumour mills were not confined to the northern hemisphere; they were also working overtime in one of rugby union's strongholds and the message generated was much the same – it wasn't a case of if the game would turn professional, but when. The demands on international players' time were becoming intolerable with an ever-expanding fixture list that encroached into the preserve of the summer months that had once been protected with such great vigilance.

The players may have been seen as the victims in the escalating issue, with the International Rugby Board, the game's governing body, handed the role of pantomime villain, but in truth the die was cast. Ken Jones didn't need to travel to the end of the world for confirmation of what in his heart of hearts he already knew, but talking with like-minded people, ex-All Blacks who also viewed the developments with much suspicion and anger, told him he should prepare for the worst.

Speaking on behalf of the IRB from a Paris hotel on Sunday 27 August 1995, Vernon Pugh QC informed the throng of pressmen filling the conference space that with immediate effect rugby union would become a professional sport. This was a desperately sad day for Ken but, even allowing for the fact that he was a staunch advocate of amateur rugby football, his reaction to the news came as a shock to many, not least those who knew him best. He wrote to Newport Athletic Club confirming his decision to stand down from the position of president with immediate effect, and any attempts to persuade him to rethink his decision fell on deaf ears.

Nobody could convince Ken that he should move with the times, swallow his pride and accept that the game had moved on. Here was an angry and upset man, one who felt a certain betrayal when the game was declared open, and it was a poignant day indeed when he eventually decided to remove all his memorabilia from the museum at Rodney Parade.

These were sad days indeed for someone whose life was so steeped in the recent history of Welsh rugby. Looking back from a distance some 15 years later it is not easy to fully understand what fuelled such an extreme reaction. Other players of Ken's era may not have endorsed the move to professional rugby, but neither would they turn their backs on the game. Bleddyn Williams and Jack Matthews were ever present at Cardiff and Wales home matches, maybe watching with some discomfort in the knowledge that the players on view were receiving financial reward for their endeavours, but still lending their support from the sidelines.

Likewise at Rodney Parade, where many of Ken's contemporaries were also not prepared to forfeit their Saturday afternoon enjoyment for the sake of a principle, even one that stuck in the craw as much as the issue of professionalism did. So why did Ken Jones take such great exception to what in the eyes of most was a natural progression, the only way forward if the future of rugby union was not to fall into the hands of the mavericks who were waiting in the wings, cheque book in hand, ready to ambush the game and turn it into a global circus? In truth it would not appear that he had a logical reason with which to argue the case other than the old chestnut: 'It wasn't like that in my day.' But to accept that simplistic view is to demean a man who held dear such strong principles.

The governing bodies of athletics had also accepted the reality that if you wanted the best performers to appear at events outside the major games then some form of payment would have to be made, and in time the sport would boast many wealthy individuals among its ranks. This would also have been difficult for Ken to rationalise and the combination of the two sports he held most dear moving away from all he stood for rested badly with him.

Perhaps there was a certain amount of envy, resentment even, that the current crop of rugby players and athletes were receiving not insignificant amounts of money for their time and effort. Nobody could put in more hours in their search for success than those with which Ken had been familiar; maybe he could not forget those eight years when one season rolled into the next, years when it was impossible for him to get off the treadmill. But that was his choice and he would have been the first to agree that he could have stopped the whole process any time he wanted to – but he didn't.

As words such as envy and resentment could never be applied to Ken Jones then we are left to assume that the reasons for his reaction to the arrival of professional rugby football in particular lay elsewhere. His working-class background was never far from his thoughts. He would visit Blaenavon at every given opportunity and as Philip remembers, 'If we went for a drive on a Sunday afternoon it didn't matter where we ended up, Dad would always make his way home via Blaenavon...'

As a young lad growing up in the 1920s and 1930s Ken was witness to much hardship. The men returning home after a day spent underground at the coal face or working the iron ore deposits, his father among them, were images that would remain with him. He knew that life could be tough, money was hard earned, and yet there was always a camaraderie between the men that showed him the real meaning of life – family and friendship. He embraced this simple ethos that was prevalent in any working society and carried it with him for the rest of his days.

The boys were never happier than when kicking around an old ball in the street or on a piece of wasteland. As one well-known blues singer recently observed, 'I started out with nothing and I've still got most of it left...' – Ken Jones would have related to that.

The word materialism was not in common use in the 1920s, if indeed it had even been introduced to the language, but there was still much to value in life, and having been brought up in a working-class environment Ken knew the meaning of fellowship and trust; honour and obedience; responsibility and reliability; all human traits that would serve him well. He also knew that after you worked hard, then the time to play hard would follow. That the two could ever be synonymous with one another never entered his head.

Adamant that his long association with rugby had ended there was, however, one connection that he did not sever. In 1985, a Black and Amber Former Players' Association was founded and Ken had been elected its first president. Its sole *raison d'être* was to bring together men who had played for the club in years gone by and on occasion meet with similar groups from other clubs whenever the fixture list allowed. Largely supported by players from the '50s and '60s, the association was one which Ken valued highly, and any personal grievances were put to one side whenever a chance to meet up with his old teammates presented itself.

In 1996, Ken celebrated his 75th birthday. The ten years since his retirement had passed all too quickly, but as was so often heard from people finding themselves in the same position, he didn't know how he had ever found the time to work. If he wasn't in the garden then he would be found in an armchair listening to his favourite operas. A regular supporter of the Welsh National Opera, frequent visits were made to the New Theatre in Cardiff to see that finest of companies perform and a long-standing ambition was satisfied when he visited Verona to attend the famous opera season held in the open air at the Arena.

In his later years, Ken also acquired an interest in modern history which took him to the First World War battlefields at Ypres, Passchendaele and the Somme. And there were many visits to Spain, where he and Irene had bought an apartment in Malaga. Ken was still very comfortable with life as he entered his 77th year. He could still carry out the everyday chores, even if he was a bit slower about it than had once been the case, and he was able to cope with the R&R as well as the next man. But all that was about to change.

On Saturday 4 April 1998 Ken attended a concert given by the Cwmbran Male Voice Choir in the nearby town.

He returned home in fine form, the hymns and arias still resonating in the depths of his mind, and headed off to bed looking forward to watching Wales play France at Wembley Stadium on the television the following afternoon. In the morning it was Irene who rose first, Ken reluctant to change the habit of a lifetime, but when she returned from the bathroom it was to find her husband collapsed at the side of the bed, unable to move or communicate, the victim of a massive stroke. She called for an ambulance before ringing Philip at his home in Cwmbran. He arrived at Tregarth shortly after, only to see his father being carried on a stretcher to a waiting ambulance.

Newport's Royal Gwent Hospital is situated on the opposite side of the town, but with little traffic cruising the roads early on Sunday morning, the three-mile journey was completed in good time. Ken Jones was handed over to the care and attention of those best qualified to cope with such emergencies and the waiting game began.

The initial prognosis was not good; Ken couldn't move and his speech was seriously impaired. So began four months of hospitalisation during which there was little cause for optimism, the immediate family left to ponder what the future may hold and whether or not Ken would ever be able to return home.

These were dark days. To see a man who once cut such a fine figure as an international athlete and rugby player now bedridden and unable to talk was heartbreaking. Ken's inability to swallow meant that food had to be drip fed directly into the stomach, a process not easily accommodated away from a hospital ward, but Irene and Philip were determined he should return home. This was one of three options available to them, the alternatives an extended stay in hospital or transfer to a care home.

If Ken were to return home then there was much to be done before the doctors would agree to the move. A living room was adapted to accommodate a large bed and the equipment needed to carry on the artificial feeding process. A walk-in cupboard was converted into a shower room and a hoist installed enabling the patient to be moved around in comfort. And professional carers would be required to visit three times a day. Undaunted by the prospect that now faced them, Irene and Philip set about getting everything in place and on 17 August Ken Jones was discharged from the Royal Gwent Hospital and taken by ambulance back to Tregarth, where he was introduced to his new living quarters. It was Philip's 40th birthday and he could not have wished for a better present.

Home Ken may have been, but Irene had taken on a task that would prove to be exhausting while at the same time very rewarding. Ken would never recover from the effects of the stroke, but knowing that he was in familiar surroundings and that friends could come and spend time with him whenever convenient was a tremendous boost to the immediate family. Knowing the demanding regime to which his mother had committed herself, Philip moved back into the family home and together with the invaluable assistance provided by the carers, a new routine was established and life carried on. Twice a year Ken would be transferred to Panteg Hospital for two weeks, allowing the medical teams to monitor him while also giving Irene a break which she would often spend at the apartment in Malaga.

Three years passed. For much of that time Ken had been far too weak to undergo any physiotherapy but when he was introduced to the rebuilding process he responded well. The encouraging signs persuaded the doctors that the patient could spend some of the day sitting in a wheelchair, a massive improvement from the interminable 24 hours spent in bed. Now there could be walks around the garden. Ken could sit outside and enjoy any good weather and, in time, Philip would become more adventurous, get him into the car and reintroduce his father to the surrounding countryside, especially that around Blaenavon.

The rehabilitation process continued to move forward following what at first was viewed as a setback. Since the stroke Ken had been fed intravenously. His inability to swallow offered little other option but when the attachment in his stomach showed signs of deterioration and would soon need replacing, medical opinion suggested he was too weak to undergo the necessary surgery. Tentative steps were taken to see if any food could be swallowed. It was a slow process, but by taking small amounts at a time Ken was gradually weaned off the drip before any decision had to be made regarding its replacement. This was a great step forward and Philip is adamant that once he had reverted to taking food by mouth, his father began to give clear signs that he was improving. Unfortunately, speech was still failing him but Irene persisted in trying to extract some meaningful communication and, perhaps because she knew him better than anybody, a rapport of sorts was established and Ken Jones was beginning to pick up the pieces and get some enjoyment out of life again.

Regular sessions of physiotherapy proved to be the hardest physical undertaking of his life. It was during these that the inner determination of the man became apparent and as time moved on so did Ken became less dependent on the equipment in place to help him move around. Small it may have been, but the overall improvement in his well-being encouraged Philip to take him to the opera at the newly opened Millennium Centre in Cardiff Bay at which the Welsh National Opera Company now staged its major productions.

And there were visits to Rodney Parade whenever the former players met up. For those who remembered him playing at a ground where he was once held in the highest esteem, seeing the frail man being pushed around in his wheelchair would have been a distressing experience. But Ken Jones was now into his eighties and notwithstanding his current unwelcome circumstances, it is doubtful that he would have changed anything about his long and full life. He had reached the heights, received great acclaim from two different audiences and in doing so, earned himself a permanent place in the record books. For those of a more recent generation, seeing an elderly man sitting quietly in his wheelchair, occasionally acknowledging a familiar face, would have meant very little but those of an earlier generation knew that there sat Wales' greatest sportsman.

With the arrival of spring in April 2006 eight years had passed since Ken suffered the stroke that impacted so heavily on his life. After a difficult few years, with the help of much love and affection he had adapted to his misfortune with admirable courage and continued to give great pleasure to those in his immediate circle of family and friends. Ken always enjoyed the company of others but in those last years one suspects that he would have cherished the time with Irene, who spent many hours sitting with her husband.

Occasional shortness of breath is a problem not uncommon with octogenarians, and when Ken felt uncomfortable he would use an inhaler: a few quick puffs and all was well. On the afternoon of Tuesday 18 April, Ken decided that he would take a nap and Irene took up her position in a chair, on hand if needed. She remembers Ken indicating that he wanted his 'puffer', which she handed to him. Settling back down in the chair Irene looked across at her husband and knew immediately that in those few short seconds he had passed away.

Ken Jones was 84 years of age when he departed this world. The last eight had been a most difficult period for all concerned, but by displaying the grit and determination that had served him so well in the past, he made the most of the cruel misfortune fate had handed him. Rarely did he despair of his lot and on the few occasions that he displayed any anger or annoyance it was with himself, simply frustrated that he was dependent on others for assistance in carrying out the simplest of manoeuvres. But that was the last eight years; the 76 that had gone before were both full and rewarding.

To reach the heights in one sport is a grand achievement but to be recognised at the highest level in two is rare. There are many examples of sportsmen who were outstanding in one arena while also performing well in another but rarely has anyone achieved such recognition in two contrasting endeavours as did Ken Jones, and it is certain that his equal is not to be found in the annals of Welsh sport.

The history books will always remind us of the 44 Welsh caps, the British Lions tour and his service to Newport RFC; the 16 Welsh Athletics titles, the medals won at the Olympic Games, the British Empire and Commonwealth Games and the European Championships. But what a trawl through the tomes that record such deeds will not confirm is what a damn fine fellow Kenneth Jeffrey Jones was. Modest in the extreme when coerced into discussing his achievements, here was a man happy to let his performances on the playing field and running track do his talking for him, but life is rarely that simple. His great deeds took him into the public domain, where he would remain for many years after his retirement from competitive sport, and even if the wider extent of his fame slowly receded he was still a man who attracted attention on his home territory – in and around Newport and on the many visits to his beloved Blaenavon.

And it was to Blaenavon that Ken was about to return. His passing was well documented in the national press, *The Times*, *Daily Telegraph* and *Guardian* among those that devoted many column inches to his obituary. Likewise the *Western Mail*, *South Wales Argus* and *Free Press* included extended pieces on the famous sportsman in the days immediately following his death ,while at the head of the valley, the people of Blaenavon prepared for the funeral of the town's favourite son.

Ken and Irene had been married in St Peter's Church on 30 December 1947, and a happy occasion it most certainly was, one that attracted much interest from the local community. The church was full on that auspicious day, every available space in each of the pews taken, with the overflow content to wait outside for a glimpse of the newlyweds. On 25 April 2006 St Peter's Church welcomed another full house; in fact the place of worship was full to overflowing, standing room only, while outside an even greater crowd stood waiting patiently for a last chance to say goodbye. Many of Ken's contemporaries from rugby and athletics were among the congregation. The Blaenavon Male Voice Choir added their vocal support in rousing renditions of 'O Love That Wilt Not Let Me Go' and 'The Day Thou Gavest Lord Is Ended'. A moving eulogy was read by Brian Jones who, at the start of his noteworthy career, enjoyed four seasons playing alongside Ken as the great man's neared its end.

Situated high up on the opposite side of the valley from Blaenavon, the cemetery offers a panoramic view over the town. Greenfield Place and Lower Hill Street can be clearly identified, as can the Workmen's Hall, the Iron Works and the home of Blaenavon RFC. An extension of the churchyard, it was only brought into use as a burial ground in the 1990s, prior to which it was simply a part of the landscape favoured by ramblers and others in search of peace and solitude. It was also where a young Ken Jones and Irene Edmunds spent some of the courting phase of their long relationship. They were together for more than 70 years and in due course the intention is that they will be reunited, back together up on the hills that they enjoyed walking as a young couple. There could be no more fitting final resting place for Ken, nowhere he would prefer to lie than at the exposed cemetery overlooking the town where he was born, was married and is now buried. There was much to celebrate in between times, many memorable days, but after an absence of almost 60 years, Ken Jones had returned home.

There is talk of a statue. One that would be positioned in Blaenavon, a permanent reminder of the lad who used to run down the street to the railway station; the young man

Ken Jones

who ran like the wind down the right wing and around the running track; and the older version who also ran like the wind down the right wing and around the running track. It would be the finest of gestures and while funding will always present problems, it is hoped that on this occasion, the necessary monies can be found. Ken Jones deserves it.

APPENDIX ONE

RUGBY FOOTBALL

Ken Jones played a lot of matches for Newport RFC. Similarly he scored a lot of tries, but how many matches he appeared in and how many tries he notched up remains open to debate. The following record does not claim to be definitive and it is necessary to point out that the figures do not concur with those set out in Jack Davis' *One Hundred Years of Newport Rugby*. In the 1952–53 season, Davis credits Jones with 32 appearances against the 33 listed below and in the following season, 1953–54, Davis has Jones playing 28 matches and scoring 17 tries, compared with the 30 matches and 18 tries noted herein. Mistakes can be made and source material is often found wanting, but the overall impact of these disparities means that for the purpose of this record, Ken Jones played 295 matches for his club and scored 146 tries together with one conversion.

NEWPORT RFC

1946–47

7 Sep	Penarth	H	w	15-6	one try
14 Sep	Llanelly	H	d	0-0	
21 Sep	Bristol	H	w	15-10	one try

28 Sep	Swansea	A	d	14-14	
30 Sep	Pontypool	A	d	0-0	
5 Oct	Cardiff	H	w	l 6-8	
12 Oct	Blackheath	H	w	11-3	two tries
19 Oct	Leicester	H	w	14-6	two tries
26 Oct	Wasps	A	w	11-0	
9 Nov	Cardiff	A	l	0-11	
16 Nov	London Welsh	A	w	16-11	one try
23 Nov	Gloucester	H	w	3-0	
30 Nov	Llanelly	A	d	0-0	
14 Dec	Cambridge Un	H	w	16-8	
21 Dec	Swansea	H	w	14-5	one try
26 Dec	Watsonians	H	w	10-0	
28 Dec	Newbridge	H	w	9-6	one try
25 Jan	Pontypool	H	w	13-3	
15 Feb	Cardiff	H	d	3-3	
1 Mar	Cardiff	A	d	l 3-13	
3 Apr	Abertillery	H	w	3-0	
8 Apr	Barbarians	H	l	l 3-19	
3 May	Neath	H	l	11-12	
10 May	Cross Keys	H	w	21-0	one try

1947–48

27 Sep	Swansea	H	w	33-16	one try
4 Oct	Cardiff	A	l	l 0-29	
18 Oct	Leicester	A	w	21-10	
23 Oct	Australia	H	l	4-8	
8 Nov	Cardiff	H	l	0-12	
15 Nov	London Welsh	A	w	11-6	
26 Dec	Watsonians	H	w	11-6	two tries
27 Dec	Wasps	H	w	25-0	one try
3 Jan	Richmond	H	w	22-0	
10 Jan	Llanelly	A	w	l 0-8	
24 Jan	Plymouth Albion	A	w	18-0	
26 Jan	Devonport Services	A	w	8-5	
31 Jan	Pontypool	H	d	3-3	
11 Feb	Oxford University	A	w	15-0	two tries
14 Feb	Leicester	H	w	32-6	one try
28 Feb	Blackheath	H	w	21-3	two tries
6 Mar	Cardiff	H	l	5-8	
20 Mar	Cross Keys	H	w	3-0	
30 Mar	Barbarians	H	w	5-3	

Appendix One

1948–49

2 Oct	Cardiff	H	l	0-9	
9 Oct	Blackheath	A	w	25-0	one try
30 Oct	Neath	H	w	6-0	
13 Nov	Cardiff	A	l	3-5	
27 Dec	Watsonians	H	w	11-3	
8 Jan	Neath	A	l	3-11	
12 Feb	Leicester	A	w	22-3	
19 Feb	Cardiff	A	d	3-3	
5 Mar	Cardiff	A	l	0-5	
19 Mar	Bath	A	w	18-0	one try
16 Apr	Bath	H	w	34-8	two tries
23 Apr	Penarth	A	w	25-5	three tries

1949–50

10 Sep	Bristol	A	w	11-8	
17 Sep	Wasps	H	l	3-11	
24 Sep	Swansea	H	l	8-11	
1 Oct	Cardiff	A	l	5-14	
8 Oct	Blackheath	A	w	11-5	
15 Oct	Leicester	A	l	8-13	
22 Oct	Neath	H	d	3-3	
29 Oct	Llanelly	H	d	3-3	
5 Nov	Plymouth Albion	H	w	9-5	
12 Nov	Cardiff	H	l	0-11	
19 Nov	London Welsh	A	l	6-8	one try
21 Nov	Cambridge Un	A	w	6-0	
26 Nov	Penarth	A	w	6-5	one try
3 Dec	Bristol	H	w	8-6	
10 Dec	Llanelly	A	d	3-3	
24 Dec	Newbridge	A	w	3-0	
31 Dec	Gloucester	H	w	11-0	one try
14 Jan	Neath	A	w	5-3	
8 Feb	Oxford University	A	w	11-6	
11 Feb	Leicester	H	w	13-3	
18 Feb	Bath	H	w	21-8	two tries
4 Mar	Cardiff	H	l	8-11	

1950–51

21 Oct	Leicester	H	w	19-6	
9 Dec	Cambridge Un	H	w	16-6	one try
26 Dec	Watsonians	H	w	9-0	

30 Dec	Penarth	H	w	12-0	
13 Jan	Newbridge	H	w	8-0	
27 Jan	Richmond	A	w	24-6	one try
8 Feb	Oxford University	H	w	21-3	
10 Feb	Leicester	H	w	16-0	two tries
17 Feb	Cardiff	A	w	8-3	
17 Mar	Harlequins	A	l	0-3	
26 Mar	London Welsh	H	w	9-0	
27 Mar	Barbarians	H	w	13-6	
31 Mar	Neath	A	w	13-0	
12 Apr	Swansea	H	w	10-0	
21 Apr	Plymouth Albion	A	w	6-5	one try
23 Apr	Torquay Athletic	A	w	15-3	one try
24 Apr	Exeter	A	l	0-3	
28 Apr	Cross Keys	H	w	8-5	

1951–52

20 Oct	Leicester	A	w	16-3	
27 Oct	Wasps	H	w	31-3	one try
3 Nov	Abertillery	A	w	3-0	
17 Nov	Cambridge Un	A	l	8-14	
24 Nov	London Welsh	A	w	9-0	two tries
1 Dec	Bristol	H	w	15-0	one try
15 Dec	Cardiff	H	l	5-6	one try
26 Dec	Watsonians	H	w	33-3	one try
27 Dec	Rosslyn Park	H	w	16-3	one try
31 Dec	Cognac	A	w	6-5	
1 Jan	Nantes	A	w	8-3	
10 Jan	South Africa	H	l	6-12	
12 Jan	Cardiff	A	l	3-6	one try
16 Feb	Llanelly	H	w	14-11	
23 Feb	Blackheath	A	w	15-8	one try
1 Mar	Cardiff	H	l	6-11	
13 Mar	Oxford University	H	w	9-0	
15 Mar	Harlequins	H	w	12-0	

1952–53

13 Sep	Bristol	H	w	14-0	
20 Sep	Neath	H	w	12-8	one try
27 Sep	Swansea	A	w	8-5	
29 Sep	Nantes-Cognac	H	w	12-11	one try
25 Oct	Wasps	H	w	17-0	one try

1 Nov	Penarth	A	w	11-3	
8 Nov	Cardiff	A	l	0-14	
15 Nov	Gloucester	H	w	8-3	
22 Nov	London Welsh	A	l	0-3	
29 Nov	Bristol	A	w	6-5	
6 Dec	Plymouth Albion	H	w	30-0	
15 Dec	Cambridge Un	H	w	25-0	two tries
20 Dec	Harlequins	A	w	8-0	one try
26 Dec	Watsonians	H	w	22-3	two tries
27 Dec	Cross Keys	H	w	16-0	one try
30 Dec	Percy Park	A	w	19-3	
1 Jan	Watsonians	A	w	6-0	one try
10 Jan	Cheltenham	H	w	6-3	
24 Jan	Richmond	A	d	6-6	one try
31 Jan	Llanelly	H	d	3-3	
14 Feb	Leicester	A	w	14-3	
21 Feb	Cardiff	H	w	6-0	
28 Feb	Blackheath	H	w	9-6	one try
7 Mar	Cardiff	A	d	5-5	
21 Mar	Penarth	H	w	14-3	one try
4 Apr	Aberavon	H	w	5-3	
6 Apr	London Welsh	H	w	8-3	one try
7 Apr	Barbarians	H	l	6-8	one try
11 Apr	Plymouth Albion	A	w	24-9	
13 Apr	Devonport Services	A	w	6-3	one try
14 Apr	Exeter	A	w	19-8	one try
18 Apr	Neath	A	w	8-0	
25 Apr	Newbridge	A	l	6-11	one try

1953–54

5 Sep	Penarth	H	d	11-11	
12 Sep	Bristol	A	d	9-9	
17 Sep	Swansea	A	w	14-3	
19 Sep	Neath	H	w	8-0	one try
26 Sep	Swansea	H	w	11-0	one try
3 Oct	Cardiff	A	l	6-15	
5 Oct	Lansdowne	A	w	20-14	two tries
7 Oct	Dolphin	A	w	13-8	
10 Oct	Blackheath	H	w	30-3	two tries
17 Oct	Gloucester	A	l	3-8	one try
24 Oct	Wasps	H	w	12-6	
21 Nov	Cambridge Un	A	l	11-15	

28 Nov	London Welsh	A	w	17-3	
12 Dec	Ebbw Vale	H	l	5-16	
26 Dec	Watsonians	H	w	18-9	one try
2 Jan	Cross Keys	A	w	14-3	one try
21 Jan	New Zealand	H	l	6-11	
23 Jan	Richmond	H	w	14-8	one try
13 Feb	Leicester	H	w	20-3	
27 Feb	Blackheath	A	w	21-11	three tries
6 Mar	Cardiff	H	d	3-3	
17 Mar	Cardiff	A	l	9-13	one try
20 Mar	Rosslyn Park	H	w	16-0	one try
3 Apr	Plymouth Albion	A	l	0-6	
12 Apr	Penarth	A	d	6-6	one try
17 Apr	Newbridge	H	w	9-3	
19 Apr	London Welsh	H	l	11-15	one try
20 Apr	Barbarians	H	w	14-3	
24 Apr	Abertillery	A	l	3-5	one try
29 Apr	Llanelly	A	l	0-11	

1954–55

23 Sep	Penarth	H	w	11-6	one try
25 Sep	Swansea	A	w	9-3	one try
2 Oct	Cardiff	H	d	3-3	
9 Oct	Blackheath	A	w	20-12	one try
16 Oct	Gloucester	H	w	16-0	one try
23 Oct	Wasps	H	w	25-0	two tries
30 Oct	Llanelly	A	l	8-16	one try
6 Nov	Penarth	A	w	8-3	
13 Nov	Cardiff	A	l	3-6	
20 Nov	Abertillery	H	w	6-3	one try
27 Nov	London Welsh	A	w	11-0	one try
4 Dec	Bristol	A	w	11-8	one try
18 Dec	Harlequins	A	w	21-0	one try
27 Dec	Watsonians	H	w	14-5	one try
28 Dec	Ebbw Vale	H	w	9-8	
29 Jan	Llanelly	H	w	12-0	
10 Feb	Oxford University	H	w	21-6	one try
12 Feb	Leicester	A	w	9-3	two tries
19 Feb	Cardiff	H	l	0-6	
5 Mar	Cardiff	A	w	11-6	one try
19 Mar	Rosslyn Park	H	w	12-11	
2 Apr	Aberavon	H	w	8-0	one try

9 Apr	Cross Keys	H	d	5-5	
11 Apr	London Welsh	H	w	13-6	one try
12 Apr	Barbarians	H	d	14-14	one try
16 Apr	Neath	H	w	17-0	two tries
23 Apr	Plymouth Albion	A	w	11-3	
25 Apr	Devonport Services	A	w	11-3	

1955–56

10 Sep	Bristol	A	l	6-11	
17 Sep	Neath	H	w	23-5	one try
24 Sep	Swansea	H	w	3-0	
1 Oct	Cardiff	A	w	16-6	one try
8 Oct	Blackheath	H	w	32-3	one try
15 Oct	Gloucester	A	l	6-11	
29 Oct	Llanelly	H	w	17-0	
5 Nov	Rosslyn Park	A	w	8-6	one try
12 Nov	Cardiff	H	w	13-0	one try
26 Nov	London Welsh	A	w	19-14	two tries
3 Dec	Bristol	H	w	16-0	one try
24 Dec	Abertillery	H	w	15-0	one try
26 Dec	Watsonians	H	w	24-0	five tries
27 Dec	Newbridge	H	w	9-0	one try
14 Jan	Swansea	A	w	6-3	
9 Feb	S A Universities	H	l	3-6	
11 Feb	Leicester	H	w	10-3	
18 Feb	Cardiff	A	w	3-0	
3 Mar	Cardiff	H	l	9-10	
17 Mar	Aberavon	A	w	11-3	
2 Apr	London Welsh	H	d	3-3	
3 Apr	Barbarians	H	w	14-3	
7 Apr	Neath	A	l	0-3	
14 Apr	Plymouth Albion	A	w	14-11	
16 Apr	Devonport Services	A	w	14-0	one try
21 Apr	Ebbw Vale	H	w	19-6	

1956–57

22 Sep	Swansea	A	d	0-0	
29 Sep	Leicester	H	w	22-3	
6 Oct	Cardiff	H	d	6-6	one try
13 Oct	Blackheath	A	w	21-3	
20 Oct	Gloucester	H	l	6-8	
27 Oct	Wasps	H	w	11-0	

10 Nov	Cardiff	A	l	5-6	one try
14 Nov	Cambridge Un	A	l	3-14	
22 Nov	Oxford University	H	w	8-3	one try
24 Nov	London Welsh	A	w	8-3	
1 Dec	Bristol	H	l	8-19	one try
15 Dec	Harlequins	H	w	8-3	
22 Dec	Plymouth Albion	H	w	31-0	one try
26 Dec	Watsonians	H	w	6-0	
12 Jan	Swansea	H	d	6-6	one try
19 Jan	Coventry	A	w	11-8	
26 Jan	Richmond	A	l	3-5	
9 Feb	Leicester	A	l	3-13	
16 Feb	Cardiff	H	l	0-8	
23 Feb	Blackheath	H	w	9-0	one try
2 Mar	Cardiff	A	w	10-0	
9 Mar	Wasps	A	w	6-0	
16 Mar	Rosslyn Park	H	w	9-6	
20 Mar	Ebbw Vale	A	w	6-0	
23 Mar	Llanelly	H	w	21-8	two tries
28 Mar	Ebbw Vale	H	w	19-8	one try
6 Apr	Plymouth Albion	A	w	19-14	
8 Apr	Devonport Services	A	w	6-3	one try
9 Apr	Exeter	A	w	19-3	
13 Apr	Neath	A	w	23-3	one try
20 Apr	Newbridge	H	w	37-3	three tries
22 Apr	London Welsh	H	w	12-0	
23 Apr	Barbarians	H	l	5-8	

1957–58

28 Sep	Swansea	H	w	19-6	
5 Oct	Cardiff	H	l	0-3	
19 Oct	Cardiff	A	d	3-3	
26 Oct	Cross Keys	H	w	5-3	
23 Nov	Australia	H	w	11-0	
30 Nov	Leicester	A	w	9-8	
7 Dec	Bristol	A	l	3-8	
14 Dec	Aberavon	A	l	8-9	one try
21 Dec	Harlequins	A	l	3-9	
26 Dec	Watsonians	H	w	21-6	two tries
27 Dec	Ebbw Vale	H	w	20-3	one try
28 Dec	UAU	H	d	3-3	one try
11 Jan	London Welsh	A	w	3-0	

18 Jan	Coventry	H	l	3-8	
25 Jan	Richmond	H	w	28-0	
6 Feb	Oxford University	A	w	18-3	
15 Feb	Cross Keys	A	w	8-5	
22 Feb	Blackheath	A	w	14-3	
1 Mar	Cardiff	H	d	3-3	
5 Mar	Neath	H	w	15-5	two tries
8 Mar	Wasps	A	w	16-0	
15 Mar	Cardiff	A	w	14-6	one try
22 Mar	Gloucester	A	w	8-6	
27 Mar	Swansea	A	w	6-3	
5 Apr	Newbridge	H	w	15-5	
7 Apr	London Welsh	H	w	8-0	
8 Apr	Barbarians	H	w	13-8	
12 Apr	Plymouth Albion	A	w	39-0	two tries
14 Apr	Devonport Services	A	w	18-6	
15 Apr	Exeter	A	w	20-6	two tries, con
19 Apr	Neath	A	l	5-6	
24 Apr	Llanelli	A	l	6-11	

WALES

1947
18 Jan	England	Cardiff Arms Park	w	16-9
1 Feb	Scotland	Murrayfield	w	22-8 two tries
22 Mar	France	Stade Colombes	w	3-0
29 Mar	Ireland	St Helen's, Swansea	w	6-0
20 Dec	Australia	Cardiff Arms Park	w	6-0

1948
17 Jan	England	Twickenham	d	3-3 one try
7 Feb	Scotland	Cardiff Arms Park	w	14-0 one try
21 Feb	France	St Helen's, Swansea	l	3-11
13 Mar	Ireland	Ravenhill, Belfast	l	3-6

1949
15 Jan	England	Cardiff Arms Park	w	9-3
5 Feb	Scotland	Murrayfield	l	5-6
12 Mar	Ireland	St Helen's, Swansea	l	0-5
26 Mar	France	Stade Colombes	l	3-5 one try

1950
21 Jan	England	Twickenham	w	11-5
4 Feb	Scotland	St Helen's, Swansea	w	12-0 one try
11 Mar	Ireland	Ravenhill, Belfast	w	6-3 one try
25 Mar	France	Cardiff Arms Park	w	21-0 two tries

1951
20 Jan	England	St Helen's, Swansea	w	23-5 one try
3 Feb	Scotland	Murrayfield	l	0-19
10 Mar	Ireland	Cardiff Arms Park	d	3-3
7 Apr	France	Stade Colombes	l	3-8 one try
22 Dec	South Africa	Cardiff Arms Park	l	3-6

1952
19 Jan	England	Twickenham	w	8-6 two tries
2 Feb	Scotland	Cardiff Arms Park	w	11-0 one try
8 Mar	Ireland	Lansdowne Road	w	14-3 one try
22 Mar	France	St Helen's, Swansea	w	9-5

1953
17 Jan	England	Cardiff Arms Park	l	3-8
7 Feb	Scotland	Murrayfield	w	12-0 one try
14 Mar	Ireland	St Helen's, Swansea	w	5-3
28 Mar	France	Stade Colombes	w	6-3
19 Dec	New Zealand	Cardiff Arms Park	w	13-6 one try

1954
16 Jan	England	Twickenham	l	6-9
13 Mar	Ireland	Lansdowne Road	w	12-9
27 Mar	France	Cardiff Arms Park	w	19-13
10 Apr	Scotland	St Helen's, Swansea	w	15-3

1955
22 Jan	England	Cardiff Arms Park	w	3-0
5 Feb	Scotland	Murrayfield	l	8-14
12 Mar	Ireland	Cardiff Arms Park	w	21-3
26 Mar	France	Stade Colombes	w	16-11

1956
21 Jan	England	Twickenham	w	8-3
4 Feb	Scotland	Cardiff Arms Park	w	9-3
10 Mar	Ireland	Lansdowne Road	l	3-11
24 Mar	France	Cardiff Arms Park	w	5-3

1957
2 Feb   Scotland   Murrayfield   l   6-9

BRITISH LIONS 1950

13 May Buller   Westport   w 24-9 one try
16 May West Coast   Greymouth   w 32-3 two tries
20 May Otago   Dunedin   l 9-23
23 May Southland   Invercargill   l 0-11
27 May New Zealand 1st Test   Dunedin   d 9-9   one try
31 May South Canterbury   Timaru   w 27-8 one try
3 Jun   Canterbury   Christchurch   w 16-5 one try
10 Jun New Zealand 2nd Test   Christchurch   l 0-8
17 Jun Hawke's Bay   Napier   w 20-0
24 Jun Wellington   Wellington   w 12-6 one try
8 Jul   Taranaki   New Plymouth w 25-3 two tries
15 Jul Waikato–King Country
        –Thames Valley   Hamilton   w 30-0 two tries
19 Jul North Auckland   Whangerei   w 8-6   one try
22 Jul Auckland   Auckland   w 32-9 two tries
29 Jul New Zealand 4th Test   Auckland   l 8-11 one try
2 Aug   NZ Maoris   Wellington   w 14-9 one try
2 Sep   New South Wales   Newcastle   l 12-17

BARBARIANS

1949
3 Mar   East Midlands   Bedford   w   24-11   one try

1952
26 Jan   South Africa   Cardiff   l   3-17

1953
28 Dec   Leicester   Leicester   w   39-11   three tries

1954
20 Feb   New Zealand   Cardiff   l   5-19

1956
30 Mar   Penarth   Penarth   w   9-6

Incomplete records are not satisfactory, therefore it is not proposed to identify any further matches in which Ken played, but the following are teams he was associated with during his distinguished career:

Blaenavon Schools; Jones' West Mon School; Monmouthshire Schools; Welsh Secondary Schools; Talywain RFC; Pontypool RFC; St Paul's College, Cheltenham; RAF (Chakeri) Cawnpore; Blaenavon RFC; Newport RFC; Monmouthshire; Wales; Somerset; Loughborough College; Universities Athletic Union; Leicester RFC; Barbarians RFC; British Lions.

Additionally, there were numerous trial matches; appearances for various invitation teams; England/Wales combined teams; and the house matches for Priestley and the junior teams at West Mon where the long journey began.

APPENDIX TWO

ATHLETICS

Beyond the major games and championships, it is impossible to produce a comprehensive record of Ken Jones' athletics career. Even as prestigious an event as the AAA Championships failed to attract any press coverage other than the finals, and as Ken rarely featured in the latter stages of the sprints, his performances in the earlier rounds could not be sourced.

WELSH AAA CHAMPIONSHIPS

100 yards
1946	Sloper Road, Cardiff	Champion	10.9
1947	Pontypool	Champion	10.2
1948	Talbot Athletic Ground	Champion	9.9
1949	Abertillery	Champion	9.8
1950	Did not compete		
1951	Maindy Stadium, Cardiff	Champion	10.3
1952	Maindy Stadium	Champion	10.3
1953	Maindy Stadium	Champion	10.2
1954	Maindy Stadium	Runner-up	10.4

220 yards
1946	Sloper Road	Champion	24.0
1947	Pontypool	Champion	24.1

1948	Talbot Athletic Ground	Champion	23.1
1949	Abertillery	Champion	22.5
1950	Did not compete		
1951	Maindy Stadium	Champion	23.2
1952	Maindy Stadium	Champion	23.1
1953	Maindy Stadium	Champion	22.7
1954	Maindy Stadium	Champion	22.5

Long Jump

1949	Abertillery	Champion	6.37m

OLYMPIC GAMES, LONDON 1948

100m

Heat	2nd	10.6
Second round	3rd	10.7
Semi-final	6th	10.9

4x100m relay

Heat	1st	41.4
Final	2nd	41.3

BRITISH EMPIRE AND COMMONWEALTH GAMES, VANCOUVER 1954

100yds

Heat	2nd	10.0
Semi-final	3rd	9.8
Final	6th	9.8

220yds

Heat	1st	22.4
Semi-final	2nd	22.1
Final	3rd	21.9

EUROPEAN CHAMPIONSHIPS, BERNE 1954

100m

Heat	2nd	10.9
Semi-final	4th	10.7

4x100m relay

Heat	2nd	41.4
Final	2nd	40.8

BIBLIOGRAPHY

Barber, Chris: *Exploring Blaenavon Industrial Landscape and Heritage Site*, Blorenge Books 2002

Billot, John: *History of Welsh International Rugby*, Roman Way Books 1999 (second edition)

Billot, John: *All Blacks in Wales*, Ron Jones Publications 1972

Chester, RH and McMillan, NAC: *The Visitors – A History of International Rugby Teams in New Zealand*, Moa Publications 1990

Chester, Rod, Palenski, Ron and McMillan, Neville: *Men in Black*, Hodder Moa Beckett 2000 (fifth edition)

Chester, Rod, Palenski, Ron and McMillan, Neville: *The Encyclopaedia of New Zealand Rugby*, Hodder Moa Becket 1998 (third edition)

Crane, Arthur: *Serve and Obey – The Official History of West Monmouth School*, West Monmouth School 1998

Davis, Jack: *One Hundred Years of Newport Rugby*, Starling Press 1974

Evans, Alan: *Lions Down Under 1950 Tour to New Zealand, Australia and Ceylon*, Stadia 2006

Fox, Dave, Bogle, Ken and Hoskins, Mark: *A Century of the All Blacks in Britain and Ireland*, Tempus 2006

Godwin, Terry: *The International Rugby Championship 1883–1983*, Willow Books 1984

Griffiths, John: *The Phoenix Book of International Rugby Records*, Phoenix/Dent 1987

Hampton, Janie: *The Austerity Olympics – When the Games Came to London in 1948*, Aurum Press Ltd 2008

Jenkins, John M, Pierce, Duncan and Auty, Timothy: *Who's Who of Welsh International Rugby Players*, Bridge Books 1991

Lovesey, Peter: *Official Centenary History of the AAA*, Guinness Superlatives Ltd 1979

More, Charles: *A Splendid College – An Illustrated History of Teacher Training in Cheltenham 1847–1990*, Cheltenham and

Gloucester College of Higher Education 1992

Sheridan, Michael: *British Athletics 1951–1959*, Michael Sheridan 2008

Shnaps, Teddy: *A Statistical History of Springbok Rugby*, Don Nelson 1989

Smith, David and Williams, Gareth: *Fields of Praise*, University of Wales Press 1980

Thomas, Clem: *The History of the British Lions*, Mainstream Publishing 1996

van Esbeck, Edmund: *Irish Rugby 1874–1999*, Gill and Macmillan 1999

Wemyss, A: *The Barbarians*, Playfair Books 1955

Williams, Clive (editor): *The History of Welsh Athletics*, Dragon Sports Books Ltd 2002

Williams, Clive: *VIth British Empire and Commonwealth Games*, Welsh Athletics 2008

The Rugby Almanack of New Zealand 1951, Sporting Publications Ltd 1951

Playfair Rugby Football Annual – Playfair Books Ltd, various editions

Newport High School for Boys School Magazine – various editions

The Westmonian – various editions

Newspapers and Magazines

Boy's Own, October 1954

Cheltenham Chronicle and Gloucestershire Graphic

Cork Examiner

Empire News

Football Argus

Ingot

Irish Independent

Leicester Mercury

Loughborough Monitor

News of the World

South Wales Argus

South Wales Echo and Express

South Wales Football Echo

The Times

The Sunday Express

The Free Press of Monmouthshire

Western Mail and South Wales News

World Sports, March 1953

INDEX

Index

Index

Thomas, WR 234
Thompson, Peter 237
Tolan, Eddie 98
Travers, Bill 'Bunner' 184
Travers, George 259
Treloar, John 83, 96
Trew, Billy 259
Twain, Mark 145

Uren, Dick 114

Vannier, Michel 264

Waddell, Gordon 270
Wakefield, Sir Wavell 201
Walters, Gwyn 184
Walthen, Councillor TH 108
Watkins, Alan 236
Watkins, Mrs Holmes 26
Watt, James 15
Webb, Jim 259
Weeks, Alan 240
Wells, Gordon 249
Wetter, Jack 158, 178
Whent, Derwyn 29-30, 50, 52
White, Duncan 118
White, Richard 153
White, 'Tiny' 213
White, William 141
Whitson, Geoff 253, 260, 271
Whittle, Harry 208
Wilde, Jimmy 236

Williams, Billy 163, 170, 187, 193,
  203, 218, 260
Williams, Bleddyn 11, 36, 52, 60-61,
  63, 74, 78, 116, 126, 131, 142,
  146-47, 163, 170-71, 189, 201, 212,
  215, 218, 220, 242, 248, 276, 284,
  293, 295
Williams, Bryn 163, 167, 170
Williams, Christopher 165
Williams, CD 170, 260
Williams, G 36
Williams, Gerwyn 213, 218, 220
Williams, Ivor 165
Williams, John L 194, 259
Williams, JPR 282
Williams, Les 63, 78
Williams, Lloyd 266
Williams, Ossie 127
Williams, Rhys 220, 260, 264
Williams, Shane 284
Williams, Stan 80
Williams, WE 59, 64
Williams, WO 81-82, 197
Willis, Councillor AE 158
Willis, Rex 131, 151, 163, 170,
  189-90, 193, 213, 218, 221, 248, 283
Wooderson, Sydney 90
Woodward, John 189
Wooler, Wilf 236-37, 276, 284
Wright, Lorenzo 101, 103-05

Zatopek, Emil 98, 233